Civil War Hostages

Hostage Taking in the Civil War

By
Webb Garrison

WHITE MANE BOOKS

Unless otherwise noted, illustrations are from the author's collection.

This White Mane Books publication
was printed by
Beidel Printing House, Inc.
63 West Burd Street
Shippensburg, PA 17257-0152 USA

In respect for the scholarship contained herein, the acid-free paper used in this book meets the guidelines for permanence and durability of the Committee on Production Guidelines for Book Longevity of the Council on Library Resources.

For a complete list of available publications
please write
White Mane Books
Division of White Mane Publishing Company, Inc.
P.O. Box 152
Shippensburg, PA 17257-0152 USA

Library of Congress Cataloging-in-Publication Data

Garrison, Webb B., 1919-
    Civil War hostages : hostage taking in the Civil War / by Webb Garrison.
        p. cm.
    Includes bibliographical references (p.) and index.
    ISBN 1-57249-199-X (alk. paper)
    1. United States--History--Civil War, 1861-1865--Prisoners and prisons. 2.
Hostages--United States--History--19th century. 3. Reprisals--History--19th century. I.
Title.

E615 .G37 2000
973.7'7--dc21
                                                                        00-031662

Contents

Preface

Militant Iranians seized 52 Americans late in 1979 and for months held them as hostages. Their detention is widely regarded as having played a significant role in Jimmy Carter's defeat when he sought a second term as president of the United States. This dramatic international case, which was news for week after week, encouraged citizens of the modern world to link hostage-taking with struggles in the Near East. Consequently, the discovery that it was an integral and significant component of the Civil War comes as a surprise to many contemporary Americans.

Seizure of hostages had been a long-established military practice when hostilities began in 1861. During the American Revolution, Virginia's royal governor pondered the risks involved in taking Martha Washington at Mount Vernon and eventually decided against making the try. George Washington castigated his foe, saying that he didn't believe a British gentleman would stoop to "so low and unmanly a part." That verdict upon the part of the "Father of His Country" was emotion-charged and incorrect; English and European monarchs and generals regarded the use of hostages as a commonplace aspect of military campaigns.

While the North/South struggle raged President Zachary Taylor's grandson, a Confederate general, condemned the taking of "unoffending men for the supposed guilt of others" as lying outside the boundaries of civilized warfare—yet he probably took a few, himself. That dichotomy in ideals/actions was consciously or unconsciously experienced by many a commander on both sides. Hardly anyone offered a defense for the practice of arbitrarily seizing innocent persons and making them responsible for the liberty or lives of men of whom they had never heard. Yet nearly everyone in a position of authority was sooner or later involved in it—sometimes heavily.

Were it not so ridiculously inaccurate, one short paragraph included in Federal instructions for armies in the field would evoke laughter. For after hundreds of hostages had been taken and the practice was increasing in intensity and frequency, commanders of blue-clad soldiers were officially advised that "Hostages are rare in the present age."

Jefferson Davis authorized a dramatic and spectacular lottery by which the war's earliest publicized hostages were selected. Abraham Lincoln never condemned and occasionally condoned the taking of hostages. Both Robert E. Lee and Ulysses S. Grant sanctioned this practice; so did future chief executive Andrew Johnson of Tennessee. This special retaliatory act was launched almost as soon as the first Confederate vessels that sailed under a Letter of Marque hit the water. It continued throughout nearly all of the estimated 1,400 days during which Americans fought, imprisoned, maimed, and killed other Americans with ever-increasing ferocity.

In many instances, official accounts of the use of hostages were squeezed into so few words that despite the barbaric cruelty involved, from the distance of generations they seem almost sterile of emotion. That certainly was not the case during 1861–65. Even the most humble and obscure hostages had kinfolk, neighbors, and friends. When a man who had done nothing to deserve such treatment was snatched up by the enemy, everyone acquainted with him must have become frightened and angry at the same time.

Soldiers who went into a battle knew that they might not come out of it. Civilians who had not knowingly harmed anyone did not expect to be arrested and used as hostages simply because they happened to be at the wrong place at the wrong time. Since this practice took place over and over in every seceded state, numerous border states, and a few states deep inside Union lines, hostage taking contributed significantly to the intensity and duration that marked America's most deadly war.

Despite the frequence with which hostages were used by men in both gray and blue, accounts of these actions are not easily and readily found. The mammoth index volume of the *Official Records* includes an entry for "hostages"—but points users to no cases except those that revolved about Confederate seamen whose captors initially labeled them as pirates. I believe this is the first of the tens of thousands of books about the Civil War that deals exclusively with hostages, their captors, and some of the results achieved through use of them. Though it is the fruit of long and diligent searching, some cases are sure to have been overlooked or omitted.

Here's hoping that the incidents treated here will enable you better to understand why less than four watershed years were marked with barbarity that we fervently hope our nation will never again experience.

Citations and Abbreviations

Because few general officers held the same rank throughout the war, all are designated simply as "Gen." Unless otherwise designated, military units to which references are made are infantry regiments of state militia bodies or of volunteers. To bypass the cumbersome and often frustrating search for endnotes that are located far from the data to which they refer, abbreviated citations are included in parenthesis at the ends of cited text material. Complete listings appear in the bibliography, however. Abbreviations employed herein consist of:

ACW   *America's Civil War.*
AL   Abraham Lincoln, *Collected Works*, 8 vols.
BG   *Blue & Gray.*
CDC   *Charleston Daily Courier.*
CM   *Charleston Mercury.*
CMH   *Confederate Military History*, 17 vols., expanded edition.
CV   *Confederate Veteran*, 40 vols.
CW   *Civil War.*
CWT   *Civil War Times, Illustrated.*
D   Dyer, *Compendium.*
DxD   Long, *The Civil War Day by Day.*
Ency.   Faust, *Historical Times Illustrated Encyclopedia.*
GB   Warner, *Generals in Blue.*
GG   Warner, *Generals in Gray.*
H   *Harper's Encyclopedia of United States History.*
JSHS   *Journal of the Southern Historical Society*, 50 vols.

M   A serial numbered volume in the 68 collections of personal experi-
        ences published by the Military Order of the Loyal Legion of the
        United States; the serial number of a reprinted volume is indicated.

NOR   *Naval Official Records*, 30 vols., and master index.

NYH   *New York Herald.*

NYT   *New York Times.*

OR   A serial number followed by a page number or numbers refers to
        the *Official Records* (Army), 127 vols., and master index.

P&C   *Charleston Daily Post/Courier.*

PH   Miller, *The Photographic History of the Civil War*, 10 vols.

RD   *Richmond Dispatch.*

RR   Moore, *Rebellion Record,* 10 vols. These volumes are divided
        into three sections: Diary (D), Documents (Doc.) and Poetry and
        Incidents (P).

WS   *Washington Star.*

WWW   Sifikas, *Who Was Who in the Civil War.*

Part I

Piracy in North American Waters

1

Three Deadly Lotteries—Ligon's Tobacco Warehouse, November 10-11, 1861

Alfred Ely of Rochester, New York, was visibly disturbed when he received word from Confederate Gen. John H. Winder, commander of Richmond's prisons, that his presence was required at an assembly that would be held on November 10, 1861. As the only civilian inmate of an improvised prison holding dozens of captured Federal officers, the congressman from New York wondered what was about to happen to him. While waiting to be escorted to Winder's meeting, he recalled earlier tumultuous events and wondered whether he had angered a Rebel official.

Like hundreds of other prominent persons who were in Washington D.C., during the previous summer, Ely had taken his carriage to Manassas, Virginia, on July 21. He wanted to be on hand in order to see Gen. Irvin McDowell's troops whip the daylights out of Confederate Gen. P. G. T. Beauregard's Rebel force. When defeat of blue-clad troops turned into a rout, the Federal lawmaker was captured about 5:00 P.M. by members of a South Carolina regiment. Though threatened, he was not harmed, but was forced to spend the night on the ground during driving rain.

On Monday, July 22, he was questioned by Beauregard, Confederate President Jefferson Davis, and Gen. William F. "Extra Billy" Smith. After giving a lengthy explanation of his presence on the battlefield, he was sent to a barn in which captured Federal officers were being held. Members of this special group of prisoners were sent to Richmond on Tuesday, and Virginians who had known him in Congress clamored for his release. Their pleas were not heeded, but the presence of the New York congressman in the Ligon Prison "was announced by the Richmond papers and the whole press of the South, by which he soon became notorious."

While in prison he had numerous prominent visitors, including governors of several seceded states and former Union Vice President John C. Breckinridge. Unionists of Richmond sent him fresh flowers almost daily,

Though dwarfed by its immediate neighbors, Ligon's Tobacco
Warehouse *(center)* was large enough to hold hundreds of prisoners.

and some families sent him "nicely prepared meals." Inside the prison, plans
were under way to form a Prison Association—and Ely's name headed the
list of potential presidents. He thought perhaps this matter had come to
Winder's attention and would lead to reprimands or worse when the scheduled assembly of inmates was held. (NYT in RR, 3, Doc. #239)

Ely's worries were groundless; when led before assembled prisoners
by a guard, he saw a tin ballot box and wondered what its presence meant.
According to 1st Lt. John Whyte of the 79th New York, six ballots "were
placed fairly in a tin or ballot box, a cap covering it, and then well shaken."
Ely was then told to draw a single slip of paper from the box. Visibly agi-
tated and wondering what on earth was taking place, the congressman nod-
ded to Winder and followed instructions. Without unfolding the ballot he
had selected blindly, he handed it to the prison commandant.

Winder glanced at the ballot and read loudly: "Colonel Michael
Corcoran of the 69th New York Militia has been selected as hostage for the
life of Captain Walter W. Smith." Corcoran, who had been sent to
Charleston's Fort Pinckney, did not know that he headed the hostage list
until mail reached him. Though a few of the men selected as pawns in the
deadly game of trying to save Rebel privateersmen were in the Ligon Prison,
most were already in other improvised prisons that were considered to be
more secure. (OR, 116, 130–32; RR, 3, Doc. #147)

Many of the assembled officers knew precisely what the congressman's announcement meant. Captured by a Federal gunboat on the high seas, Smith had been convicted of piracy—a verdict that carried an automatic death sentence. The deadly lottery in which Ely was a major participant had resulted in the potential execution of Corcoran by a firing squad or the hangman's noose. Rebels had selected from their prisoners of highest rank a hostage for the life of the highest-ranking seaman who had been convicted of piracy. (OR, 116, 38–120)

Winder ignored shouts of indignation from the ranks of his prisoners and calmly announced that the remaining colonels in his custody would be held liable for the fate of five other Rebel seamen among captured privateers. This meant that Col. Milton Cogswell of the 42nd New York Zouaves faced the same fate as Corcoran. So did Cols. William Raymond Lee of the 20th Massachusetts Volunteers, William E. Woodruff of the 2nd Kentucky, Orlando B. Wilcox of the 1st Michigan, and Alfred M. Woods of the 14th New York.

His demeanor having already suggested that the Rebel commandant had not concluded his business, Winder proceeded to announce that all additional field officers in his custody would also be held responsible for the safety of privateers who were on trial. Five more names were read solemnly but quickly, making hostages of Lt. Cols. George W. Neff of the 2nd Kentucky and Samuel Bowman of the 8th Pennsylvania plus Majs. James D. Potter of the 38th New York, Paul J. Revere of the 20th Massachusetts, and Israel Vodges of the 1st Union Artillery.

With the lives of 11 Federal officers having been laid on the line, Winder was not quite through. Since 14 Rebel privateers faced the gibbet, he was forced to resort to line officers in order to supply the number of hostages needed. With the names of all captains held by Confederates having replaced those of their superiors in rank, Ely was instructed to draw three more ballots. The second lottery put Capts. Hugh McQuaide of the 38th New York, George W. Rockwood of the 15th Massachusetts, and James B. Ricketts of the 1st U.S. Artillery among the hostages. Since Ricketts was seriously wounded, Thomas Cox of the 1st Kentucky offered to take his place but Winder said that the lottery was binding and refused to make the exchange.

Before another day passed, Winder decided to remove McQuaide and Ricketts from the list of 14—possibly because one or both seemed likely to die before trials of privateers could be concluded. Another lottery was held, and from the captains in the prison Francis J. Keffer of the 1st California and Henry Bowman of the 15th Massachusetts were selected to take the place of their wounded comrades. The third ceremony within 36 hours ended by making the number of able-bodied hostages—14—exactly equal to the number of privateers held in Northern prisons. (OR, 116, 740)

On-the-spot accounts and lists of men condemned to die unless Lincoln or Davis wavered were prepared by participant Cogswell and observer Whyte. Winder's official list was relayed to Benjamin on November 11. To Lee—who was one of his West Point classmates and a prewar close personal friend—the prison commandant expressed regrets that if the hostages should hang, "so must you." (OR, 116, 130–32; RR, 3, Doc. #147; OR, 116, 739; JSHS, 3, 88)

These deadly rituals took place as a result of a series of events at the highest levels of government. Evacuation of Fort Sumter by the Federal garrison headed by Maj. Robert Anderson took place on Sunday, April 15, 1861. On Monday, Abraham Lincoln issued a proclamation calling for 75,000 volunteers to serve in Federal forces for 90 days. Since that number of volunteers would represent approximately six times the effective force of the Union army on the day of the call, the president expected repentant secessionists to scurry back into the Union. (CW, #4, 331–32)

Confederate President Jefferson Davis reputedly showed no signs of fear or any other emotion when he learned of the action taken in Washington. A West Point graduate and a former Union secretary of war, the chief executive of Rebels was much better acquainted with military history and international law than was Lincoln. In 1856, Davis remembered, the United States had refused to sign the Treaty of Paris—one provision of which outlawed the ancient and honorable practice of privateering on the high seas.

Davis correctly reasoned that under international law, the brand new Confederacy was free to license privateers who would be expected to prey upon Yankee shipping. Forty-eight hours after his counterpart called for an immense army of volunteers, the president who was situated in Richmond made public a proclamation of his own. He offered to issue Letters of Marque by which persons owning and operating "private armed vessels" would be authorized to "aid this Government in resisting so wanton and wicked an aggression [as that announced two days earlier from a distance of about 100 miles]."

Operators of small vessels operating under a Letter of Marque would be required to post a bond in the sum of $5,000—a sum that would be doubled in the case of a vessel with a crew of 150 or more men. Vessels of all sizes would be required to pay to the Confederate Treasury a portion of the value of prizes they took, he pointed out. His tediously lengthy proclamation ended with an exhortation to "the good people of these Confederate States" to exert themselves in preserving order and supporting all measures adopted for defense. Davis said he hoped that "Under the blessing of Divine Providence," such measures would bring about "a speedy, just, and honorable peace." (OR, 5, 796–97)

Two days after the Confederate chief executive invited his adherents to become privateers, Lincoln responded with an equally lengthy countermeasure. Unwilling then or ever to concede that secession had taken place,

President Jefferson Davis personally interrogated Congressman Alfred Ely of New York, who had gone to Bull Run in order to see the Rebels take a licking.

the chief executive of the United States stipulated additional steps he felt needed to be taken in order to quell what he termed "an insurrection." He stressed that so-called secessionists had been invited by Davis "to commit assaults on the lives, vessels, and property of good citizens." Hence Lincoln proclaimed a blockade of the ports in each of the seven states he had enumerated earlier. What is more, he warned that anyone operating under the "pretended authority" of these states who molested a Union vessel or its cargo or persons aboard it would be "held amenable to the laws of the United States for the prevention and punishment of piracy." Strangely, this emotion-charged document does not appear in Lincoln's *Collected Works*. (OR, 122, 89–90)

In Washington and in Richmond as well as throughout both warring regions, it was widely known that if a jury convicted a man of piracy, the presiding judge did not have to deliberate concerning the resulting sentence. Statutes of the day required that a convicted pirate should hang by the neck until dead; under the law, there was no alternative or option.

Distinguished newspaper correspondent William Howard Russell had earlier covered the Crimean War. Smelling the likelihood of civil conflict in North America, he had come in order to report to British readers what was happening three thousand miles to their west. Three weeks after the trio of challenges had been fired from bitterly divided capitals his readers were told that

> Today the papers contain a proclamation by the President of the Confederate States of America, declaring a state of war between the Confederacy and the United States, and notifying the issue of letters of marque and reprisal. Mr. [William H.] Seward [the Union secretary of state] told me that but for Jefferson Davis, the secession plot could never have been carried out. No other man of the [secession] party had the brains or the courage and dexterity to bring it to a successful issue. (*London Times*, May 6, 1861)

Russell probably did not then suspect that the United States would never declare war on the Confederacy—claiming instead to "quell an insurrection" at a cost of more than 620,000 lives.

On the heels of Lincoln's announcement that privateers would be treated as pirates, Davis ordered Col. Richard Taylor of the 9th Louisiana personally to take to Washington a lengthy July 6 message that was addressed to the president. A proposal had been made to the officer in charge of the blockading squadron whose vessel captured the privateer *Savannah* that prisoners should be quickly exchanged, he wrote. Lincoln was then informed that by the time his Confederate counterpart found that an exchange would not be accepted, he learned from New York newspapers that captured privateers were being treated as criminals rather than as prisoners of war.

Col. Richard Taylor hand delivered to Washington the Davis warning that the Confederacy would not permit captured sea-men to be treated as pirates.

"It is the desire of this Government so to conduct the war now existing as to mitigate its horrors as far as may be possible," the Davis dispatch continued. Using carefully chosen words, he then warned that "painful as will be the necessity this Government will deal out to prisoners held by it the same treatment" accorded to captured privateers. He then renewed his proposal for an exchange of prisoners of war in equal number and "according to rank." Taylor was refused admission to the Executive Mansion and was told by Gen. Winfield Scott that a written reply would be made "as soon as possible." (OR, 119, 5–6)

Old timers in Washington derided the Taylor mission, which in the newspaper was ridiculed as a transparent ruse aimed at "communicating with enemies in our midst." The uniformed officer was mocked as having come under a white flag with a 12-man escort. Admitting that Lincoln refused to see the man representing Davis, newspaper readers were told that the letter went to Lincoln, "who communicated its exact contents to none besides his constitutional advisers and Gen. Scott." Arrival of the dispatch from Richmond was dismissed as amounting "to nothing of earthly importance in the present crisis."

We repeat, editors wrote:

> the whole affair amounted to little more than a ruse or trick of Uncle Sambo's [a widely used label for the Confederacy] to communicate "on the sly" with traitors in Washington, which failed entirely, owing to the careful watch kept over this Uncle Sambo's instrument in the matter while here, and the precaution taken not to permit him to remain over night in Washington. (WS, 7/9/61)

Overseas, some notables had earlier condemned the notion that privateers were pirates. On May 16, the earl of Derby went on record as holding that "if *one thing was clearer than another, it was that privateering was not piracy,*" and that no nation could enact a law contrary to the "law of nations." Lords Brougham and Kingsdown had quickly echoed the verdict of their colleague, and Lord Russell had gone so far as to brand the execution of "a duly authorized privateersman" as murder. Distinguished

British leaders could have saved their breath; their opinions had no effect upon Washington. (JSHS, 1, 155; *Columbiad*, vol. 1, no. 1)

When it became apparent after three months that he would receive no reply to his message that had been hand delivered to the Federal capital, Davis directed Confederate Acting Secretary of State Judah P. Benjamin to send an order to Winder. Issued from the War Department in Richmond on November 9, 1861, it did not include the emotion-charged word "hostage." Yet it instructed the provost marshal to "choose by lot" a captive officer of the highest rank. When selected, he must be "confined in a cell appropriated to convicted felons," Benjamin wrote. This officer must then "be held for execution in the same manner as may be adopted by the enemy for the execution of the prisoner of war, [Walter W.] Smith, recently condemned to death in Philadelphia."

So far as the Rebel cabinet officer was concerned, selection of a hostage for the life of Smith would end the lottery. He did not know that it would prove impossible for Winder to select 13 additional field officers who would be held responsible for the lives of remaining captured privateers. The decision to choose three line officers by lottery and then to select substitutes for two of them by the same process was made by the Rebel commandant of prisons. (OR, 116, 738)

When news of the life-and-death lotteries in which a New York congressman played a central role reached the Northern public, an immense furor resulted. Officials of the War Department in Washington received a constant stream of angry and emotion-charged messages from relatives and friends of the hostages. These men were temporarily transferred to Richmond's public jail, since it was the only facility that met specifications of the Davis proclamation; soon plans were made to disperse them to other prisons. (PH, 9, 36; NYH, 7/61; WS, 7–8/61)

Each of the 14 hostages was by then fully aware that his plight had come about as a result of a power struggle between two warring sections of what had once been a single nation. Responding to the blockade proclaimed by Lincoln, civilian-owned and -manned vessels that had been licensed by Confederates had gone to sea. Some of their crewmembers who were labeled pirates were staring death in the face—and a band of anxious hostages wondered what might happen next.

2

"Easy Money"—The Confederate Privateersmen

Businessmen of New Orleans habitually congregated about 1:00 P.M. at a tavern in the French Quarter. Usually they talked about incoming and outbound vessels, the tide, and their own affairs. On or about April 20, 1861, they were joined by veteran seaman John Wilson. He went from table to table, breaking into conversations by announcing: "Easy money!" As soon as he had a few listeners, he informed them that he had "absolutely sure proof" that Jefferson Davis was offering to commission vessels as privateers. Strictly speaking, the term applied only to armed vessels under commission; in practice, it was widely used to designate members of a privateer's crew. When a little Yankee trader was spotted, Wilson explained, even a lightly armed vessel could take her and her cargo as a prize. What's more, it would take only a small amount of capital to get started.

Some of the men who were in the tavern that day put their heads together, made a few quick calculations, and decided immediately to form a stock company in order to equip a ship and put her to sea. They congratulated themselves on getting an old 500-ton pilot boat at a bargain price, renamed it the *J. C. Calhoun*, and shopped around for guns. By the time a Confederate commission arrived early in the third week of May, their side-wheel steamer named for South Carolina's famous "father of the nullification theory" was armed with one 18-pounder, two 12-pounders, and two 6-pounders. With Wilson as master, the first Confederate privateer slipped into the Gulf of Mexico in search of prey. (NOR, 1, 818–19; *Columbiad*, vol. 1, no. 1)

Wilson and his men initially found the pickings to be as easy as he had promised. His first prize, the *Ocean Eagle*, was so covered with barnacles that she was barely able to move at a slow pace; but her cargo of lime was worth more than $20,000. Within days the privateer captured the schooners *John Adams* and *Mermaid* along with the bark *Panama*. Every man-jack in the crew of 150 began dreaming of a life of leisure devoted to spending his share of the fast-mounting prize money.

11

A nation in every sense except diplomatic recognition, the Confederate States produced its own great seal.

They did not know that Union Secretary of the Navy Gideon Welles had already put Federal warships on their trail. On June 17, Welles notified Acting Rear Adm. James L. Lardner that vessels of the West India Squadron should be on the lookout for "the steam privateer *J. C. Calhoun.*" The Confederate vessel was believed to be headed toward the region in which the coal-laden *Whistling Wind*, bound for New Orleans out of Philadelphia, had been burned by Rebels. (NOR, 2, 354)

As soon as he spotted big frigates headed in his direction, Wilson decided to put into port and lie low until warships left these waters. From other masters, he soon learned that instead of decreasing in number, vessels of the Union navy were heading into the Gulf in droves. Their presence made it foolhardy to leave New Orleans again, so when the Crescent City was captured by David G. Farragut's warships one year after the start of hostilities the *Calhoun* was burned in her berth.

The fall of New Orleans on April 29, 1862, blew at least eight other steamers and the bark *Matilda* out of the water. Numerous citizens of Charleston had already begun to outfit privateers, so the center of activity shifted far to the east. In the city where the Civil War began, the steamers *Gordon* and *Rattlesnake* were quickly converted. At least four schooners and the bark *Jefferson Davis*—whose name was customarily slightly abbreviated—also left Charleston in search of Yankee merchantmen. Residents of Mobile, Baltimore, Wilmington, and Norfolk celebrated when their privateers took to sea, but of more than two dozen ships that received Confederate commissions only the little *Davis* and her sister ship, the *Savannah*, became widely known in the North as well as the South. (NOR, 2, 818–20)

From the temporary Confederate capital a Letter of Marque and Reprisal was issued that led to selection of hostages nearly seven months later. It said:

> Know ye that by virtue of the power vested in me by law, I Jefferson Davis have commissioned and do hereby commission, have authorized and do hereby authorize the schooner or vessel called the *Savannah* (more particularly described in the schedule hereunto annexed) whereof T. Harrison Baker is commander, to act as a private armed vessel in the service of the Confederate States on the high seas, against the United

When chasing prey, the privateer *Savannah* displayed the Union flag
until within range of its target.

States of America, their ships, vessels, goods, and effects, and those of
their citizens during the pendency of the war now existing between the
said Confederates States and the said United States.

This commission to continue in force until revoked by the President
of the Confederate States for the time being.

Schedule of descriptions of the vessel: name, *Savannah*, schooner;
tonnage, 53 41/95 tons; armament, one large pivot gun and small arms;
number of crew, 30.

Given under my hand and the seal of the Confederate States at Montgomery, this eighteenth day of May, A. D. 1861.

JEFFERSON DAVIS

By the President:

R. Tombs, *Secretary of State* (NOR, 5, 691–92)

Soon after this commission was issued, Confederate authorities prepared and circulated a set of detailed instructions to men handling "private
armed vessels." Masters of privateers were assured that they could take
prizes within Union waters, but were warned to stay three miles away from
coasts of countries "at peace both with the United States and the Confederate States."

Vessels of neutral powers were to be left strictly alone, privateersmen were told. Except for contraband of war, even property belonging to the enemy and carried on neutral vessels was not to be seized. In a move to make sure that men planning to prey upon enemy shipping understood precisely what property could be seized in most instances, a formal list of contraband items was included:

> All arms and implements, serving for the purposes of war by land or sea, such as cannons, mortars, guns, muskets, rifles, pistols, petards, bombs, grenades, ball, shot, shell, fuses, pikes, swords, bayonets, javelins, lances, horse furniture, holsters, belts and generally all other implements of war.
>
> Also, timber for ship building, pitch, tar, rosin, copper in sheets, sails, hemp, cordage, and generally whatever may serve directly to the equipment of vessels, unwrought iron and planks only excepted. (NOR, 28, 340)

Investors plus masters of privateers were required to fill in the blanks of a pre-printed form by which they provided bond that they would "observe the laws of the Confederate States, and the instructions for the regulation of their conduct." (NOR, 28, 241–42)

After sailing from Charleston on June 3, the little *Savannah* took the sugar-loaded brig *Joseph* as a prize on her second day out of port. Since no havens except those of the Confederacy were open to any privateer, Rebel seamen were put aboard the captured vessel and it was ordered to Beaufort, South Carolina. In waters about 60 miles east of Charleston, the *Savannah* exchanged fire with the USS *Perry* soon after dark the next day. Only a few shots came from guns of the *Perry*, but after about 20 minutes Commander Baker and his remaining 19 seamen gave up the fight and surrendered. Their capitulation made the *Savannah* the first privateer to be captured. (NOR, 1, 28–29)

Baker and his men were put aboard the southbound *Perry* as prisoners, but most of them were soon transferred to the northbound USS *Minnesota*. Before the month ended, 13 men from the *Savannah* were in New York City's notorious Tombs Prison. After spending a month in irons the prisoners were taken to the Federal Circuit Court for a trial over which Justice Samuel Nelson presided. A 10-count indictment against them was based largely upon statutes enacted in 1790 and 1820. Since the defendants faced the likelihood of conviction and death sentences, the plight of these men from the *Savannah* led Davis to pen his lengthy July 6 challenge to Abraham Lincoln. (JSHS, 1, 153–54)

Counsels for the defense pointed out that several captives were not citizens of the United States, hence were not covered by the Act of 1790. Their removal from this portion of the indictment left only Baker, John Harleston, and Charles S. Passalaigue to defend themselves against charges of piracy on the high seas. After one week of hearings the case went to the jury, whose members were hopelessly divided in their views. It took the court just one day to acknowledge the existence of a hung jury and to bind the defendants over to its next session. (Davis, *Short History of the C.S.A.*, 128–30)

Another Charleston-based privateer, the *Jeff Davis*, put to sea three weeks later than the *Savannah*. Its first prize was the brig *John Welsh*, but the schooners *Enchantress* and *S. J. Waring* soon fell prey to its 75 men and five guns. On July 9 the brig *Mary E. Thompson* and the schooner *Mary Goodell* were captured. The *Jeff Davis* then roamed until July 21, when she took the brig *Alvarado*. Early in August the brig *Santa Clara* and the *John Carver*, whose type was not recorded, fell prey to the *Jeff Davis*. During six weeks she made eight captures—twice as many as any other privateer regardless of how long it cruised—and became feted throughout the Confederacy and hated in the Union. (NOR, 1, 818–19)

In seafaring cities of the North, the Lincoln administration was widely castigated for failing to put a stop to depredations of privateers. Near hysteria that did not subside for years gripped much of the Union, and was especially acute in and near major seaports. Gen. Benjamin Alvord warned Washington that the Union consul stationed at Victoria, Canada, was believed to have plans to "fit out a privateer." In order to prevent this, Alvord wanted the USS *Saginaw* or some other naval vessel sent to Puget Sound at once. (OR, 109, 677–78)

From Portland came news that three conspirators had tried to seize the Union revenue cutter *Shubrick* in order to turn her into a privateer. M. B. Duffield, Union marshal of Arizona, notified the Union vice consul at Guaymas, Mexico, that "certain parties from the valley of the Mississippi" had come into the region. They were believed to be seeking a ship or ships that could be stolen, armed, and put to work for the Confederacy, he said. From San Francisco, provost marshal Capt. Robert Robinson notified Gen. John S. Mason that a man known only as Frazier should be watched carefully. He was described as "about five feet ten, weight 175 or 180, about fifty-five years of age, a little stoop shouldered." According to Robinson, Frazier was on the West Coast seeking to find ships that could be used as privateers. (OR, 106, 323–24, 907–8, 957)

Though Rebel privateers had been driven from the sea much earlier, in November 1864, Union Secretary of State William H. Seward had reason to voice fears that a new international crisis might be in the making. Writing to Secretary of War Edwin M. Stanton, he sent a translation of a document believed to have originated in the French legation to the United States. According to it, President Benito Pablo Juarez of Mexico seemed to be following in the footsteps of Jefferson Davis. He was alleged to be having privateers constructed at New Orleans and San Francisco—presumably in order to prey upon French shipping. About the same time,

New Orleans was by far the largest city in the Confederacy.

Gen. Irvin McDowell seized in San Francisco a vessel that Peru was believed to be fitting out as a privateer. (OR, 106, 1068–69, 1105)

Perhaps as a result of a discernible swing in public opinion about the dangers posed by privateers, numerous officials seemed to feel it necessary to demonstrate their patriotism and their zeal for the war effort. In this climate, the case of Walter W. Smith became the most celebrated of many that revolved around privateersmen.

As a petty officer of the *Jeff Davis*, on July 16 he was put aboard the captured *Enchantress* as prize master. Six days later, less than three hundred miles from Charleston and safety, he was overtaken by the USS *Albatross*. A fourth-rate wooden screw steam of only 378 tons, the battery of the Federal vessel consisted of four 32-pounders and one 12-pounder rifle. Once his prize was within range of Federal guns, Smith realized that his merchant vessel did not have a chance.

Consequently he surrendered on the day after Bull Run; the *Enchantress* became a Federal prize and Smith was heavily ironed and treated as a pirate. Four other seamen from the *Jeff Davis* who were aboard the *Enchantress*—Eben Lane of Massachusetts, Daniel Mullins of Charleston, Edward Rochford of Liverpool, and Thomas Quigley of New York—knew that their lives were also in jeopardy. After a brief stop at Hampton Roads, the *Albatross* took her prisoners to Philadelphia. Meanwhile, the *Jeff Davis*—which had earlier been a slaver—was wrecked near the southern tip of Florida. (NOR, 28, 30; RR, 2, D, 51; RR, 3, Doc. #10)

Prize master Smith was arraigned on October 22 "in the district court of the United States in and for the eastern district of Pennsylvania in the third circuit, of August sessions." The extremely long bill of indictment that was read by the clerk of court charged that the defendant:

> did with force and arms piratically, feloniously and violently set upon board, break and enter a certain American vessel, to wit a schooner called the Enchantress, the same being then and there owned in whole or in part by Benjamin Davis, jr., Richard Plummer, John T. Page, Ezekiel Evans, J. B. Creasy, J. W. Creasy and E. M. Read, citizens of the United States of America, [taking] 75 sacks of corn, 100 barrels of mackerel, 170 grindstones, 50 boxes of candles, 23,000 feet of white pine boards, 200 covered hams, 30 tierces of lard, 50 barrels of clear pork, 200 quarter boxes of soap and package of glassware of the value of $5,000 . . . (OR, 116, 58–59)

After three days the trial over which Justice Robert C. Grier presided ended with a verdict of guilty. It took four more days for the court to deal with three of Smith's subordinates, however. This time, their places of birth or residence made no difference to the judge, and the trio were also given death sentences on October 29.

Eben Lane pled that as steersman of the prize vessel he had secretly handled the wheel in such fashion that the *Enchantress* was kept on the

Tens of thousands of men in blue ate and drank at the Union Volunteer Saloon in Philadelphia, Pennsylvania.
F. B. Schell, *The Soldier in Our Civil War*

open sea long enough to be captured. In the light of evidence that supported this testimony, he was found not guilty. As a result the Philadelphia trials ended with four privateersmen facing the gallows. Much of the arguments and testimony as well as examinations and cross-examinations of the accused and of witnesses has been preserved. (OR, 116, 58–121)

In the aftermath of one of the most celebrated jury trials of the century, authorities in Richmond tried to count the heads of men who faced execution for having taken a Confederate commission at face value. Walter W. Smith's name was by now familiar throughout much of the North and of the South, so he headed the list. He and his three subordinates, along with Baker and his men, were clearly in danger; so were other men who had been captured aboard privateers. Yet at the time Richmond decided to hold hostages, no Rebel seamen except those from the *Savannah* and the *Jeff Davis* were taken into account.

Richmond apparently did not know the full truth about events that took place in a Philadelphia courtroom. Though Lane was found to be innocent and did not face the gallows, he must have been included in the count made by Davis or Benjamin. Their error meant that 14 captured officers were held hostages for 13 Rebels—most of whom were ordinary seamen. One surplus hostage plus deliberate failure to observe the "rank for rank" provision of later exchange cartels made Confederate handling of this matter stink in the nostrils of Federal officials who knew the whole story. Still, they could not avoid recognizing that their president's proclamation triggered the series of actions that were taken in Ligon Prison.

On May 30, 1862, the roll of "privateer prisoners confined at Fort Lafayette" in New York harbor included all of the men for whom hostages had been chosen. In addition, the Federal installation held three men from the *York*, seven from the *Sumter*, six from the *Dixie*, and 30 from the *Petrel*. Dramatic lotteries held in Libby Prison in order to select Federal officers as hostages had riveted the attention of the world upon the piracy issue. Yet the choice of 14 men who were considered "liable for the safety of Rebel seamen in northern prisons" had failed to put an end to the issue. (OR, 116, 611)

Hostages having been deliberately selected, their fate—and the fate of "pirates" who also faced death—was yet to be determined. In the light of this torturous dilemma, perhaps it was natural that there should be no single act by which the long-drawn drama would come to an end. Instead, the officers whose names had been drawn by Congressman Ely soon found that their cases seemed almost to be treated on an individual basis.

3

Somehow, Hostages Made It

613 SPRING GARDEN STREET, PHILADELPHIA

December 13, 1861

HON. SIMON CAMERON, *Secretary of War.*

SIR: Here is my husband and a number of other brave men now confined in a damp jail. As my husband writes to me he is of the firm opinion that if something is not done soon that some of these gentlemen will not be able to bear up under their weight of trouble, not being able to enjoy even a walk when the days are so clear and lovely. . . .

And now would it not be best to release those men called pirates and give them a chance to be good citizens again? Probably they never would commit another crime. They have not been forgiven, ninety and nine times; no, not even once have they been forgiven, which is dreadful to think of. Their families certainly are in deep sorrow at the dreadful suspense which they are kept in; days and nights of intense anxiety must prevail among all of us unhappy wives and mothers and children of those unfortunate hostages and so-called pirates. . . . my child comes home from school and cries whenever he thinks of his kind and indulgent father whom he has not seen for five months.

He left home July 15 as Capt. Francis J. Keffer, Company H, First California Regiment, the late Col. E. D. Baker's brigade, and was taken prisoner at Ball's Bluff, October 21. He does not complain for he knows he is not the only one who is suffering, but he wishes me to appeal to you and President Lincoln in his behalf. . . .

Will you please give an answer to this if it is only a few words that I may know you received this.

Mrs. A Keffer.

P.S.—Mr. Cameron, please let the President read this or have it read to him, and as I cannot appear in person before Congress to plead let me beg of you or some one else to plead for me and suffering humanity in this deplorable case. Do not throw this aside as of no use, but do all that lies in your power. You can show this letter to any one you choose; print it, publish it or anything, only so justice is done to the poor prisoners everywhere through the land which gave them birth. (OR, 116, 160–61)

Keffer and his comrades, most of whom were from Pennsylvania, named their regiment in honor of distant California—where Colonel Baker had been a prominent political leader. There is no record that his wife's appeal, here considerably abbreviated, ever reached the eyes of the president who had declared that privateersmen must be treated as pirates. Neither is there any record that Cameron replied to the wife of one of the hostages who were selected in Richmond.

Keffer's case was exceptional in only one respect: his wife wrote long letters in his behalf and some of them have been preserved. The date of his capture was such that he had been a prisoner of war less than one month before his status abruptly changed and he became a hostage. Col. William Raymond Lee was in the same predicament, for he was also taken during the battle that claimed the life of Col./Sen. Edward D. Baker, a friend of Lincoln so intimate that the future president named one of his sons Edward Baker.

At least two of Keffer's fellow hostages, Cols. Michael Corcoran and Orlando B. Willcox became prisoners at Bull Run. Maj. Israel Vodges was taken in early October, when Rebels made an unsuccessful attempt to storm Federal works on Santa Rosa Island, Florida. Scarey Creek, Virginia (now West Virginia) was the most obscure point at which a hostage was captured; Lt. Col. George W. Neff fell into the hands of secessionists there just four days before Bull Run. (OR, 116, 136; DxD, 852, 1073, 1074)

In the early summer of 1862, Keffer's wife dispatched another letter to Stanton that has been preserved. After having identified her husband, she wrote that

> I think he is confined in the jail with six other officers, or rather speaking, a place where rats inhabit the room, and damp, too, but he does not complain to me, but I know this to be a fact and I expected when Mr. [Alfred] Ely came he would try to do something, and I hope he will use all the means in his power to have every prisoner released. Cannot anything be done to have all the prisoners released at once? Does it acknowledge the Southern Confederacy any more to have a large number released than a small number? Will you let me know if I shall write to the Tombs [prison in New York City] and ask if there is any one there that they would exchange for my husband, or must I not do it?
>
> I have written twice to Secretary Cameron and to President Lincoln and to Mr. Ely and to Fort Warren, but it does seem that none have answered but the one at Fort Warren, and the commanding officer tells me that the South will not give up one for any other than a privateer, but this does not satisfy a woman. May I write to the mayor of New York on this

subject? I will do whatever you think proper. If you can send me a few lines I will be very thankful for it.

Mrs. ADELINE KEFFER

No. 613 Spring Garden Street, Philadelphia (OR, 117, 100–101)

Again considerably abbreviated, this letter that was sent to Cameron's successor in office seems to have been ignored in spite of being preserved. Matters that appeared logical and simple to a female civilian were viewed as convoluted and extremely complex by leaders in the North and in the South.

Adeline Keffer's husband's name again appeared in the record on February 1, 1863. That is when Lt. Col. George Sinister, commanding a detail of paroled prisoners whose status was quite different from that of hostages, made a formal report to Col. William Hoffman. Keffer, he wrote, "has been detailed in accordance with your request." By November of that year, Adeline's husband was again in a blue uniform and was serving in the office of the provost marshal at Annapolis, Maryland. (OR, 118, 332; OR, 119, 536)

From the instant that his name was drawn from a ballot box by Congressman Alfred Ely, Col. Michael Corcoran's status was different from that of the 13 other men who were selected in Libby Prison. He was specifically designated as hostage for Capt. Walter W. Smith of the *Savannah*—the captured privateersman of highest rank at that time. The native of Ireland who was a prewar officer of the New York Militia was better prepared than other hostages to be at the center of a storm of controversy. At the time Maj. Robert Anderson decided to evacuate Fort Sumter, Corcoran was facing a court-martial. When England's Prince of Wales and future king visited the state in 1859, the fiery Irishman refused to call out his regiment in honor of the royal Englishman. Charges went into limbo upon the outbreak of war, and were never pursued. (WWW, 143–44)

Corcoran's earliest wartime duties were performed near the Arlington House mansion of Mrs. Robert E. Lee. Since he and his men helped to build an early set of fortifications for the Federal capital, admirers dubbed the installation Fort Corcoran. After having led his regiment to Bull Run he was captured

Here depicted after having become a general, Irish-born Col. Michael Corcoran was the first man whose name Congressman Ely drew in the Richard lottery.

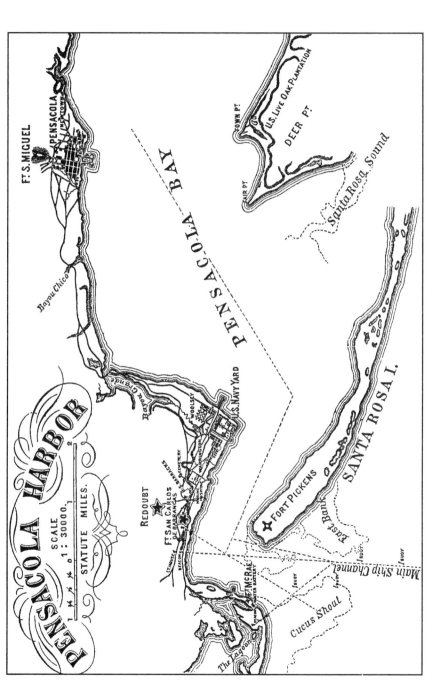

An island in Pensacola Bay housed the only important fort except Sumter that lay within a seceded state.
The Rebellion Record

on the field of battle and sent to the prison at which he became one of the most celebrated hostages of 1861–65.

Early in December 1861, the Confederate secretary of war notified Gen. Benjamin Huger that some rules concerning prisoners of war would be relaxed a bit. But he added that this relaxation "will not apply to those who are held confined in cells as hostages for our privateers captured by the enemy." (OR, 116, 749)

Corcoran was sent to Charleston, South Carolina, where he was imprisoned when Capt. Benjamin Huger, Jr., declined Gen. J. E. Wool's offer to exchange privateersman Smith for the Federal officer. From the port city he reached the jail in Columbia, South Carolina, on January 2, 1862. Fellow inmate Maj. James D. Potter, who was not a hostage, confided in February to a friend that inmates "neither expected an

Among the 14 hostages for privateersmen, Maj. Israel Vodges had been captured at the southernmost point.

Photographic History

exchange or release from our present most unpleasant position until the privateers are placed in the same relation as other prisoners of war."

From Columbia, the man noted for having led an all-Irish regiment into battle was sent to Salisbury, North Carolina. Finally paroled in August 1862, he received a commission as a brigadier that was retroactive to July 21, 1861. After having survived months of torturous imprisonment as a hostage, he was killed at Fairfax Court House when his horse fell. (RD, 1/62; OR, 116, 216, 242; WWW, 143–44)

Col. Alfred M. Wood had influential friends and relatives. On December 3, 1861, the House of Representatives noted that after having been wounded and captured he was confined "in a felon's prison." Hoping to effect his release, lawmakers suggested that the president order his exchange for John Slidell, a Rebel envoy who was central to the *Trent* case that threatened to bring Great Britain into the war. (OR, 116, 1115)

Maj. Israel Vodges, third among men of his rank in John Whyte's list of hostages, graduated from West Point at age 21 as #11 in the class of 1837. Future generals Joseph Hooker, Jubal Early, Braxton Bragg, and John Sedgwick were among the classmates of the Pennsylvania native. Captured while helping to defend Fort Pickens, he had earlier been stationed at Fort

Moultrie in Charleston harbor. His wife also tried to intercede for him, suggesting without avail that he be exchanged for Confederate Maj. G. B. Cosby. Three months after being exchanged in August 1862, he became a brigadier general. (OR, 116, 563; GB, 529–39)

Along with Col. W. Raymond Lee, Maj. P. J. Revere of the 20th Massachusetts was lodged in the Henrico County, Virginia, jail on January 1, 1862. Revere was brought back to Virginia late in February 1862, and was immediately forwarded to Baltimore. Gen. George B. McClellan personally penned a request for his immediate exchange on February 25, but he had no influence in Richmond. Two months later, Gen. Lorenzo Thomas suggested that he be exchanged for Maj. E. W. Alexander of the 27th Alabama. Details of an exchange were worked out on April 4, at which time Confederate Col. George S. Patton of the 22nd Virginia reported that he had also been exchanged for Revere or Lee. The Rebel officer was mistaken, the agreement to exchange Revere for Alexander was implemented. Patton was somehow involved, but did not know exactly what his role had been. (OR, 116, 174, 334, 414–16, 424, 840)

In Richmond, Atty. Gen. Judah P. Benjamin had gone on record three weeks earlier as being pleased to have unofficial word that "privateers previously treated as felons" were now to become prisoners of war. His pleasure was premature; Gen. Howell Cobb warned him to hold on to the hostages, since he believed policy makers in Washington "intend to back out from their own proposition" to make exchanges. Cobb was right; Wool did not make a firm promise to deliver the privateersmen for exchange until May 19. Some exchanges took place—quietly and without notices being sent to newspapers—before the month ended. Other exchanges were delayed, and the transactions were not completed until late in the summer. (OR, 116, 553, 789–90, 808–9)

Col. Orlando B. Willcox of the 1st Michigan also went to the South after spending a period in a Richmond jail. In February, Thomas told Mrs. Marie L. Willcox that "three-fold more trouble" had been taken by his office "to effect the release of Colonel Willcox than in the case of any other of our captive officers and men." Late in the winter of 1861–62 he and six other hostages were among 372 prisoners who were returned to Virginia on a single steamer. Union Gen. John E. Wool, who was already giving broad hints that all charges of piracy would be dismissed or ignored, made a special request for the exchange of Willcox on April 25. Three weeks later he intimated willingness to exchange or parole all of the privateersmen if the same terms could be extended to all hostages selected during the previous November. (OR, 116, 323, 514, 552, 595, 884–85)

Suddenly negotiations that had been proceeding smoothly became tangled. Two weeks passed before Willcox and other hostages went aboard the steamer *Massachusetts* for a short trip to City Point, Virginia. Wool, who based his agreement upon a simultaneous exchange of hostages for privateersmen, cited "the cartel agreed upon between the United States and Great Britain" at the close of the War of 1812—during which the Union made great use of privateers and their crews. Almost as an afterthought, Wool added a postscript to his dispatch of June 1. In it, he said that "After the above delivery on parole of privateersmen and hostages I presume there will be no difficulty as regards future exchanges." Fog delayed the arrival of the *Massachusetts*, but after additional bickering and bargaining, some of the planned exchanges were made. (OR, 116, 654–57)

Numerous privateersmen were still confined at Fort Hamilton in New York harbor, however, and they were becoming extremely restless. On June 25 Lt. Col. Martin Burke of the Confederate 3rd Artillery reported to Thomas that prisoners had refused to police their quarters and had shouted their approval of Jefferson Davis. As a result of these and other "evidences of insubordination," the noisemakers had been clapped in irons. (OR, 116, 65–66)

By a strange coincidence, a long report drafted at Martinique bore the same date as Benjamin's directive to Winder. Summarizing his voyage to date, Cmdr. Raphael Semmes of the raider CSS *Sumter* detailed his capture of 18 Yankee vessels. When he stopped at Trinidad on July 30, he wrote, he learned about the plight of Smith and men from the *Savannah,* who had been seething with fury for days. Upon making port, he learned that hostages had been chosen to guarantee the safety of men aboard the *Savannah* and other privateers, so recorded his satisfaction by saying that

> it had been my intention, had the Government of the United States dared to carry out its barbarous threat of treating the prisoners of the privateer Savannah, who had fallen into its hands, as pirates, to retaliate on them and their crew by hanging man for man [of prisoners held on the Sumter], but I was glad that this unpleasant duty had not, as appeared by late intelligence, been imposed upon me. (NOR, 1, 633)

On April 7, Wool asked for positive confirmation that Revere could be released from his parole. Evidently that came quickly, for the former hostage was cited by Gen. E. V. Sumner for distinguished conduct at Antietam. (OR, 116, 430–31; OR, 27, 276)

Washington never made a formal announcement that charges of piracy lodged against privateersmen had been dropped. Instead, small groups of men whose lives were long in jeopardy were quietly transferred to the category, "prisoner of war." This procedure meant that the Lincoln administration was never faced with public humiliation at having to make a major change in its announced policy. It also meant that all of the 13 privateersmen who were endangered in November 1861 and the 14 hostages held for them, lived through the ordeal.

When each exchange had been effected, every man had a separate story to tell. Records do not indicate whether hostages realized that they were in extremely rare and distinguished company. Some of them were aware that Confederate Maj. George S. Patton was positive he had been exchanged for one of the hostages, but did not know which Federal officer was involved.

If they made any written comments about the fact that Maj. P. J. Revere was a grandson of Revolutionary hero Paul Revere, their notes and memos about him and his ancestor have disappeared. Not a man who played a key role in the long-drawn hostage drama imagined that George S. Patton, Jr., would play a key role in World War II and would briefly succeed Dwight D. Eisenhower as commander of United States forces in Europe.

Men aboard the privateer CSS *Tacony* (*right*) burned some of the ships they captured, and Federal officials said they faced the death penalty for piracy.

4

Zarvona—7 for 1

Capt. George N. Hollins of the Confederate navy took off his uniform before going to the Point Lookout wharf at which he planned to board the side-wheel passenger steamer *St. Nicholas*. His story of what soon took place differs somewhat from that told by others who were present on June 28–29, 1861. Union Secretary of the Navy Gideon Welles later reported that he had received information that a spectacular hijacking had been planned by James C. Hurry of Baltimore, "a man of notoriously bad character." Dozens of newspaper correspondents and editors attributed a chain of dramatic events to the colonel of a Virginia militia unit. (NOR, 4, 569)

According to Hollins, a band of his men—also dressed as civilians—accompanied him aboard the little passenger carrier. Within minutes after boarding they spotted Col. Richard Thomas, a soldier of fortune who began calling himself Zarvona while fighting in Europe. Now a Virginia officer, Zarvona was disguised as a female whom fellow passengers believed to be Madame La Force. At the instigation of Hollins, he had gone into the North and had spent about $1,000 securing a supply of arms and ammunition. His purchases were aboard the steamer, packed in a number of "high, large trunks such as milliners use."

When Hollins gave a signal to his men, they pulled the trunks open and extracted the weapons. Taking a Sharps rifle and two pistols, the naval officer raced to the wheel house and told the captain that his boat had been captured. Bound toward Washington, the course of the vessel was changed to a landing on Coan River in Virginia. At this rendezvous point, Capt. Henry H. Lewis led a body of Maryland Zouaves in colorful Near Eastern uniforms aboard.

While the captured steamer was being made secure, Hollins picked up a Baltimore newspaper and read an account of the death of Union navy Capt. James H. Ward. Killed while leading an assault upon Mathias Point, Virginia, according to the newspaper all of the Federal warships "had gone

Richard Thomas, who preferred to be called Zarvona, boarded the *St. Nicholas* at a landing close to Baltimore's Federal Hill.

Frank Leslie's Illustrated Weekly

up the [Potomac] river to Washington to the funeral." This news meant that the goal of the hijacking—capture of the mighty USS *Pawnee* at its berth in Aquia Creek—could not be accomplished.

Hollins therefore put in to land early on Sunday and told civilians aboard that they could return to Baltimore if they wished. According to him, his offer had only a few takers "as nearly all were on their way South." He seems to have been a bit disconcerted when ladies on the captured vessel spent much of the Sabbath "amusing themselves by making Confederate flags out of the Yankee flags I had captured."

Knowing that the *Pawnee* was at Washington and having no cannon aboard, Hollins decided to put into Fredericksburg and turned into Chesapeake Bay. He soon spotted and took as a prize the brig *Monticello*, "bound for Baltimore out of Rio" with a full cargo of coffee. Lt. Robert D. Minor and a number of seamen were put aboard the *Monticello* and told to take her to Fredericksburg. Less than an hour later, the Rebel-held *St. Nicholas* captured the schooner *Mary Pierce* out of Boston and headed for Washington with a cargo of ice. Another officer and prize crew were put aboard and ordered to Fredericksburg, where Hollins knew that wounded men would rejoice at getting ice.

According to the Confederate naval officer's story, the captain of the ice freighter soon came to him with a proposition. He would gladly go back to Boston and get another cargo of ice, he said. He could then meet Hollins at a prearranged point, where his ship could be captured so they could "sell the ice and divide the proceeds." To some men the offer might have been tempting, but Hollins dismissed it, asking himself only, "Would anyone but a Yankee have been guilty of such rascality?"

A third capture was soon made; the north-bound *Margaret*, steaming from Baltimore toward Boston, proved to have 270 tons of coal in her hold. When he learned what he had taken Hollins was overjoyed, since he was on his "last bucket of coal in the *St. Nicholas*." Using steam produced by captured coal, he ran his passenger vessel to Fredericksburg, where "the Government bought the *St. Nicholas* for about $45,000 and turned her into a gunboat." Though raiders had not come near the USS *Pawnee*, they considered their mission to be a splendid success and quickly began to plan another one like it. (NOR, 4, 553–55)

Despite the fact that Hollins claimed to have originated the scheme in company with Gov. John Letcher of Virginia, most newspaper headlines were devoted to the Rebel officer who had posed as a female. Artists who had never seen the raider who was being called "The French Lady" produced sketches that featured heavy veils. One editor after another picked up accounts of the Virginia colonel's exploits and quickly made him famous in the South and infamous in the North. Had Washington then issued posters offering rewards for "most wanted men," the name of Zarvona—or Richard Thomas—would have been at or near the top of the list.

Disguised as "The French Lady," Zarvona reputedly attracted the interested attention of other males aboard.

Harper's Weekly

Having been given the credit for the *St. Nicholas* affair, Zarvona decided to strike again, this time without the guidance of Hollins. He chose the steamer *Columbia*, a sister ship of the *St. Nicholas*, and in order to start from an unexpected point crossed the Potomac on a privateer. Backed by only four or five of his men, the raider took passage on the Baltimore-bound *Mary Washington* on July 8. He would have waited for another vessel had he known that several members of the crew of the *St. Nicholas* were aboard. These seamen spotted him almost instantly and alerted fellow passenger John Horner, a Baltimore police officer who was accompanied by Lt. Thomas H. Carmichael of the Middle District police.

Neither of the police officers had given Zarvona a thought before they learned that he had come aboard. They were headed for Fair Haven, Maryland, in Anne Arundel County, hoping to arrest barber Neale Green, who was charged with having taken a leading part in the April 19 Baltimore riot in which soldiers clashed with civilians. With Green in custody and his wife accompanying them, the guardians of the law decided to use the *Mary Washington* for their return trip to their base.

Near Annapolis, both men became convinced that Zarvona was aboard, so Carmichael ordered Capt. Mason L. Weems to take his vessel to Fort

McHenry. Smelling trouble, Zarvona threw off his veil and confronted the police officers with a brace of pistols. With "female passengers running about screaming," it looked as though there might be a standoff. When the *Mary Washington* came alongside the wharf below Fort McHenry, however, Horner dispatched a male passenger to inform Gen. Nathaniel P. Banks that the famous Zarvona was being held at bay.

An entire company of infantry hurried aboard the ship and quickly secured Zarvona's subordinates without having located him. After a 90-minute search the wanted man was discovered "concealed in the drawer of a bureau in the ladies cabin, in the aft part of the boat." The small valise he carried was found to contain "a full uniform of a Zouave, including a cap." With Zarvona and his followers in the custody of Banks, Green was taken to Baltimore's middle police station. After admitting that he had committed an assault upon a soldier, he "was locked up for examination." (*The Baltimore American*, 7/9/61; NOR, 4, 570)

Since there was no positive way to know whether Zarvona's act of "piracy of the worst form" was committed in Maryland or in Virginia waters, Banks was not sure that the trial could proceed in "this criminal district alone." According to the section on "Arrests for Disloyalty" of the Union State Department's record book, military authorities at Baltimore wanted to try their prisoner as a spy as well as a pirate and traitor. During months spent at Fort McHenry awaiting trial, Zarvona managed to get a number of messages smuggled to Virginia newspapers. Publication of them brought public interest in the raider who posed as a European female to new heights. Consequently his July 8 arrest came to be regarded by Federal officials as one of the principal events of the period. (OR, 114, 586–87; OR, 115, 1, 379)

Thomas C. Fitzpatrick, who was charged with having taken part in the seizure of the *St. Nicholas*, was arrested late in July and was soon transferred to Fort Lafayette. Protesting that he was a British subject, he won a brief release and was last heard from on February 15, 1862, when still at Fort Lafayette. Another Zarvona follower, 1st Lt. G. W. Alexander of the Confederate provisional army, was captured and spent about 70 days at Fort McHenry before making his escape. Gen. John A. Dix, who replaced Banks

Admirers of Gen. John A. Dix lauded him as "the very best."
Harper's Pictorial History of the Great Rebellion

Prisoners being landed at Fort Lafayette in New York harbor.

as commandant at Fort McHenry, was soon tired of hearing about his notorious prisoner and wrote to Seward that "It would be a great convenience
if all these prisoners including Thomas (Zarvona) could be sent away." Perhaps as a result of this viewpoint by Dix, the prisoner was transferred to
Fort Lafayette on December 2. Dix soon responded to an inquiry from Washington by saying that in his opinion, the famous captive's name "ought not
to be transferred to the list of prisoners of war." (OR, 114, 738–39; OR, 115,
151, 226, 291, 384; OR, 116, 725)

Before Zarvona had been in New York harbor a week, some members
of the U.S. Congress were beginning to urge the administration to adopt a
system of prisoner exchange. Fellow Fort Lafayette inmate William H.
Psidium addressed a letter to Congressman M. F. O'Dell. Protesting that he
had been arrested and jailed without evidence, Psidium pointed out that
though he was not "a prisoner of war taken with arms," such a person was
confined in the room next to his. Insisting that his suggestion should be
kept secret, the civilian prisoner in Fort Lafayette said that for "Richard T.
Zarvona" Rebels would give up Col. A. M. Wood and all members of the
80th New York who had been captured at Bull Run. (OR, 115, 383–84)

By March, conversion of the *St. Nicholas* into a Confederate gunboat
was well under way. In Baltimore, the wealthy and influential mother of
the famous captive was beginning to become restless. On April 3 she addressed a letter to a prison official in which she said that earlier inquiries
had not been answered and protested:

> Excuse a mother's anxiety in requesting you to inform me of the situation
> of my son; also the state of his health. Knowing the active mind that my
> son has I fear much the effects of solitary confinement on his mind. Please

let me know if he received my several letters and a suit of clothes sent by Adams Express March 22.

About the same time, Edward B. Cuthbert sent to Confederate Secretary of War George W. Randolph a long and passionate plea that a Federal colonel be held hostage for the celebrated Rebel officer. (NOR, 5, 759; OR, 116, 396; OR, 117, 774–76)

About the middle of June, Letcher decided that it was time for him to get busy. He reminded Randolph that Zarvona was a West Point graduate that he, the governor, had authorized to raise a regiment for state service. "Upon my own responsibility," he continued, "I took occasion to inform Colonel Zarvona that if the threat of Lincoln's Government to hang him upon the charge of piracy and treason was carried out I would see that two of his grade should hang for him." (OR, 117, 781)

By September, Richmond was beginning to take interest in the case of the man who seemed likely to be executed as a pirate. Robert Ould, agent for exchange, sent a lengthy message to his Federal counterpart in which he called special attention to "the case of Colonel Thomas [Zarvona]." According to information that had reached the Rebel capital, this prisoner was "compelled to endure unusual hardships and cruel privations." It was therefore hoped, said Ould, that "Colonel Thomas will be delivered to us as speedily as it can be done." (OR, 117, 552–53, 555)

Hopes for the prisoner were raised early in the following month, when Ould received a letter from Union Lt. Col. William H. Ladle, an acting commissioner in charge of prisoner exchanges. The Federal official wrote to Richmond that

> The case of Zarvona is yet under advisement. There is every disposition to be lenient. I shall take great pleasure if [it is] in my power and consistent with the public interest in responding to your personal appeal on his behalf.

By October, Randolph was sure that a hostage would be retained for Zarvona, thereby guaranteeing that he would not receive the death penalty. (OR, 117, 909, 914)

William Percher Miles, who had been an aide to Gen. P. G. T. Beauregard during the artillery duel that ended with the surrender of Fort Sumter, was now an official of the Confederate government. Writing from Richmond to his former commander in November, he said that a one-time Federal commissioner of exchange had fallen into disfavor "with the abolition government in Washington." This official had earlier hinted that Zarvona might be exchanged for "a Yankee spy whom we have here under sentence of death," he noted. Unhappily, it no longer seemed likely that such a proposal would be approved by Lincoln, Miles reported. (OR, 117, 934)

Two months later Virginia's chief executive directed a message to the Executive Mansion in Washington. He went to considerable length in telling the president what Maryland-born Zarvona had done, but stressed that he was not to be regarded as a felon since he held a military commission from the state of Virginia. Fuming that the celebrated prisoner had been held for 18 months during which he insisted that no provision of the Union Constitution had been complied with, the governor minced no words in telling Lincoln what he had done.

Virginia state forces, separate from those of the Confederacy, were headed by Gen. John B. Floyd, he said. They presently held 201 prisoners "most of whom have been brought to the city of Richmond for safe custody." From these prisoners Letcher had selected seven men: Capt. Thomas Damron, Lt. Wilson Damron, and Pvts. John W. Howe, Isaac Goble, David V. Auxier, Samuel Pack, and William S. Dils. All of them, the governor warned the president, were to be kept in the penitentiary in solitary confinement, "there to remain until Colonel Zarvona is properly exchanged under suitable agreement or [is] discharged and permitted to return to this city." (OR, 115, 401–3)

Auxier, Goble, and Howe lost no time in sending an urgent plea to the Union secretary of war. Under date of January 5, 1863, they told him that they were in the state penitentiary "as a means of retaliation for the confinement of one Colonel Zarvona." Their brief message ended on a plaintive note: "We beseech you to effect an exchange for us as soon as possible." Before the month ended, Union Col. Wickham Hoffman, commissary general of prisoners, communicated with Ladle who was now at Fort Monroe. He told Ladle that Rebels held seven officers in close confinement for "Zarvona, *alias* Mr. Thomas," whom he identified incorrectly. Urging a general exchange of "those who are suffering in their horrible prisons," he offered to send full rolls if they were needed. (OR, 118, 218–19, 223)

Congressman James R. Morris sent Stanton a newspaper clipping enumerating the hostages held for Zarvona, but refrained from offering comments or suggestions as to a suitable course of action with respect to the matter. Men whose letter was headed "Penitentiary of Virginia, Richmond," were not so reticent. A February 5 letter, signed this time by all seven who were being held responsible for the life of Zarvona, noted that the group included not two but four officers. Characterizing their place of confinement as "loathsome," the Federal soldiers wrote to Congressman G. W. Dunlap because "several letters to Secretary Stanton upon the subject" had brought no reply. Imploring the lawmaker to aid them in their "present suffering condition," they emphasized that the entire matter was at the discretion of Washington since "Governor Letcher has long since notified our Government of his readiness to exchange us." (OR, 115, 407)

When an agent for exchange of prisoners consulted the Union secretary of war about the increasingly tense Zarvona affair, Stanton declined to authorize an exchange. Members of the Confederate Senate suggested to a military leader that Confederate, not state officials, should "set apart hostages for Colonel Z." There is no record that Rebel lawmakers received a reply, but no observer saw any signs of movement concerning Zarvona in Washington. Yet an April 4 dispatch from the Federal agent for exchange of prisoners dealt with the matter in two sentences: "The secretary of War has authorized me to exchange Zarvona. Will you also please have him sent from Fort Lafayette to Fort Delaware?" (OR, 115, 413; OR, 118, 323, 415, 433–34)

Along with 32 other prisoners held by the Union Navy Department at Fort Lafayette, Zarvona started south to Fort Monroe on April 16 "by direction of the Secretary of War." Upon reaching his destination, he was formally exchanged for four Federal officers and three privates. After nearly two years in prison, the flamboyant soldier of fortune wanted no more to do with the Civil War in North America. Perhaps influenced by newspaper publicity about his exploits in disguise, "The French Lady" immediately sailed for France and never returned to the country that was reunited by unconditional surrender of Confederate forces. (OR, 118, 460, 465, 522)

5

Pirates plus Hostages, 1863

CONFEDERATE STATES OF AMERICA, WAR DEPARTMENT
Richmond, Va., December 15, 1863
Brig. Gen. S. A. Meredith, *Agent of Exchange:*
SIR: The Confederate Government has received authentic information that Acting Master John Y. Beall and Edward McGuire, of the Confederate Navy, and fifteen regularly enlisted seamen of the same service,
are now closely confined in irons at Fort McHenry, awaiting trial as pirates. They were recently captured in Virginia. They were engaged in open
warfare and are entitled in every respect to the treatment of prisoners of
war.

With whatever regret retaliatory measures may be adopted, the
course of your authorities leaves no other alternatives. In the hope, therefore, of inducing your Government to accord to these parties the treatment due to prisoners of war, I inform you that Lieut. Commander Edward
P. Williams and Ensign Benjamin H. Porter and fifteen seamen, all of the
Union Navy and prisoners in our hands, have been placed in close confinement in irons and held as hostages for their proper treatment.

Respectfully, your obedient servant,

RO. OULD
Agent of Exchange

Though it employed the language of a gentleman and an officer, this
dispatch almost reads as though its recipients in Washington had never
heard of seamen being charged with piracy and hostages being held for
their safety. All of the Rebel privateersmen plus the Federal officers held as
hostage for them had been exchanged at least two months before the message of December 15, 1863, was penned. The change of policy in classifica-
tion of the early "pirates" was made as quietly as possible, it is true. But all
high-level officials on both sides knew precisely what had taken place.

John Yates Beall managed to escape death as a pirate, but was executed as a convicted spy.
U.S. Naval Historical Center

Why, then, did 15 members of the Confederate navy face the charge of piracy instead of being treated as prisoners of war? Every reader will have to reach a personal conclusion at this point, for there is little or no evidence in the record. It is tempting to blame the 1863 impasse upon slow and unreliable communication, but news of the new batch of Federals who were being held hostage hit the *Richmond Examiner* on December 17—and smuggled copies were scanned daily in Washington. When Beall's life was again laid on the line in 1865, word of his predicament spread very, very rapidly. From Virginia to Canada, interested persons—some of them more than locally notable—quickly did their best to help the accused officer.

By today's standards, communication was intolerably slow. Yet it was fast enough for everyone in the loop to get word within a few days. Well before Christmas, it was widely known that another showdown was in the offing.

Beall was born and reared in Richland County, Virginia (now West Virginia), locally known as part of the Potomac Highlands. Residents delighted in telling newcomers that in 1794 James Madison had taken Dolley Payne Todd as his bride in their county. At age 21 John inherited a large estate from his father and took over its management. Three years later John Brown staged his famous raid at Harpers Ferry, after which he was tried and executed for treason against the state of Virginia in Charles Town. Like the Ferry, the county seat was only a few miles from the Beall estate, and its museum still displays the wagon in which Brown rode to his trial. In the aftermath of the fear of a slave uprising created by Brown's raid, young gentry of Richland organized a self-defense body and called themselves the Botts Grays. (CV, 35, 300–301; CWT 11/61, 23; JSHS, 33, 72; Internet, Richland County history)

Beall may have been the only charter member of the Grays who graduated from the University of Virginia, whose buildings were designed by Thomas Jefferson. While a student he met and became a close friend of aspiring actor John Wilkes Booth, with whose name he is connected in widespread oral traditions. Yet his life was described as "without interest" until most of the Grays went into the 2nd Virginia regiment and became part of the Stonewall Brigade.

His career as a soldier was short, however. After having taken part in the action at Bull Run, he went home on leave and soon after arriving there learned that action was expected close to the plantation. Beall—whose relatives and friends pronounced his name as though it were spelled Bell—hurried to join a force led by Col. Turner Ashby. In an ensuing skirmish he took a bullet that left him permanently impaired. Having been discharged from Confederate forces for medical reasons, he went to Iowa for a couple of years and then migrated into Canada.

At the Queen's Hotel in Toronto, he met and soon became a close friend of North Carolina native Jacob Thompson, 15 years his senior, who was the chief Confederate commissioner to Canada. From Thompson, Beall learned that a treaty between the United States and Great Britain permitted only one warship on the Great Lakes. Thompson probably pointed out to his young friend that if the 14-gun USS *Michigan* could be captured, her battery could be turned upon cities along coasts—and the course of the war might be affected. Beall made several trips between Toronto and Richmond, where he presented a proposal for action against the Federal vessel, plus other water-related ventures. Policymakers gave token approval to his daring and imaginative schemes, but were slow to authorize any plan of action based on them. (CV, 7, 66–67; PH, 8, 208)

Though he already had early symptoms of tuberculosis, linked with the bullet lodged in his lung, Beall wanted to get back into action; in Richmond he pled for a chance to fight again. In February 1863, Confederate Secretary of the Navy Stephen R. Mallory named him to a naval rank that no longer exists— acting master—that carried the courtesy title of captain. That made him a member of the very small group of men who had both military and naval careers during 1861–65.

With Scottish-born Bennett G. Burley as his second in command, he took over two tiny boats, the *Raven* and the *Swan.* As soon as they were ready for action the former member of the Stonewall Brigade began hunting for prey in

Partly because he had no warships when he took office, Stephen R. Mallory was a highly innovative Confederate secretary of the navy.

Artist's conception of a Federal advance at Bull Run.
The Soldier in Our Civil War

Chesapeake Bay. Among the prizes he took only the *Alliance* was large, but nearly a dozen vessels that he captured and destroyed created significant problems for Yankee shippers and their clients. He succeeded in cutting a major telegraph line leading into Baltimore and temporarily made fast communication with other cities impossible. On the heels of having destroyed several lighthouses on Maryland's eastern shore, he became a wanted man in October 1863. (CWT, 11/61, 63)

One of his many admirers, James H. M'Neilly, later insisted that Federal authorities "sent out quite a large expedition of infantry, cavalry, and artillery, with gunboats, to capture him." Jaws of a trap set for him snapped on November 15; he and all of his men were captured. Lt. John W. Conner, Sgt. Robert R. Christopher and a detail of men from Co. B, 1st Eastern Shore Maryland Volunteers, were credited with having taken the man they called a pirate. Taken to Fort McHenry and held in irons, Lt. Col. Wm. H. Chesebrough surveyed the captives and decided that "they will probably be tried as pirates or as robbers, either in the United States court or the local court, unless ordered to trial by military commission." (OR, 48, 639; CWT, 11/61, 23)

Records fail to indicate who ordered the Rebel seamen to be treated as prisoners of war rather than as pirates, but the change took place—without an official announcement concerning it. This time, the hostages selected by Richmond had a comparatively short period of segregation from other captives. After just six months, an exchange was perfected that freed 34 men—half of them Confederates and half Federals.

Though the case of Beall and his crew was the last spectacular instance in which Rebels were charged with piracy and were freed because of leverage exerted by Richmond's use of hostages, they were not the only Southerners who were compared with Blackbeard and Edward Teach in 1863.

Near Pass a l'Outre on the Mississippi River, Confederates aboard a converted towboat captured the bark *Lenox* in June. Members of the Northern press castigated them as pirates, but there is no record that they were formally charged with the crime that could have led to death sentences. During the same month, the bark *Tacony* and the schooner *M. A. Schindler* were taken by the brig *Clarence* at a point "about forty miles off Cape Virginia." Still another vessel, the *Kate Stewart*, soon fell into the hands of privateers. Since there were a number of ladies aboard, captors assented to a practice that was then common. After the master of the *Kate Stewart* gave bond for $7,000 his ship was "ransomed," or permitted to go on her way. Both the *Tacony* and the *M. A. Schindler* were set on fire and abandoned, and the privateersmen were publicly condemned for having committed piracy—but seem never to have gone on trial. (RR, 7, D, 6–7)

Beall, Thompson, and other expatriates concocted a plot by which several targets would be struck nearly simultaneously. Johnson's Island, Ohio, where numerous Rebel officers were imprisoned plus sprawling Camp

Douglas at Chicago were central to their scheme, which is often dubbed the Northwest Conspiracy.

Effectively to strike at Johnson's Island, Beall insisted that he needed the *Michigan*. Preparing to take over the warship, he captured the steamers *Philo Parsons* and *Island Queen*, then decided he did not need the latter and sunk her. Hoping soon to train guns of the warship upon the Lake Erie prison, the attempt at its capture was bungled and his entire plan of operations had to be scrapped. The Northwest Conspiracy, whose importance is frequently challenged today, came to nothing as a result of a plotter having turned informer. (JSHS, 33, 72–74)

Knowing that trains regularly took prisoners from Johnson's Island to Fort Warren in Boston harbor, the Virginia raider turned his attention to the railroad between Dunkirk, New York, and Buffalo, New York, that was used for such traffic. Three attempts to derail the train failed, and on the heels of the final effort Beall was captured at Suspension Bridge, New York, not by soldiers in blue but by local police. Since he was arrested in civilian clothing, he was automatically charged with being a spy. When directed into a room at Fort Lafayette, he found that Gen. Roger A. Pryor, recently captured in Virginia, would share the space with him. Knowing his life to be in jeopardy, the raider tried to persuade captors to permit Pryor to represent him at his trial. Gen. John A. Dix, noted as a strict disciplinarian and stickler for the letter of regulations, said that no prisoner of war could act as counsel for another inmate of a Federal facility. (CWT, 11/61, 23; Internet, John Yates Beall)

Incorrectly suspected by Federals with having had a part in the recent bungled attempt to burn New York City by use of Greek Fire, two charges made up of nine specifications were lodged against him. Attorneys for the prosecution carefully avoided the charge of piracy this time, despite the fact that he admitted seizing vessels on the Great Lakes and trying to take over a Union warship. Noted New York attorneys James T. Brady and Algernon S. Sullivan offered a spirited defense, but they later told Confederate officials that the outcome of the hearings was determined before they started. Moving speedily, the court found Beall guilty on most charges and on February 21, 1865, Dix ordered that he "be hanged by the neck until dead" at Fort Columbus three days later. (OR, 101, 1166; OR, 116, 11; OR, 121, 279–80, 282; CV, 7, 68)

The story that speedy action by Federal officials was prompted by fear that Richmond would take another hostage if they knew what was taking place was widely circulated, but is without foundation. Many persons in Richmond and in Washington knew within 36 to 48 hours every detail of events in the drama that was unfolding at Fort Lafayette.

According to documents that were not made public until much later, influential persons in Washington tried to intervene in order to save Beall's life. Senator Orville H. Browning, a close personal friend of Lincoln, took to the president at least two sets of petitions asking for executive clemency. One of them carried the signature of Speaker of the House Schuyler Colfax—later U. S. Grant's vice president for one term. The other petition insisted that Beall's actions on the Great Lakes were done "under the authority and direction of Jefferson Davis." Future President James A. Garfield and a host of other dignitaries insisted that Beall was a soldier rather than a spy, but no appeal or argument conveyed to the Executive Mansion had any effect. (CV, 7, 69; Internet, John Yates Beall; CMH, 3, 227)

Logically, that should end the saga of the man hailed as a martyr in much of the South—but little about the persons and events of the Civil War is logical. While the trial was still in progress far to the North, it became widely known that Lincoln had refused to exercise clemency in the Beall case. Hence a story immediately surfaced according to which Booth's assassination was an act of retaliation for the president's failure to intervene on behalf of his college friend. Though no documentary or oral evidence supports the story, it was widely circulated and believed. Even the Virginia Historical Society authorized publication of one version of it. (M 28, 259–61; JSHS, 32, 99–101; JSHS, 33, 75–79; CV, 3, 3–4)

The last prominent Rebel who was formally charged with piracy but was in 1863 saved by a hostage held in Richmond died as a convicted spy shortly after 1:00 P.M. on February 24, 1865.

Part II

~~~~

Civilians — Usually Sitting Ducks

6

Big Nets and Banner Hauls

John Brown seized numerous hostages at Harpers Ferry, but did not make effective use of them. The first significant hostage event after war broke out was spontaneous and unplanned. The seemingly insoluble issue of how to save the lives of Rebel privateersmen triggered the lottery that was held in Richmond in mid-November 1861. Though the number of Federal officers involved was small by later standards, the ploy worked. Policies announced in a formal proclamation by Abraham Lincoln were quietly altered in order to save the lives of 14 men in blue.

With civilians being the victims far more often than military officers, use of hostages continued throughout the conflict. Even when significant numbers were involved, their names were not always preserved. Numerous states saw actions roughly equivalent to casting out nets and trawling for fish until nets were full. Such large-scale events became so taken for granted that top-level policy makers in Washington made almost casual references to this method of dealing with the enemy.

General Lorenzo Thomas, the Federal adjutant general, sent to the Union secretary of war on October 14, 1862, one of many papers dealing with exchange of prisoners. His paragraph 5 treated briefly the case of more than 100 "citizen prisoners" who had just been exchanged. He then turned to the matter of hostages and as though Edwin M. Stanton didn't already know it, wrote that "In a number of instances citizens have been arrested and held as hostages for the delivery of Union citizens." Reverting to this topic in paragraph 9, he noted that "In some cases our authorities have arrested rebel citizens and held them as hostages for the delivery of Union prisoners." (OR, 117, 621–22)

Joseph Holt, the veteran Federal judge advocate general, sent Stanton lists of political prisoners on June 9, 1863. He referred to the use of hostages in such perfunctory fashion that the document reveals how frequent and casual the practice was by then. Lists his office had compiled, said Holt, included "prisoners held as hostages."

Union Gen. Lorenzo Thomas, easily identified by his white hair, seemed to be fully at ease in the company of younger females.

More than a year later Holt sent to Stanton a lengthy and detailed report concerning Copperheads—or Southern sympathizers in the North. This time, he pointed to Rebel practices, noting that in border regions the capture of guerrillas often resulted in the seizure of "prominent Union citizens" who were held as hostages for the release of captured men. (OR, 118, 765–66; OR, 120, 948)

Arrest of innocent parties who were used to exert leverage upon Confederates was taken for granted at the highest level of the world's greatest democracy. Hence it was inevitable that there should be many instances in which substantial numbers of civilians were taken hostage. Dozens of cases involving less than a dozen hostages are summarized in chapter 11.

Florida, more remote from the center of action than many spots in what was then the far West, saw only one banner haul. On March 20, 1863, Confederate Gen. Joseph Finegan reported to Gen. Thomas Jordan about Union activities. Men in blue then stationed in Jacksonville consisted of "two regiments of black troops." Their white officers included Col. Thomas Wentworth Higginson, he wrote. Aided by "troops supposed to be white," Finegan said that "They are making prisoners of all male citizens found in Jacksonville, on the Saint John's River, who refuse to take the oath of allegiance, and holding them as hostages for their negro troops." (OR, 20, 837–38)

Louisiana also saw only one instance in which scores of innocent persons became hostages. Capt. Howard Dwight, an assistant adjutant general in the occupation force, was murdered on May 4, 1863, while riding to the Union front. Though the killers were not known, they were believed to have been guerrillas. Gen. Nathaniel P. Banks acted promptly and decisively when he learned what had happened to his captain. He ordered Gen. William Dwight, Jr., who was in command of the advance, "to arrest 100 of the white male persons in the vicinity of the murder and to send them to New Orleans, there to be kept in close confinement as hostages for the delivery of the assassins into the hands of the military authorities of the United States." (OR, 21, 312, 1119)

Gen. Richard Taylor, who was in command of Confederate forces in western Louisiana, dispatched a formal protest to Banks, who replied nearly a month after the murder. Dwight, he explained, had been following the Federal column at some distance. Unarmed and attended only by a body servant, he was set upon and killed in bayou country. To his enemy, Banks patiently explained that he had ordered the release of the 100 hostages soon after they were taken. He took this action for two reasons, he said. First, the residents of the affected region had not been warned of punitive action.

Union Judge Advocate Joseph Holt was widely respected for his legal knowledge.

Century

Second, the arrest and brief confinement of 100 hostages served to notify the people of the area about the consequences of forcible resistance. (OR, 119, 253–54)

No other hostage incident involving a large number of persons was resolved so quickly and so relatively painlessly. Yet despite fierce fighting in Mississippi for many months, civilians in the state across the river from Louisiana seldom suffered arbitrary imprisonment. Acting upon orders of Gen. H. J. T. Dana, Col. Embury W. Osband at Port Gibson took "13 of the most prominent and wealthy citizens to be held as hostages." Their capture was effected on October 30, 1864, but what Dana did with them is not recorded. (OR, 77, 569, 878)

Late in 1861, an unspecified number of Yankee prisoners were held as hostages in the state from which Jefferson Davis went to Montgomery to become president of the Confederacy. When 900 Rebels who had been captured arrived at Vicksburg late in 1862, Maj. N. G. Watts assumed that he was expected to exchange for them the majority of the captives that he held. In a terse memo to Gen. John C. Pemberton, a Pennsylvania native then in command of Rebels at Oxford, Watts explained that he knew he was not expected to release the unspecified number of hostages he had on hand. (OR, 118, 774)

Civilians in bitterly divided Missouri did not fare so well in this respect. In several instances groups were seized without provocation or warning; some of these instances were the work of Gen. Ulysses S. Grant.

During his brief tenure as commander at St. Louis, Gen. Henry W. Halleck received unsolicited advice from Gen. William T. Sherman's foster brother, Gen. Thomas Ewing. Writing from Lancaster, Ohio, early in January 1862, Ewing suggested that "railroad destroyers" in Missouri should be treated as military criminals. He believed life and property could best be protected by subjecting a few ringleaders among enemy civilians to courts-martial and then publicly hanging them. Hostages who would face death if sabotage continued, urged the Ohio native, should be taken "from each neighborhood, family, and clique." (OR, 8, 824)

Confederate partisan leader M. Jeff. Thompson, whose men referred to him as "General," needed no prompting from Ohio or anywhere else. By August 1861, he and his band had about 20 unidentified hostages in captivity. Not knowing how best to make use of them, he inquired of Gen. Gideon J. Pillow whether to send them to New Madrid "where they can be used" or to the Bloomfield, Missouri jail. (OR, 3, 647; OR, 114, 540)

Maj. J. B. Kaiser, in command at Licking, Missouri, showed in May 1863, that some Federals needed no coaching in order to use the hostage ploy. To the assistant adjutant general of the Rolla district, he reported that 17 horse thieves seized five Unionists on April 29. Kaiser promptly arrested "5 of the most prominent rebel sympathizers in that vicinity" and held them as hostages for the safe return of pro-Union civilians. (OR, 33, 267)

Slightly more than a year later, a much more complex hostage situation developed at Mexico, Missouri. On July 22, Capt. J. H. Davis of the Enrolled Missouri Militia was taken from his home by men presumed to be bushwhackers. Isaac Gannett, an assistant provost marshal, arrested four Rebels as hostages for the safety of Davis—then learned that he had been killed. A guerrilla force responded by moving close to Mexico and taking hostages of their own. They warned that they'd kill 25 Unionists unless Gannett released his hostages by 7:00 P.M. on July 23. Instead of bowing to pressure, the Federal officer "at once placed in close confinement about twenty-five rebels" of Mexico and let it be known that he'd put them to death if guerrillas carried out their threat.

Abolitionist Thomas W. Higginson was a pioneer commander of units then known as colored regiments.
National Archives

Two days later, Gannet received a warning that bushwhackers, who abounded in the region, threatened to kill 10 Union men for every hostage the Federals put to death. Desperate, the Union officer dispatched an emergency call for more troops. He planned soon to release the 25 hostages taken a few days earlier, he reported, but would not release the initial band of four hostages without orders. He recommended that "a few citizens be held for a certain time till the rebels surrender the murderers of Davis." There is no record that the killers were ever identified and apprehended, however. (OR, 84, 395)

Logic suggests that Pennsylvania should have been insulated from the incessant process of hostage taking and bargaining over them, but it was not. When Confederate Gen. J. E. B. Stuart and his riders were preparing to invade the Keystone State in October 1862, one of his aides issued an order telling cavalrymen that

> As a measure of justice to our many good citizens who, without crime, have been taken from their homes and kept by the enemy in prison, all public functionaries, such as magistrates, postmasters, sheriffs, &c., will be seized as prisoners. They will be kindly treated and kept as hostages for our own.

Stuart's official report of the famous ride acknowledged that "A number of public functionaries and prominent citizens [of Maryland and Pennsylvania] were taken captives and brought over as hostages." These captives constituted part of the "250 Union men" held by Richmond early in 1863. Arrangements for the release of all of them were completed on February 2. (OR, 28, 54, 56; OR, 118, 244; JSHS, 3, 75; OR, 14, 481–83)

East Tennessee, heavily Unionist in loyalty, was much smaller than the state of Missouri but was about as badly divided. Some Federal forces reached the region fairly early, and by October 1862, had taken four hostages at Jackson. The prisoners, who were held to guarantee the safety of some of the 11 Tennesseans held at Holly Springs, Mississippi, were taken to Oxford, Mississippi. From their place of imprisonment, they beseeched Pemberton to see that the "deluded wretches" who held views opposite to theirs should be released. This ought to be done, said the civilians, "not for their sake but for ours and the cause we have at heart." (OR, 117, 928–29)

While stationed at Maynardville, Tennessee, in August 1864, Union Capt. J. W. Branson of the 1st Tennessee urged the wholesale arrest of Rebel citizens so they could "be held as hostages, that the return of our [loyal citizens] may thereby be secured." At Knoxville, Gen. S. P. Carter wanted to send a small force into Union County to arrest hostages, and won the qualified approval of Gen. J. M. Schofield for such an expedition.

Meanwhile, civilian John Vaughn had a lengthy appeal on the way to Richmond. Addressing Davis, he told him that "a large number of the best citizens of East Tennessee are held by the Federal authorities as hostages for citizen prisoners of East Tennessee now confined in different prisons of the Confederacy." The Morristown resident urged that men in Confederate prisons were "a low-down, vagabond set" while civilians held by Federals were "of the wealthiest and most influential class." Vaughn therefore suggested an immediate exchange of "all citizen prisoners of East Tennessee." He wasted his paper and ink; many hostages were held for weeks and some were not freed for months. As late as March 10, 1865, Col. L. S. Trowbridge of the 10th Michigan Cavalry expressed delight at being able to forward 17 hostages for an exchange. (OR, 77, 461; OR, 121, 377)

Winchester, Virginia, is widely believed to have changed hands more times during 1861–65 than any other town. Yet the record for hostage-taking belongs to Fredericksburg. Major incidents linked with the latter town are treated elsewhere, but other parts of the Old Dominion were not without incidents involving 10 or more civilians.

A Federal prison was established in Columbus, Ohio, more than a month before Bull Run. Its first large batch of inmates had been taken as hostages in the Kanawha Valley—very early deeply involved in the North/South struggle plus the move to carve Virginia into two states. This group, alleged by J. M. Bennet who was first auditor of Virginia to number more than 100, attracted the notice of a Columbus newspaper. In its issue of July 6, 1861, the *State Journal* published the names of 23 hostages:

> R. B. Hackney, A. B. Dorst, A. Roseberry, H. J. Fisher, R. Knupp, Jacob C. Kline, Frank Ronsom, J. N. McMullen, J. W. Echard, David Long, G. D. Slaughter, A. E. Eastham, J. F. Diltz, Robert Mitchell, S. Hargiss, E. J. Ronsom, T. B. Kline, Alexander McCauseland, O. H. P. Sebrill, James Johnson, W. O. Roseberry, Benjamin Franklin, and James Carr.

According to the newspapers, "The majority of them are wealthy and influential citizens" who were taken in an effort to guarantee the safety of Unionists who had been seized by secessionists. Bennett charged that these and many other civilian Rebels were being held at Columbus in cow sheds, but the *Ohio Journal* did not include a description of facilities that constituted the hastily improvised prison. (OR, 115, 1390–91)

In the city that was the capital of both Virginia and the Confederate States, in January 1863, Capt. T. P. Turner received 29 men from the Shenandoah Valley who were to be held as hostages. Possibly, but not positively, because the military prison he headed was already crammed full and Richmond's food supplies were dangerously low, Turner quickly paroled all of these hostages except Lt. Anderson Dawson and sent them home. Retention of Dawson may have stemmed from the fact that he was captured while serving in a unit known as the 1st West Virginia Cavalry. Every knowledgeable person east of the Allegheny Mountains knew that their elected leaders still denied that the state of West Virginia had been created. (OR, 118, 819, 821)

In the region that Richmond's leaders called "the bogus state of West Virginia headed by F. H. Peirpoint as bogus governor," a party of 50 mounted men raided Point Pleasant late in June 1861. Several "prominent Union men" were seized, so men of the 1st Regiment of State Troops "scoured the countryside" and took 30 prominent secessionists as hostages. Some of these civilians may have been among the "dozen citizens held as hostages by the Governor's order" at an unspecified later date. (OR, 115, 15; OR, 119, 662)

Incidents in which 10 or fewer civilians became hostages were much more frequent than cases in which "big nets resulted in banner hauls," yet the number of civilians involved in the larger incidents is impressive. With Fredericksburg, Hole-in-the Day, doctors, and other special categories included, seizures of 10 plus hostages involved hundreds of civilians, most of whom were white males.

7

The Champion—Fredericksburg

Three months before the bloody battle of Fredericksburg in December 1862, serious troubles of the small city began with its occupation by soldiers in blue on April 19. Late in July, a captain serving under Union Gen. Rufus King arrested four civilians upon orders of Gen. John Pope. Chosen because they were known to be influential and "taken from their beds late at night," they became hostages for four Unionists arrested quite a bit earlier by Rebels and imprisoned at Richmond. Within 24 hours, resident S. M. Carpenter identified the hostages as: Thomas S. Barton, Beverly T. Gill, Thomas F. Knox, and Charles C. Wellborn. On July 24 the Fredericksburg quartet, who were then in Old Capitol Prison, learned the reason for their seizure. Pope sent word to them that day that they would be given their liberty when "Union citizens shall have been released from their confinement in Richmond." (OR, 117, 272, 274, 275; RR, 5, D, 46)

Asst. Adj. Gen. John P. Shelburne soon provided names of the Unionists for whom the Fredericksburg quartet were hostages: Maj. Charles Williams, Moses Morrison, Thomas Morrison, and Peter Cause. He notified the superintendent of Old Capitol Prison that four other Fairfax County men, loyal to the United States, were also imprisoned by Confederates. Hence four additional hostages were being held for George Rayless, Abraham Lydecker, Mr. Murphy, and Julius Visser. (OR, 117, 287)

On July 30 Fredericksburg captives wrote to the Confederate secretary of war, asking him to arrange for release of the four men named by Shelburne, whom they identified as residents of Spotsylvania County. This action on the part of the Confederacy, they told George W. Randolph, would assure their own release from Federal clutches. Barton's name was not appended to the petition, but his son wrote from Petersburg to ask for his release. In addition to three men identified by Carpenter, the petition was signed by James McGuire, James H. Bradley, and W. S. Broaddus. Since they were also residents of Fredericksburg, seven leading citizens were now hostages. (OR, 117, 828–30)

54

Confusion was compounded by Union Gen. James S. Wadsworth. It had come to his attention that Peter Cause was not a prisoner of Confederates but was "at large in Richmond." Uncertain as the authenticity of this report, on August 7 he requested Lewis McKinzie to locate F. I. Cause, brother of the man in question, and find from him the truth of the matter. (OR, 117, 351)

Union Judge Advocate L. C. Turner had no doubt that Peter Cause was in a Rebel prison. On August 9 he notified Lafayette C. Baker to "arrest, convey to and detain in the Old Capitol Prison" 14 more citizens of Fredericksburg. Turner had informants inside the city, since he specified that these new hostages must be: G. H. C. Rowe, Montgomery Slaughter, John J. Berry, Michael Ames, Edwin Carter, J. H. Roberts, John F. Scott, William H. Norton, W. Roy Mason, John Coakley, Benjamin Temple, Abraham Cox, James Cooke and Lewis Wrenn.

Though his municipal office was not mentioned, it was widely known that Slaughter was mayor of Fredericksburg. All 14, Turner told Baker, were to be held for seven "prisoners of war, citizens of the United States, who have been arrested and now imprisoned in Richmond, Va." According to the judge advocate, the "Union men" for whom the 14 new hostages were to be held were Cause, the two Morrisons, and Williams—plus Squire Ralston, Burnham Wardwell, and A. M. Pickett.

As though he was not sure the Turner directive carried sufficient weight to guarantee obedience to it, P. H. Watson sent a nearly identical message to General Wadsworth. As military governor of the District of Columbia, Wadsworth had plenty of manpower to see that the directive by the Union assistant secretary of war would be obeyed. By August 10 Wadsworth was able to report that he held 30 hostages "citizens of Fredericksburg and that part of Virginia in front of Washington." All of them, he said, were imprisoned because Rebels held an equal number of persons who were "confined simply because they are Union men." Most or all of those not from Fredericksburg were residents of Fairfax County. (OR, 117, 366, 369, 376, 383; CW, #59, 77)

Wadsworth, who seems to have had his fill of hostages from Fredericksburg, indicated on August 13 that he was willing to exchange them for "men who were taken at Savage Station while engaged in aiding the sick and wounded" of the Federal force that was engaged there. These Unionist civilians were:

J. W. Wightman, Oliver L. Miller, W. H. Smith, W. E. Gosling, John Veltzhoover, John Bryant, Legrand Hart, Thomas G. Smythe, Isaac Brown, Thomas McCombs, John Haney.

Gosling was, however, soon separated from the rest. Grilled by Rebels, he claimed to be a citizen of Tennessee and as a result his case was made a special one. Before the day ended, Wadsworth had a talk with the secretary of war and changed his mind. He now "deemed it inexpedient to send these men south via Fredericksburg." (OR, 117, 382–83)

Forty-seven Fredericksburg residents who had not been made hostages sent a long letter to Jefferson Davis on August 21. Citing the Confederate arrest of the four men from Spotsylvania as the precipitating cause, they declared that seven of their fellow citizens were made hostages prior to the seizure of 14 ordered by Turner. Writers said that the seven who seemed to have been entirely overlooked by Federal authorities were the four who were arrested on July 22, plus James H. Bradley, James McGuire, and the Rev. William S. Broaddus.

Gen. James S. Wadsworth, military governor of the District of Columbia, soon had 30 residents of Fredericksburg under detention.

The petition to the Confederate president explained why the name of Barton had dropped from lists of hostages. Because of infirm health, he had been discharged on a parole that required him to stay in Baltimore. Some of their 19 fellow citizens who had become hostages were "among our oldest and most esteemed citizens," said George Aler, J. Harrison Kelly, and 45 other Fredericksburg residents. Three of the men taken in Spotsylvania County, they told Davis, had emigrated from Delaware and Pennsylvania.

As for Charles Williams, the petitioners said he had lived in Fredericksburg since birth and held "or affected to hold opinions opposed to the common judgment of the community." He was prone to engage in controversial conversation, they said, and "assumed oddity and originality of views" that caused him to be regarded as "a wild talker, but a kind-hearted man." They were positive, they told Davis, that "no consideration of public policy" called for continuing to hold the two Morrisons, Cause, and Williams. Hence they urged that these men, taken by Confederate authorities, should be released in order to make possible "the return to their homes of many of our friends now in custody as hostages for them." (OR, 117, 861–62)

Wadsworth now held 41 Virginian civilians, not all of whom were from Fredericksburg. Some correspondence may not have reached its destination, and prison records were not carefully kept. Hence it had become impossible for anyone in a position of authority positively to know who was

Secret Agent Lafayette C. Baker, who often disguised himself as a general, was given a list of 14 persons whom he was told to arrest.

hostage for whom. This much was certain in Washington, however; the Confederate secretary of war had ordered the release of seven men and they were on their way home from prison. Wadsworth reciprocated by giving their freedom to seven of his captives. (OR, 117, 417)

About the same time, Mayor Slaughter sought the help of the congressman in whose district Fredericksburg lay. He arrived at the same total of hostages from the city that was reported to Davis—19. Congressman D. C. de Jarnette was asked by Slaughter to try to effect the release of the seven imprisoned Unionists for whom the 19 were being held. In a postscript he noted that Wadsworth was likely to demand that Confederates free, not seven but 19 prisoners. (OR, 117, 866)

Davis evidently read and possibly reread the long communication from 47 men of Fredericksburg, for his secretary of war took a decisive step on August 27. Addressing the private secretary of the Confederate president, he reported that "The persons for whom the gentlemen arrested in Fredericksburg are held as hostages are to be released."

That was the final word that has been preserved about the 1862 incident that set all Fredericksburg agog. Voluminous and detailed as are the accounts about arrests, nothing concerning the release of the hostages went into the record after Randolph dispatched his terse memorandum. No one in the city destined to become famous as a battle site then imagined that actions taken in 1864 would make those of 1862 seem mild. (OR, 117, 865)

Though more hostages were involved than during the lengthy 1862 sets of captures the second big Fredericksburg incident was resolved comparatively rapidly and easily. It all started after the battle of the Wilderness, when sick, wounded, and worn-out men in blue scattered across the Virginia countryside. On May 8 a band of them that numbered about 60—more or less—found their way into Fredericksburg, situated about 50 miles from the Federal capital.

Since these soldiers carried their weapons with them, residents feared "some sort of Yankee trick" might be pulled. Town officials hurriedly got a band of armed men together, confronted the strangers, and gave them the choice of surrendering or being driven across the river to face Rebel partisans. Too fagged to fight, the Federals handed over their weapons and were soon shipped to Richmond and imprisoned. (Quinn, *Fredericksburg*, 96–112)

Perhaps because so many hostages were soon involved, but also because it was a spectacular example of the way both North and South used raw power when possible, this incident was treated by Mark A. Neely in a 1991 volume.

Word of the capture soon reached Washington, and the secretary of war wasted no time in inquiring about possible reprisal by Federals. Stanton, who remembered that Slaughter had been taken hostage two years earlier while mayor of the city, blamed him for the seizure of soldiers. Writing to

R. F. Zogbaum sketched Federal activity as the bombardment of Fredericksburg began.

Gen. Montgomery C. Meigs, he ordered that if Slaughter "has been guilty of any disloyal act and has not escaped, have him placed in irons and forwarded here to General Augur under guard." Meigs delegated handling of the matter to Col. Edmund Schriver who commanded occupation forces in Fredericksburg. (OR, 68, 770, 839)

Hence Stanton sent Schriver a May 19 telegram directing him to arrest and send to Washington under guard 60 "principal male citizens in Fredericksburg and its vicinity." These men would serve as hostages "for the persons captured by Mayor Slaughter and sent to Richmond," he stipulated. He then scolded Schriver for having allegedly issued rations to residents of Fredericksburg and its environs. His message ended with a blunt demand for immediate action and a prompt reply.

Schriver said he would immediately look after making the 60 arrests, but denied that he had issued Federal rations to hungry civilians. Slaughter, he reported, was said to be in Richmond; hence his house was being watched every night "for the purpose of arresting him, should he secretly attempt to enter it." (OR, 68, 934–35)

Despite the fact that the occupied town was widely considered to have a population of at least five thousand before the war started, Schriver found it difficult to do as he was told. On May 20 he rather lamely reported to Stanton that

> In relation to the apprehension of prominent citizens of this city, as ordered by you, I have to report that on account of the very few males who

are now present it has been impossible to get that number ready to dispatch to-day, but I hope to send them to Washington to-morrow. There are 30 in custody, 9 of whom are suspected of having been engaged in conveying our wounded [that is, the band of 60 men who surrendered to civilians] to Richmond.

On the same day, Schriver sent to Washington a set of commissary statistics showing that the charge of having dispensed rations without orders had no foundation. Testily, he ended his message by saying that "I take this occasion to assure the Department that whenever I fail to perform my whole duty I shall cease to wear the Government livery and will not eat its salt." (OR, 69, 26–27)

Schriver must have immediately rounded up the required 60 hostages—perhaps with Slaughter not included—and sent them to Fort Monroe. Union Lt. George Mitchell, who was intimately acquainted with Fredericksburg and its citizens, soon registered a protest at what Stanton had done. He insisted that the soldiers who meekly surrendered in Fredericksburg were stragglers who had deliberately cut loose from their units. It was his considered judgment that only three citizens should be held as hostages. (Neely, *Fate*, 156)

Abraham Lincoln, who handled an astonishing quantity and variety of paperwork, got wind of "the big affair in Fredericksburg." As soon as he looked into it, he discovered that one of the hostages, John M. Chew, was known to have ministered to wounded men in blue during and after the 1862 battle in which the city was central. The president therefore directed Stanton immediately to discharge Chew and permit him to return home. (AL, 7, 358)

Lincoln's personal intervention may have caused the wheels of military justice to move much faster than usual. Six weeks after the spotlight was again turned upon the city, Col. James A. Haddie issued an order that emanated from the War Department. "The Secretary of War directs that the Fredericksburg hostages be sent to Washington [from Fort Monroe] to be turned over to Major-General [Christopher C.] Augur for the purpose of exchange," he wrote. That message went to Gen. Alan F. Schoepf, a native of Hungary who was in command of the only military installation in Virginia that Federals held throughout the war. (OR, 120, 424)

Instead of ending with a mighty bang, the 1864 hostage incident fizzled out. As was the case two years earlier, the order directing that the 60 Fredericksburg captives be exchanged was the last that was heard of them. Presumably the Federal stragglers who had reached the city early in May were released simultaneously—but records do not indicate whether any of them promptly returned to their units for duty.

8

John Brown Uses Lewis Washington

"John Brown of Harpers Ferry," as he is widely called in order to distinguish him from scores of other men who had the same name, considered himself to be something of a military expert. As a wool producer in Ohio, he traveled to England and Europe in 1849 to sell wool and while there made an extensive study of fortifications. Earthworks especially interested him, since he seems already to have had vague ideas about waging a defensive war in the mountains of the eastern United States. For years, he read all the books he could find on what he called "insurrectionary warfare." Yet he must have had some gnawing doubts about his leadership ability, since he later briefly employed English mercenary Hugh Forbes as a military advisor. (Anderson, *Voice*, 417–18; Davis, *Brother*, 84)

Better than the 21 followers whom he had gathered, Brown was aware on Sunday, October 16, 1859, that he would need all of his skill as well as numerous hostages in order to implement his ambitious plans for the week. On the Maryland farm very close to the Virginia border that he had rented as "cattle buyer Isaac Smith," he had already made an inventory of his stock of weapons. Most of them were stored in a one-room schoolhouse that he expected to be a command center, but some would be needed for the raid that was about to begin. Finding that he had accumulated nearly two hundred rifles and an equal number of revolvers and about 950 pikes with sharp iron tips, he felt that he and his anticipated army of slaves would be able to meet all comers. (Davis, *Brother*, 87; Anderson, *Voice*, 420–24, cited at Harpers Ferry National Historic Park)

Brown selected three of his men to remain at the farm as guards. Then followed by a mixed band of whites, free blacks, and a slave he set out that Sunday morning for nearby Harpers Ferry, Virginia (now West Virginia). Located at the confluence of the Potomac and Shenandoah Rivers, the town of 2,500 population was nearly 60 miles from Washington and about 80 miles east of Baltimore. To Brown, its importance stemmed from the fact

61

that it held the only major Union armory in the deep South, along with privately owned Hall's Rifle Works. The armory alone held enough weapons to supply his army for many months. (Wood, et al., *America*, 427)

It was easy to take over the arsenal plus the town that was mostly asleep on Sunday evening. Many residents fled at the first sign of trouble, but a few took cover and fired an occasional shot at the intruders. Some of Brown's men fanned out to gather hostages, among whom a great-grand-nephew of George Washington was the most prominent. Having planned in advance to use Lewis Washington for bargaining purposes, Brown instructed the band that captured him to be sure to bring along a famous sword that tradition said was given to the first president by Frederick the Great. (Davis, *Brother*, 87; Garraty, *America*, 532)

Raiders encountered no significant trouble until an express train from Wheeling to Baltimore was forced to stop soon after midnight because barricades had been erected. Baggage master Haywood Shepherd, one of approximately one thousand free blacks who lived in Harpers Ferry, ignored shouts to surrender and tried to run. Shot about midnight, he was the first fatality of the expedition designed to give freedom to thousands of slaves. Possibly because he wanted news of the takeover to be disseminated quickly, Brown soon permitted the train to proceed to its destination. (Anderson, *Voice*, 430–37)

With nearly a dozen hostages on hand by Monday morning, Brown strapped the Washington sword to his side and selected the sturdy brick fire station as headquarters. Once inside he supervised the moving of engines to points at which he thought they would stop any attempt to break into the building from outside. Telegraph wires having been cut, the leader of the raid was so confident that he sent to the nearby Wager House hotel and got breakfast for those in the engine room—hostages included. When a town official asked what he was about and why, he shouted that he and his men were there "to free the slaves by the authority of God Almighty."

News of Sunday evening's events having spread swiftly, members of the Virginia Militia converged upon the town during the

At midlife, John Brown did not display the flowing beard that he later cultivated.

afternoon. Soon they began exchanging shots with the intruders and several, including two of Brown's sons, were hit. Partly because he now held about 30 hostages, Brown's self-assurance never wavered. Lewis Washington was widely quoted as having said of his captor that

> With one son dead by his side and another critically wounded, he felt the pulse of his dying boy [Watson Brown] with one hand, held his rifle with the other, and issued a stream of commands to his men with all the composure of a European general in his marquee.

Late in the afternoon the raider sent out a note saying he would free all of the hostages in return for a guarantee of safe conduct from the region for his little band. Though no one later seemed to know who had taken the responsibility to respond, it was universally agreed that the offer was instantly rejected by town officials. Mayor Fontaine Beckham did not make that decision; earlier in the afternoon he had been killed in an exchange of rifle fire. (Anderson, *Voice*, 421–31)

Lt. J. E. B. Stuart happened to be in Washington on leave, having come to the capital to negotiate selling to the War Department his patent for a sabre attachment he had devised. Authorities picked him as courier to take to Lt. Col. Robert E. Lee a message about whose contents the lieutenant knew nothing. He sensed, however, that something of importance was afoot, so after reaching Arlington House he offered to serve as aide to Lee and was promptly assigned to that role.

With about 90 Union marines as their fighting force and armed with two pieces of light field artillery plus carbines and muskets, Lee and Stuart took the first train to Harpers Ferry. By first light on Tuesday morning, Brown could see that a body of uniformed men whose rifles were equipped with bayonets were lined up close to the engine house. Soon Stuart appeared at the door and learned that he was expected to deal with a man who identified himself only as Smith. According to the professional soldier's account, Smith opened the door of the engine house about four inches, just enough to permit the soldier to hand him a memorandum demanding immediate and unconditional surrender.

Holding a cocked carbine so that the officer could see it, "Smith" demanded and got a lengthy parley. It continued until the leader of the raiders said that "the only condition upon which he would surrender was, that he and his party should be allowed to escape."

According to Stuart, some of the hostages "begged me with tears to ask Col. Lee to come and see 'Smith.'" Stuart managed to inform the fast-talking man whom he barely glimpsed through the opening in the doorway that no concessions would be made and no bargain could be struck.

"As soon as I could tear myself away from the importunities [of the hostages]," Lee's aide later wrote, "I left, waved my cap [in a signal for marines to attack] and Col. Lee's plan was carried out." (JSHS, 8, 438–39)

Raiders dispatched by Brown to other buildings had already been captured, but the band inside the engine house held out. Men who had come from Washington had been ordered to use nothing but edged weapons inside the building, for fear that hostages would be shot and killed or wounded. With an estimated two thousand civilians watching what was taking place, a party of a dozen marines who had seized a ladder used it as a battering ram and quickly broke down the heavy oak door. Led by Lt. Israel Green, they then swarmed into the impromptu command post after having suffered one fatality.

Green managed to hit Brown with a light sword, but his blade was deflected when he tried to run him through. With Brown now on the floor, Green beat him with his sword until he collapsed and lost consciousness. Green's men killed two raiders with bayonets and wounded others, so their comrades who were able to do so soon lifted their arms in surrender. The fight inside the engine house having lasted less than five minutes, marines took Brown and other injured men outside and bandaged their wounds as best they could. (Anderson, *Voice*, 440–46)

Before launching his attack upon Harpers Ferry, Brown had expected slaves to flock to his banner by the thousands. Hence he had sent three more men to the Maryland schoolhouse to muster newcomers into his army and supply them with weapons. No slaves came to the designated spot, but marines soon appeared and captured the remaining uninjured members of the expedition. All of the prisoners were soon taken to Charles Town, the county seat, and locked up in its jail.

Though all of the raiders knew that they were charged with treason against the state of Virginia and that their lives were in jeopardy, the spotlight was on their leader from the moment hearings began on October 27 until the verdict of the court was carried out.

Attorney Lawson Botts, a native of Virginia, was ordered by the presiding judge to act as defendant for all of the accused. News of this development initially created a ground swell of vocal complaints by prominent abolitionists. They quit protesting, however, when they learned that Botts intended to argue that his chief client was insane and was therefore entitled to the mercy of the court. Newspaper correspondents flocked to Charles Town, and Virginia officials received a barrage of letters and telegrams asking or demanding leniency for the raiders.

From distant New York City, where there were already some rumblings of possible secession from the state, Mayor Fernando Wood wrote a lengthy letter of advice to Gov. Henry A. Wise, who later became a Confederate brigadier. Wood urged Virginia's chief executive to ignore the clamor for Brown's blood that had been heard from throughout the South. Though the accused man was clearly guilty of a capital crime, Wood said, his life should be spared because he had so many prominent and vocal sympathizers in the North. (WWW, 728)

Though Wise interviewed the chief raider at length, he did not act upon the suggestion of Wood. Sen. James Mason interviewed Brown and questioned him about the source of money he used to buy weapons. Instead of admitting that prominent abolitionists had funded him, Brown insisted that he used only his own funds. There is no reason to believe Wise ever seriously thought of exercising executive clemency, so by the time Brown adamantly refused to have an insanity plea entered the fate of the man ordained by God to free the slaves was sealed. After having deliberated less than an hour, on October 31 the jury found Brown guilty of all charges.

When the condemned man went back to the courtroom on November 2 to be sentenced, he requested permission to speak briefly. He emphatically denied having made plans to do anything but free slaves. "I never did intend murder or treason, or the destruction of property, or to excite or incite slaves to rebellion, or to make insurrection," he insisted. "If it be deemed necessary that I should forfeit my life for the furtherance of the end of justice, and mingle my blood further with the blood of my children and with the blood of millions in this slave country whose rights are disregarded by wicked, cruel, and unjust enactments—I submit; so let it be done!" Almost as though he had not heard a word the convicted man said, the judge impassively sentenced him to be hanged by the neck until dead after the passage of one month. (H, 1, 419; Anderson, *Voice*, 443–59)

At Charles Town, Virginia, Brown refused the customary hood given to a condemned man and climbed the gallows with his eyes wide open.
Leslie's Illustrated

Frederick Douglass, a powerful orator on behalf of abolition, refused to have anything to do with Brown's Harpers Ferry expedition.

That verdict, which he had expected from the moment he was captured in the Harpers Ferry engine room, almost seemed to please Brown. "I am worth inconceivably more to *hang* than for any other purpose," he wrote in one of the last in a stream of letters he dispatched from prison. Taken to the gibbet on December 2, he calmly said to those nearby that "I, John Brown, am now quite certain that the *crimes of this guilty land* will never be purged away but with Blood. I had, *as I now think vainly*, flattered myself that without *very much* bloodshed it might be done."

To those who listened to Brown at Charles Town and to multitudes who soon read these and other last words, it was clear that the life-shaping mission he had launched had failed. Some of the men who had financed the raid plus Frederick Douglass who had been approached but declined to become involved left the country in fear of bodily harm. Almost immediately, however, men of prominence in the North came to the conclusion that Brown's abysmal failure as a military leader had led to triumphant success as a martyr for the cause of abolition.

Many echoed the sentiments of Henry David Thoreau, who virtually elevated the raider to the level of a member of the Godhead, saying that "Some eighteen hundred years ago, Christ was crucified; this morning, perchance, Captain Brown was hung. These are the two ends of a chain which is not without its links. He is not Old Brown any longer; he is an angel of light." Ralph Waldo Emerson echoed this idea, declaring that upon his execution Brown became "a new saint who will make the gallows glorious like the cross." (Bragdon, *Free Nation*, 403)

Abraham Lincoln instantly saw potential political repercussions in the nationally celebrated case and hastened to put distance between the raider and the young Republican party. "John Brown," he insisted, "was not a Republican, and not a single Republican [was involved] in his Harpers Ferry enterprise." Democrat Stephen A. Douglas countered with the charge that though no Republicans followed Brown, his plan and his raid were "natural, logical, inevitable results of the doctrines and teachings of the Republican party." (Wood, et al., *America*, 428)

Numerous contemporary analysts considered Brown's martyrdom to be an epochal event that would split apart a nation already torn asunder by sectional differences. Editors of the *Richmond Examiner* told readers that "The Harpers Ferry invasion has advanced the cause of Disunion more than any other event since the formation of the Government." Washington, the most articulate and respected of the more than two dozen hostages at whom Brown regularly waved a rifle or revolver said simply that the incident "fanned the already-fiery flames of sectional discord."

George Templeton Strong, soon to become a founder of the U.S. Sanitary Commission that played a vital role in the Civil War, pondered for weeks before putting into his diary a notation about "the Charles Town martyr." He noted that Brown was already being hailed as "the Hero or Representative man of this struggle" that began 13 months after his death when Maj. Robert Anderson moved his garrison into Fort Sumter.

"A queer rude song [about Brown] seems to be growing popular," the New Yorker observed. He was referring, of course, to "John Brown's Body," which was sung to the melody of "The Battle Hymn of the Republic." Strangely, this music was a Northern adaptation of a camp meeting song that was popular among the slaves of South Carolina—where artillery shells took the place of words in April 1861. Templeton's early observation was accurate; during 1861–65, "John Brown's Body" was a favorite marching song of Federal troops.

John Brown had been a perennial failure for most of his life. According to Allan Nevins he had tried "farming, tanning, land-speculation, and wool-brokerage" with remarkable lack of success. His only significant achievement before age 50 was that of having sired 20 children. Following five of his sons to Kansas, he had become notorious as a brutal killer who led "the Pottawatomie (or Osawatomie) massacre" that triggered what many observers called "civil war in Kansas." (Nevins, *Ordeal*, 2, 474–74; Wood, et al., *America*, 423)

Far the most distinguishing characteristic of the man who drifted from one failure to another was his early and passionate hatred of slavery. He wrote a long and highly intimate letter to his brother, Frederick, from Randolph, Pennsylvania, late in November 1834, a full quarter century before his Harpers Ferry raid. He had been trying some practical way to help his "poor fellow-men in bondage," he said.

He and his wife had considered trying to "get at least one negro boy or youth, and bring him up as we do our own." That is, he meant to go through the highly informal adoption process of the period and give at least one black-skinned adolescent "a good English education" that would include history and business. Above all, young Brown would have liked to fill such a boy's mind with "the fear of God." Education of blacks had been a favorite theme of his for years, he told Frederick, writing that "If the young blacks of our country could once become enlightened, it would most assuredly operate on slavery like fire powder confined in rock, and all slave-holders know it well." (H, 1, 414–15)

Fierce fighting in "Bloody Kansas" led to the sack of Lawrence by raiders led by William Quantrill.

Leslie's Illustrated

Though Brown and his wife did not take a black youngster into their home and keep him there for years, his analysis of the effect of education upon slavery was acute and accurate. In 1834 he probably did not dream that he would some day become "fire powder confined in the rock of the south's legal system" that, when ignited, would help to blow the nation apart.

Analysts of this man who sometimes seemed dominated by demonic traits vary widely in some of their views. To many, he is dismissed as a member of a family "tainted with insanity" who got more than a normal dose of it. To others, he remains an enlightened and God-fearing crusader who was somewhat like the prophets of the Old Testament who railed against the ills of their society. (Garraty, *America*, 533)

Regardless of whether he is considered to have been a near lunatic, a crank, a bold crusader, or a saint without benefit of beatification, one thing about the Harpers Ferry raid and the final weeks of Old John Brown is beyond dispute. The nation's perception of the man who seized many hostages but failed to make good use of them underwent dramatic change the instant his body began dangling from a hangman's noose. Because the South's view of Brown and that of the North were diametrically opposed, he became a major force goading the North and the South into the war that cost more lives than all other American armed conflicts combined.

9

Phoebe Munden and Elizabeth Weeks

Two North Carolina housewives were central figures in a hostage saga that was as complex as that in which Confederate Gen. William H. F. ("Rooney") Lee was a central figure. Like the case that involved the son of the commander of the Army of Northern Virginia, the North Carolina instance was initiated by the deaths of two soldiers. It differed from the highly publicized Kentucky/Virginia drama, however with respect to the persons who suffered. Both Tar Heel hostages were ordinary civilian females who had no personal ties with a famous military commander.

No one in occupied New Bern, North Carolina, had any idea that a full-blown hostage incident would soon develop. Trouble began to brew in June 1863, when Union Gen. Edward A. Wild and the black troops he led were ordered back to the river town after brief involvement in the siege of Charleston. While at the North Carolina river town earlier, Wild had begun the organization of a new black brigade and superiors wanted the job finished because the additional manpower it would provide was badly needed. (WWW, 713)

A native of Massachusetts, Wild was a physician's son who had an impressive academic background: Harvard, the Jefferson Medical College, and post-graduate study in Paris. Even his closest acquaintances—for he had no intimate friends—described him as combative and pugnacious. These traits propelled him to Turkey, where the sultan made him a medical officer and sent him into the Crimean War. When civil war erupted in Italy, he hurried to join revolutionary forces led by Giuseppe Garibaldi. (Faust, *Encyclopedia of the Civil War*, 825)

After spending months as a participant in the most famous European conflicts of the period, Wild returned to civilian life and again briefly resumed his medical practice. In the aftermath of Fort Sumter, he was snorting for another chance at combat. He was among the first officers appointed by Gov. John A. Andrew to serve in Federal forces as a captain in

As a captain in the 1st Massachusetts regiment, Wild waded across the river at Blackburn's Ford because the bridge had been burned.

Harper's Weekly

A wound which he suffered at Fair Oaks caused Wild to take off his uniform, but he put it back on when Gov. John A. Andrew approved his idea to raise a black regiment.

the 1st Massachusetts. He and his men were engaged at Blackburn's Ford just prior to Bull Run, but the outfit experienced only one casualty there.

The right hand of the surgeon who was a combat captain was sufficiently damaged at Fair Oaks to cause him to be mustered out late in July 1862. Already locally renowned and feared as a diehard abolitionist, he persuaded Andrew to let him raise a unit of black fighting men from among freedmen of the state. Reentering military service and jumping two grades in rank, he became colonel of the 35th Massachusetts. Leading a charge at South Mountain, he was again hit and this time lost his left arm at the shoulder but was soon rewarded by another promotion.

General Wild's severe handicaps did not seem to make his temper any worse; those who knew him were of the opinion that such a development was impossible—he was already known as a terror, even when in a placid mood. Despite his strong military interests, he was prone to buck the system, so was twice arrested and tried by court-martial for refusal to obey superiors or to follow standard procedures. While stationed in New Bern, North Carolina, he launched but did not complete the organization of a new unit of black troops. (GB, 558)

He and his men played a brief and unimportant role in the siege of Charleston, after which superiors decided the manpower to be gained by formation of "Wild's African Brigade" was more important than his leadership in combat. Back in the Tar Heel state, the one-armed martinet enrolled the last of more than nine hundred men—mostly North Carolina natives who had been slaves—late in June 1863. Having been transferred to Norfolk and put in charge of all black troops in the department commanded by Gen. Benjamin F. Butler, Wild nourished a dream. He badly wanted to "clean out some of eastern North Carolina's guerrillas," and waited only a few months to strike at them.

By the time he shoved off in early December for a 19-day foray into the state where he earlier spent quite a bit of time, Wild's command was augmented by the 5th Colored infantry regiment. Engineers who made up the Union's first black regiment, formed at Camp Parapet, Louisiana, late in April 1863, were initially assigned to the Corps de Afrique but this nomenclature was soon dropped in favor of "Colored Volunteers."

It took four months to complete organization of the 5th Colored at Fort Delaware late in 1863. Attached to the Department of Virginia and North Carolina, the regiment gained experience at Yorktown and other bases. Men of the 5th took part in Gen. Isaac J. Wistar's expedition against Richmond during February 1864, plus Butler's operations against Petersburg and Richmond four months later. Having served briefly in North Carolina late in 1863, members of the 5th who joined Wild's 1864 expedition into the state were seasoned veterans. (D, 3, 1718–24)

Since the goal of the foray was to reduce the number of guerrillas in some counties, anything approaching a battle was not expected. Operations

Fort Delaware was the site at which men of the 5th Colored regiment were organized and trained.

around Shiloh before and after September were the only military moves, but in this period Samuel Jordan of the 5th Colored was taken prisoner. Wild undoubtedly relayed word of the loss to Butler, but at his headquarters the commander thought for some time that the man who had been captured was Samuel Jones of the 5th Ohio. He later offered a plausible but lame excuse for his error by saying that since the 5th Colored was recruited in Ohio, its members often spoke of it as an Ohio unit. Within a month after coming under Wild's command, this regiment was involved in a minor skirmish at Sandy Swamp—near Indiantown—in which three of its members were killed and one was wounded. (*Guide-Index to the Official Records*, vol. 2.)

Daniel Bright, characterized by Wild as a Confederate deserter who had turned guerrilla, was hanged on December 18 immediately after having been captured. In a dispatch of December 28, Wild rather casually noted that he had attached to the body a placard announcing that the work was done by Federal troops. (OR, 48, 912)

Though the pertinent correspondence is missing, Rebels must have immediately notified Wild that Jordan would suffer the same fate as Bright at an undetermined time in the future. Reaction of the Union commander was swift and characteristically violent. Probably within 24 hours of the time that he learned that enemies had threatened retaliation for the death of Bright, Wild had two female hostages in captivity.

Mrs. Phoebe Munden, wife of a lieutenant in North Carolina state forces, was taken "at her own home in the presence only of her three children, of whom the eldest was ten years of age." Reportedly tied hand and foot, the 35-year-old housewife was conveyed to Elizabeth City and after a few days of captivity there was shipped to Norfolk. From the beginning of her ordeal, she was told that if Jordan should hang she would suffer the same fate. (OR, 119, 1128)

Mrs. Elizabeth Weeks, wife of a private in the company that Capt. John T. Elliott insisted belonged to state troops but Wild termed guerrillas, was captured on or about the same day—later incorrectly listed by W. N. H. Smith as December 12. On December 17 Wild notified Elliott that

> I still hold in custody Mrs. Munden and Mrs. Weeks as hostages for the colored soldier taken by you. As he is treated, so shall they be; even to hanging. By this time you know that I am in earnest. Guerrillas are to be treated as pirates. You will never have rest until you renounce your present course, or join the regular Confederate Army. (OR, 119, 1128)

From outlying Pasquotank and surrounding counties, more than five hundred citizens converged upon Elizabeth City during the middle of the month. After having listened to speeches, they adopted a set of resolutions—purportedly unanimously—by which they said they preferred Wild's troops to guerrillas. That was good news to Butler, who two weeks later notified the Union secretary of war that Wild and his men had taken "the most stringent measures." Apparently not aware that only one man in blue was a prisoner, Butler said that Wild burned "the property of some of the officers of guerrilla parties, and seized the wives and families of others as hostages for some of his negroes that were captured." (OR, 49, 596–97)

Butler seems never to have learned that on December 22 Wild notified guerrilla leader Willis Sanderlin that he held a "Major Gregory as a hostage for the colored soldier captured near Shiloh [that is, Samuel Jordan]." Though Gregory is described in some secondary documents as having been a military officer, he was actually an "aged" civilian whose title may have been honorary. No more was heard of him then, despite the fact that Wild promised to hang him if his black soldier should be executed by those who captured him. (OR, 48, 912; OR, 119, 1130)

An apparent stalemate had developed, for it appeared that no Rebel officer would be willing to risk the necks of Phoebe Munden, Elizabeth Weeks, and Major Gregory. North Carolina Gov. Zebulon Vance, who did not have it in his power to save or rescue the hostages, unleashed a torrent of verbal abuse upon Robert Ould, who was serving as commissioner of exchange in Richmond.

Vance was not welcomed or respected in the Rebel capital. Along with Georgia's Gov. Joseph E. Brown, he was a constant thorn in the flesh of Jefferson Davis, the Confederate Congress, and Rebel officials and lawmakers in general. Both governors were dyed-in-the-wool proponents of states' rights. Their views were so extreme that neither of them had much more use for Richmond than for Washington. Both chief executives did their best to shield members of their defensive forces from Confederate conscription,

Gov. Joseph E. Brown of Georgia
was so strong an advocate of states'
rights that he opposed Richmond
almost as stubbornly as Washington.
Library of Congress

and both regularly upbraided anyone with whom they had a difference
of opinion or a matter to discuss
heatedly—almost never in any other
fashion.

Writing from Raleigh on December 29, Vance raged about actions of "a Yankee general by the
name of Wild." This fellow, said the
governor, refused to treat members
of North Carolina state defensive
forces as prisoners of war despite the
fact that they were "commissioned
by law." Having some but not all of
his facts straight, Vance railed that

They have also murdered several
soldiers and have arrested two respectable ladies, whom they keep
handcuffed as hostages for two
negro soldiers and declare their purpose to hang them if the negroes are
hung. I must ask you to see if some
arrangement cannot be made to include these troops within the cartel
of exchange, and repress, if possible, this horrible, cowardly, and damnable disposition on the part of the enemy to put women in irons as hostages for negro soldiers.

The commissioner of exchange had nothing whatever to do with events
in North Carolina. Vance knew that Ould's hands were tied by complicated
regulations that governed the exchange of prisoners. Hence it would have
seemed that the man from Raleigh had said enough. Not so; the governor
stormed in writing that

Such men as this Wild are a disgrace to the manhood of the age; not
being able to capture soldiers, they war upon defenseless women. Great
God! what an outrage! . . . If these outrages upon defenseless females
continue, I shall retaliate upon Yankee soldiers to the full extent of my
ability and let the consequences rest with the damnable barbarians who
began it. (OR, 119, 776–77)

Vance could have saved his paper and ink; a Confederate commander
who may not have known that Munden, Weeks, and Gregory were held by
Wild took characteristic decisive action. From White Mills on Dismal
Swamp, Col. Joel R. Griffin notified Gen. George E. Pickett about the Bright
hanging and the seizure of female hostages. (OR, 48, 883)

On January 13, 11 citizens of Pasquotank County signed a letter that notified Union Gen. George W. Getty of a gruesome discovery. That morning, they wrote, they found a dead man hanging in their neighborhood with a message pinned to his back. They "prepared a suitable box" and put the corpse "into the ground near the place he was hung." His friends could come and get the body if they wished to do so, they added. It was their considered judgment that the Union soldier they found had been brought across the Chowan River. Once he was dangling from the limb of a tree, they believed the party that brought him had gone back across the river. The message pinned to the body of the dead man read:

> Here hangs Private Samuel Jones, of Company B, Fifth Ohio Regiment, by order of Major-General Pickett, in retaliation for Private Daniel Bright, of Company L, Sixty-second Georgia Regiment (Colonel Griffin's), hung December 18, 1863, by order of Brigadier-General Wild. (OR, 116, 846)

Pickett, whose name will forever be linked with misnamed "Pickett's Charge" at Gettysburg, had entered the obscure North Carolina struggle for reasons he did not divulge. The message suggests that he was eager to impress upon Wild that he was not dealing with a guerrilla leader, but with a distinguished Confederate officer who outranked him.

From Deep Creek, Virginia, a detachment of cavalry under the command of Capt. Justinian Alman went to the turnpike where Jordan—still incorrectly identified as Jones— was buried. They retrieved the corpse, which was sent in an ambulance to division commander Col. S. P. Spear. This officer also received from the recovery party "a pair of handcuffs which were taken from [Jordan's] wrists, which are rather ugly things." (OR, 116, 846–47)

A dispatch from Murfreesborough, North Carolina, went to Butler at Fort Monroe on January 15 but probably had not been received when fellow soldiers went to recover the body of Jordan. Col. James W. Hinton, commander of the 68th regiment of North Carolina State Troops, was more measured in his language than was his governor. He sent along one of Wild's letters that intimated officers and men of Hinton's command were to be treated as guerrillas. This and other state units were "organized under authority obtained from the Governor of the State," he wrote, adding that "its officers are regularly commissioned by the Governor."

Demanding to know Butler's views concerning plans announced by Wild, he made a temperate reference to having captured "a goodly number of the officers and men of the Union Army and Navy." He had uniformly treated them as prisoners of war in the past, Hinton said, but their future treatment would be guided by Butler's reply to the inquiry. "I desire further to call your attention to the fact that the ladies whose names are mentioned in General Wild's letter are, as I am informed, still held in close confinement in the city of Norfolk. I want to know whether it is your purpose to hold these ladies as 'hostages' for a soldier legitimately captured?" (OR, 119, 847)

As late as January 17, Butler did not have the dead Union soldier correctly identified. He wrote to General in Chief Halleck that day that "Private Jones, Company B, Fifth Ohio Volunteers" was apparently "taken from among the Prisoners of war at Richmond" and turned over to Pickett for execution. He not only made this mistake; he failed to know or to remember where Jordan was captured. At the time he contacted Halleck, the commander of the department was of the opinion that reaction to Pickett should be made by the government, not by him. Three days later he correctly identified Jordan and explained that use of "Fifth Ohio instead of Fifth Colored" stemmed from the fact that members of this unit were recruited in Ohio (OR, 119, 845, 858)

Responding to Hinton's challenge, Butler's long and argumentative letter was characteristic of the man who was called "Beast" soon after he took command of occupied New Orleans. His actions in what had been the largest city of the Confederacy were such that Rebel leaders formally branded him an outlaw and put a price on his head—probably not expecting ever to hand over the reward that was offered for his capture, dead or alive.

Though he knew only a trifle about the man for whom Jordan was hanged, Butler fumed that Daniel Bright was a deserter who was "carrying on robbery and pillage in the peaceable counties of Camden and Pasquotank [North Carolina.]" These facts, he said, "appeared to the court-martial before which Daniel Bright was tried." Then he added a promise to Hinton:

> if your men are met in the field, in the usual duty of soldiers, under your command or that of any other duly qualified officer carrying on war in any form that war has been carried on by any Christian nation, except the English against the Chinese, they will be treated whenever captured as prisoners of war, and all the more tenderly by me because they are North Carolina troops, most of whom I believe [serve] unwillingly in the service of the Confederate Government.

Characteristically ending his lengthy communication with a threat, Butler said that warfare such as that in eastern North Carolina would be "stopped by the most stringent measures." (OR, 119, 883–84)

About the same time Butler received an appeal that has not been preserved. Responding to it, he made one of the most unusual proposals put forward in a hostage situation. To Lieutenant Munden and Pvt. Pender Weeks of North Carolina defensive forces, he wrote:

> Messrs: In answer to your application in regard to your wives held as hostages by General Wild for the treatment of his colored soldier, Samuel Jordan of the Fifth U.S. Colored, . . .
>
> First. [Wild's order] for the execution of the women in retaliation will be revoked.
>
> Second. I will return the women to Northwest Landing with a copy of this note, as direction to the officer there that upon your placing yourselves in his hands in their stead, to be treated as prisoners of war unless some outrage not justified by civilized warfare is perpetrated by the men

of your commands, the two women, Mrs. W. J. Munden and Mrs. Pender Weeks, will be delivered to their friends.

Concerning Daniel Bright's summary execution by Wild, he wrote to the distraught husbands about the same thing he wrote to Hinton earlier. This time, however, he added what—for Beast Butler—was a conciliatory note: "... the execution of Private Jordan in retaliation for that act [the hanging of Bright] will be made the subject of other and different measures from any that relate to yourselves and your treatment." (OR, 119, 877–78)

Military records concerning use of two housewives as hostages by a Union general end at this point. Scattered allusions in documents held by the University of North Carolina and the North Carolina State Archives indicate that Munden and Weeks went to Norfolk and took the places of their wives, who were then released. Gregory, the "aged citizen of more than sixty years," had developed serious heart trouble while in prison; released, he soon died. Lieutenant Munden and Private Weeks were freed at an undetermined date, and there is no record that the retaliatory action threatened by Butler in his letter to them was ever undertaken.

The *Official Records* include a few other scattered references to use of women as hostages, but all of them are tantalizing. In St. Louis in October 1864, Union acting provost marshal general Joseph Darr, Jr., sent a notice to Capt. R. C. Allen at the local military prison. "Mrs. Hardesty and children and the young boy Woods, with his nurse, are held as hostages," he reported. Since this is the only reference to Mrs. Hardesty, nothing is known about the motive for holding these hostages or what happened to them. (OR, 120, 1019)

An equally enigmatic case involved William ("Bloody Bill") Anderson. In July 1864, copies of a warning letter he addressed to Gen. Egbert B. Brown were sent to newspapers of the region. Anderson said in part that

> I do not like the idea of warring with women and children, but if you do not release all the women you have arrested in La Fayette County, I will hold the Union ladies in the county as hostages for them. I will tie them by the neck in the brush and starve them until they are released, if you do not release them. . . . General, do not think I am jesting with you. I will have to resort to abusing your ladies if you do not quit imprisoning ours. (OR, 84, 75–77)

Like the St. Louis incident, nothing more is known about events involving female hostages in the region where Anderson and his men were virtual rulers for a time.

Federal troops operating near Berwick, Louisiana, in May 1863, heard that a nearby planter had a supply of sugar on hand. A party was dispatched to impress part or all of the sugar, and men were soon loading it into a wagon. Suddenly the proprietor of the place, Wilcoxen, took a shot at the men in blue. Private Loomis of the 90th New York fell to the ground, badly wounded, and Wilcoxen fled across a bayou to safety.

Lt. Joseph S. Morgan of the 90th took quick and decisive action. Reporting about the incident, he wrote that

> I ordered a detachment of mounted infantry to the place, to arrest all persons found thereon, in compliance with which they arrested the wife of Wilcoxen, whom I have brought to this place and hold as a hostage until Wilcoxen delivers himself up, or she be released by order of the major-general commanding. Secreted upon her person was found a loaded revolver . . . (OR, 40, 41–42)

Whether or not Morgan's holding of a dangerous female hostage induced her husband to surrender is unknown.

Far to the east, concerns about women believed to be used as hostages proved groundless. Edwin M. Stanton, Union secretary of war, was alarmed and outraged by a brief notice he found in the June 26, 1863, issue of the *Richmond Dispatch*. According to it, "Eleven Yankee ladies captured at Winchester" had been taken to Richmond and imprisoned. Stanton immediately instructed Col. William H. Ludlow to look into the matter and to take "rebel ladies as hostages for the Yankee ladies" if he deemed it necessary.

This time, there was a quick and happy ending to the story. On July 2 Ludlow reported to Stanton from Fort Monroe that

> Forty-seven of our women and children, being all that were captured at Winchester, have just arrived here from Richmond via City Point and go to Annapolis to-night. The rebels say that they did not intend to retain them, but did not wish to send them through our lines to any other point. . . . Files of Richmond papers from the 23rd of June to this date just received. Will be forwarded to you by the first mail. (OR, 119, 62–63, 72)

Despite the time and energy devoted to them by military leaders, nothing is known about the post-hostage lives of Phoebe Munden and Elizabeth Weeks. Logic suggests, however, that the saga of their seizure and period of imprisonment while threatened with the noose is still very much alive among their descendants.

10

Irrepressible William P. Rucker

At Lewisburg, Virginia, on August 1, 1862, Federal cavalry arrested three citizens. Samuel McClung, Samuel Tuckwiler, and Austin Handley insisted that they had done nothing wrong, but their protests were useless. Soon they learned that they had been taken as hostages for "Mr. William P. Rucker," who had just been seized at Summersville by Rebel cavalry.

On the day the trio were arrested, Col. George Crook ordered C. R. Hines of Palestine to report immediately to Meadow Bluff. He would be required, said Crook, to choose one of two unpalatable alternatives. He could take the oath of allegiance to the United States, posting as bond to guarantee faithfulness to that oath everything he owned. If he chose not to pursue this course of action, he would be forced to move his family south of the Green River. Should he choose a total move as the lesser of two evils, Hines was warned that if again found on the north side of the river he and his family would be "regarded as spies and treated accordingly." (OR, 117, 840)

High-handed treatment of Hines because he had ventured across a small river, plus the taking by Federals of three hostages for a single man seized by Rebels, indicates how tense the region was one year after Bull Run. Virginia had numerous Unionists who strongly opposed secession and civil war, but most of them stayed very quiet and tried to avoid being forced to express opinions. Rucker was cut from entirely different cloth; he seems to have dared openly to boast about his pro-Yankee views. Since his name may have already been familiar in Washington, men in blue did not think their enemies would agree to an even swap of captives. Caution prevailing on their part, they reasoned that three hostages for one prisoner would guarantee his safety. The three civilians in Federal hands were told that they would be treated by their captors precisely as Rebels treated Rucker.

In a dispatch to G. W. Randolph, the current Confederate secretary of war, Gen. W. W. Loring reported that "a recent dash by our cavalry" led to the capture of "the notorious spy and bridge burner, Dr. Wm. P. Rucker."

79

Loring suggested that all of the prisoners taken in a recent Confederate raid should be held for the three Rucker hostages. Randolph referred the issue to Jefferson Davis, whose response must have disappointed Loring. "Retaliation by hanging our disloyal citizens," Jefferson Davis ruled, "does not seem to me a remedy which should be adopted [by] which we may hope to inflict punishment on Yankees." (OR, 117, 839)

Union Col. George Crook, who was in command at Meadow Bluff, sent an August 4 dispatch to Capt. G. M. Bascom, an assistant adjutant general. Crook was careful to use "Flat Top Mountain, W. Va." in addressing Bascom. All officers on both sides knew that Washington had aided and abetted the secession of West Virginia from Virginia—and that leaders in the Old Dominion still claimed the huge region west of the Allegheny Mountains.

Had Crook sent his dispatch to Flat Top Mountain, Virginia, he would have risked censure, for officials in Washington, Richmond, and Wheeling took "the West Virginia matter" extremely seriously. Abraham Lincoln had approved the admission of West Virginia into the Union on December 31, 1862, but Congress did not act until July 20—a trifle more than 10 days days before hostages were taken in a bid to guarantee the safety of Rucker.

To his colleague in what Rebels called "the usurped government under Francis H. Peirpont." Crook noted that the man captured by Rebels should have been listed as "Dr." rather than as "Mr." Rucker was "a gentleman of property and influence" who had done a great deal for the Union cause, he noted. As a result secessionists of Virginia were extremely bitter toward him. Gen. John Charles Fremont had taken great interest in the physician, Crook wrote, and had offered him "a high position" that Rucker probably would have taken had Fremont remained in command. Aware that three hostages had already been taken, the colonel suggested that "Mr. Price, at Charleston, [should] be placed in close confinement and held as hostage for the doctor." (OR, 117, 33)

At Flat Top Mountain, Bascom apparently consulted Gen. Jacob D. Cox about the hostage situation, and with his commander's approval moved the Rucker case into phase two. Following the suggestion of Crook, Mr. Samuel Price of Lewisburg was selected to "be held responsible in his person for any cruel or unusual treatment of Dr. William P. Rucker." Two days later Crook notified the unidentified "Commanding Officer of Confederate Forces, at or near Union, Monroe County," that Price had been paired with Rucker. (OR, 117, 351, 847)

On August 11 William Skeen, attorney for the Commonwealth of Allegheny County, interjected himself into the hostage situation. He reported to Gov. John Letcher that he had issued a written demand that Loring turn his celebrated captive over to civil authorities to be tried for treason, murder, and larceny. He held warrants for the latter two charges, Skeen said, and was sure that treason would be easy to prove. He added that in his opinion, every native of Virginia captured in a blue uniform should be prosecuted for treason "and every Yankee who has stolen a negro made to answer the laws of Virginia." (OR, 117, 856)

Loring, who ignored the Skeen demand, was incensed that "an unarmed and peaceful citizen" such as Price should be used as a hostage. Hence he suggested to the secretary of war that Lt. Col. William C. Starr plus other Federal officers captured at Summersville should be retained as hostages for Price. Confederate Gen. John S. Williams, commander of troops in southwestern Virginia, considered it an outrage that Price had been seized and called actions of Federal soldiers "manifestly a violation of the usages of civilized warfare." Davis pondered reports that had gone to the War Department and suggested that since Rucker was not "avowedly in the employment of the enemy," he might be subject to trial on charges listed by Skeen. (OR, 117, 843, 848)

Letcher, who may have discussed the case with the Rebel president, suggested on August 19 that the secretary of war should instruct Loring "to deliver Rucker to the sheriff of Allegheny, that he may be indicted and tried for violations of the laws of this state." For his part, the commander who had the wanted man in his clutches had no intention of turning him over to someone else or treating him as a prisoner of war. Though doubtful that Rucker could be successfully tried as a spy, Loring wanted him "prosecuted for the treason of leading the enemy into our settlements and burning the bridge over Cow Pasture River while he was a citizen [of Virginia]." (OR, 117, 855–56, 867)

Rucker was soon characterized by Union Col. S. A. Gilbert as "a loyal citizen of the United States." Gilbert was troubled by reports that the prisoner was now "kept in close confinement and in irons" as well as "treated otherwise with unusual and unnecessary harshness and rigor." Mrs. Rucker and their children, who seem to have been living in Layette County where Gilbert was in command, went to Monroe County under a flag of truce and requested to see her husband. (OR, 117, 869–70)

Late in January, Col. William H. Ludlow suggested from Fort Monroe that the Rucker case should enter phase three. State and Confederate authorities were continually clashing in Virginia, he told Gen. E. A. Hitchcock, commissioner for exchange of prisoners.

In his opinion, Letcher—who badly wanted Rucker sent to him by Rebel military leaders—was "assuming power and performing acts in gross violations of the cartels [that governed prisoner exchange]."

In this complex situation, wrote Ludlow, he earnestly recommended that a Confederate medical officer or prominent citizen of Virginia be "immediately set apart as hostage for Doctor Rucker." Simultaneously, he suggested designating Confederate Asst. Surg. J. C. Green as a suitable man to be held for Rucker. Lincoln himself, he noted, had read a report about the Rucker case on January 20 before referring it to Gen. Henry W. Halleck. (OR, 118, 212, 216)

**Fort Monroe was the base from which Col. William H. Ludlow conducted
some of the negotiations about the noted hostage.**

Federal and Confederate agents of exchange having been drawn into
the case, Green was formally designated as the latest in a series of hostages
for Rucker. From Richmond, Robert Ould told his counterpart in Washington that "There is much difficulty in the case of Dr. Rucker. He is charged
with such crimes as you could never say were ordered to be perpetrated by
your Government." In Ould's opinion, this made the prisoner subject to be
tried, not by a military tribunal, but by a Virginia civil court. Two official
reports by Ould about the celebrated prisoner may have been read in Washington, but if so they were eventually lost. (OR, 118, 236, 244, 257)

Union Gen. Ethan A. Hitchcock, who had been interested in Rucker
for some time, began to exert strong influence for his immediate release.
Believing the prisoner now to be held at Liberty in Bedford County, he told
Hoffman to renew demands concerning him.

He authorized the commissary general of prisoners to warn Rebels
that "if he is treated otherwise than as a prisoner of war I shall recommend
retaliation and in the strongest terms." He closed by ordering that Green
be put into close confinement.

Ould, who probably had an informant in Washington, soon interjected
an idea of his own. Almost a year after the physician's capture he suggested
that a suitable captive Union officer should be set aside to retaliate for Federal treatment of "Surgeon Green, held as a hostage for the infamous
Rucker." This idea surfaced at a time when the power struggle between
Confederate military leaders and Virginia's elected officials was accelerat-
ing. Hence Ould recognized that Rucker was likely to be tried first on charges

of having broken civil laws rather than facing a court-martial as a spy. (OR, 118, 356, 941; OR, 119, 13)

By the middle of June 1863, the impasse over Rucker had become insoluble. Ludlow offered to exchange all Rebel surgeons in his custody except Green. Late in the month, Ould pointed out to Washington that Rucker was expected to be tried on Virginia state charges "not sanctioned by any military code." What is more, wrote the Confederate exchange agent, the physician's trial "has been delayed for two terms of the court, at his own instance." Under these circumstances, declared the Richmond official, the continued detention of Rucker was justified by Federal as well as Confederate principles and practices.

Ludlow pondered the complex situation until July 4, by which time he seems to have consulted Halleck again. The Federal general in chief was of the opinion that civil offenses allegedly committed by the physician took place in West Virginia—placing the case within "the military occupation of the United States." Ludlow accordingly notified Ould that he favored "the discharge of Dr. Green" as hostage for Rucker, and was ready to approve the exchange of six Rebel surgeons held at Norfolk for 11 Federal surgeons still in Richmond. (OR, 119, 18, 27, 35–36, 81)

At Fort Monroe, Col. William Hoffman requested a summary of the case that was now more than a year old. From Ludlow, who did not have an official copy of the charges against Rucker, he learned that Ould had said Virginia wanted to try the physician on three major charges: horse stealing, murder, and "acting as a guide for bodies of armed men [soldiers in blue]." Having pondered technicalities involved, on July 8 Halleck told Ould that if the physician's alleged offenses were committed in West Virginia, "by the laws and usages of war the authorities at Richmond have no jurisdiction in his case." Ould immediately notified Richmond that if Rucker had been "improperly retained and punished," Washington would retaliate for his treatment. (OR, 119, 85, 93, 109–10, 165)

Concurrently with this exchange between the two capitals, Hoffman finally put together for Halleck the principal captive's own summary of the events that led to his seizure. He said he was taken at Summersville, in West Virginia's Nicholas County, on July 25, 1862. Earlier he had led a Federal cavalry detachment from Jacksonville Depot to Cow Pasture bridge, which was burned. According to Rucker, he was guilty of no other offenses. Though Virginia did not recognize the existence of West Virginia, authorities who had been involved with Rucker for many months agreed early in August to exchange all captured surgeons except Rucker and the Confederate—Green—who was being held as hostage for him. (OR, 119, 88, 185)

Prodded by the Hoffman findings, Ould for the first time thoroughly investigated the charges against Rucker. He reported to Washington on August 16 that the now-famous captive was charged with having committed murder at Covington in Allegheny County, Virginia, on July 23, 1861. "At that time," Ould pointed out, "no Federal force was there or ever had been; invasion of the region did not take place until May, 1862." Months prior to Federal takeover of this portion of the so-called state of West Virginia, wrote Ould, Rucker was indicted for having stolen a horse.

Rucker's attorney later pinpointed all of the charges. His client was indicted for the murder of Michael Joyce in Allegheny County on July 23, 1861, he noted. A second indictment charged him with "the larceny of a horse of Joseph A. Porringer on the 17th of January, 1862." Eight indictments charged Rucker with treason in connection with his activities on behalf of Federal forces during May 17–19, 1862. The case against the Virginia Unionist had been deferred by the circuit court of Botetour in April 1863, after which it was referred to Danville and continued until the next spring term. (OR, 119, 318)

According to Richmond officials, the physician had no connection with Federal military forces at the time he allegedly committed other crimes. Green, Ould charged, had for months been "wrongfully retained in retaliation." Going far beyond Washington's suggestion that all surgeons except Rucker and Green be immediately exchanged, the Richmond official proposed that the exchange be broadened to include "nurses and members of sanitary commissions."

Gen. S. A. Meredith, now commissioner for exchange in Washington, countered with a demand that officers commanding black troops plus "Negro troops themselves" should also be included in a general exchange. Before placing this radical new proposal before Ould, the Federal general officer knew what the Rebel reply would be. Ould, he reported to the War Department, declined to exchange captured black fighting men. In doing so he said that Rebels "would 'die in the last ditch' before giving up the right to send slaves back to slavery as property recaptured." Richmond was, however, "willing to make exceptions in the case of free blacks." (OR, 119, 109–10, 208–9, 319)

Nathaniel Harrison, Rucker's attorney, had kept a very low profile for months. Now he boldly challenged Confederate authorities. Put the facts of the case before the Confederate public, he suggested, by publishing them in the *Richmond Examiner*. Secretary of War James A. Seddon perused Harrison's letter to the newspaper editor and refused to approve its publication. He said that

> I see no benefit that could result to the Government from the publication of this communication. Mr. H. may be discharging only a duty to his client, but I have to consider only the effect upon the Government, and in that view the publication can do no good and may prove mischievous. (OR, 119, 319)

Relegated to limbo for more than a month, the Rucker case surfaced again on October 2. In Washington that day, Meredith expressed his personal conviction that Rebels had no legitimate reason to hold the physician. Ould immediately responded with passion. "We are either right or wrong in the retention of Rucker," he wrote. "If right, you ought not to hold [Surgeon Green as] an equivalent. In no aspect of the case should Doctor Green or any other equivalent be retained."

Letcher reiterated his demand that the Confederate government turn the physician over to the state of Virginia. George W. Randolph, again the Confederate secretary of war, sifted through conflicting claims and decided that Virginia's governor had offered valid arguments. On October 2, he told a subordinate to notify Letcher that Rucker would be delivered for trial for murder and horse theft. This procedure, he ruled, made it "unnecessary to discuss the policy of our initiating trials for treason."

Before the month ended, in Washington it was charged by Hitchcock that Rebels had held three surgeons in addition to Rucker as hostages for Green. Ould had earlier observed that when Federals began holding Green for the Richmond prisoner, "Surgeons were afterward held in captivity on both sides." Hence it appears that Rucker exceeded Zarvona's record of causing seven men to become hostages. Though not all of them were involved at the same time, at least eight persons—probably more—were imprisoned by Richmond or Washington because of "the infamous Dr. Rucker." (OR, 117, 876; 119, 337–38, 382, 656)

Since the charge of treason was dropped and civil charges were remanded to Allegheny County, military records say nothing about decisions made concerning Rucker by a jury or juries. If the man accused of aiding and abetting Federal troops was convicted on any charge, he did not remain a prisoner for any length of time. In October 1864, a detective grilled George Fellows, who was charged with belonging to the secret "Order of Heroes of America." A black shoemaker warned the Federal agent that local citizens were planning to form a band and seize him. During their conversation, the shoemaker "inquired of us about Doctor Rucker and his command. Said his wife had a ring which was given to her by Doctor Rucker with his name on it."

Brief as it was, this allusion suggests that Rucker, now a free man, was holding a responsible position in Federal forces operating outside Virginia. This supposition about one of the Old Dominion's most irrepressible Unionists is confirmed by a terse November 27, 1864, dispatch from Tullahoma, Alabama. In it Asst. Adj. Gen. John O. Cravens informed Maj. John F. Armstrong of the 5th Tennessee Cavalry that "the general commanding received your report last night by Doctor Rucker."

11

"Minor Incidents" Abounded

Compared with numerous hostage cases that involved dozens or scores of persons, an incident in which no more than 10 men were seized was minor—at least in size. It was not minor to the persons who became hostages or to their families, however. Small-scale incidents took place in at least 18 states and the District of Columbia. Collectively, they involved large numbers of persons, most of whom committed no offense except that of being in the wrong place at the wrong time.

Near Stevenson, Alabama, Maj. Lewis R. Stegman of the 102nd New York found two young males lounging on a riverbank. Needing a local guide, he impressed—or forcibly secured—one of them to act in this capacity. Seeking to guarantee that his guide would not lead him up a blind alley, the Federal officer took his brother as hostage "for his good behavior."

Alabama Unionist Dixon Chitty having been arrested by Rebels, Col. R. F. Smith seized "known secessionists" David Harris and James H. Bell. At Bridgeport he penned a report in which he recommended that both be held "as hostages for the safe and prompt return through our lines of said Chitty."

At Huntsville, C. C. Clay, Sr., and "another prominent gentleman" were arrested and taken to Nashville. There they were held as hostages for the safety of Judge West H. Humphreys of Madison County, earlier arrested by Confederates for "disloyalty." (OR, 53, 219; OR, 57, 659; OR, 121, 86–87)

Incidents of this sort were as numerous in Arkansas as in Alabama. Confederate Gen. T. C. Hindman was provoked when he learned that men under Gen. John S. Marmaduke had made prisoners of Federals who were hospitalized at Fayetteville. Before he could secure their release, Union Gen. James G. Blunt made hostages of "a number to citizens" in order to guarantee that the sick men would not remain in captivity.

At Helena, Capt. C. O'Connell of the 15th Illinois Cavalry received stern orders from Gen. N. B. Buford to lead a raid into a region drained by Big

Nashville, Tennessee, was a sprawling river town under Federal occupation when hostages were sent there for safekeeping.

Creek, where he was warned that a loyal citizen named Hobbs might have been a victim of secessionists. Should that prove to be the case, directed Buford, "You will seize as hostages two of the most influential rebels you can find who have given aid and comfort to the enemy."

Not far from Fayetteville, A. Drury McMinn was found shot through the head after having been tied to a tree. When he learned of the tragedy, Lt. Col. T. H. Baker rejoiced that he already held as prisoner L. Burnett, who had earlier been sent to him as a hostage for McMinn. (OR, 59, 746; OR, 62, 240; OR, 117, 949)

In the District of Columbia, military Governor James S. Wadsworth did not ask for approval of a plan by the U.S. secretary of war. Without authorization from above, he seized Alfred Leigh, Joshua C. Gunnell "and one or two other disloyal citizens of Northeastern Virginia as hostages for the safe return of certain Union citizens of the same region now imprisoned in Richmond." (OR, 117, 28)

Florida residents first saw black soldiers in blue when Col. T. W. Higginson took the 1st South Carolina on an expedition up the St. Mary's River. Reporting to Gen. Rufus Saxton, he described his men as having "a fiery energy about them beyond anything of which I have ever read." They seized ship loads of railroad iron and lumber, and took six male hostages whom they brought to Hilton Head, South Carolina. In the same state, Confederate Asst. Surg. William Wilson was held as a hostage for a period before being exchanged. (OR, 20, 195–96; OR, 66, 244)

There is no record that men under the command of Gen. William T. Sherman took hostages during their move through the state of Georgia. His foes, however, took H. G. Tibbals of Macon as a citizen prisoner and held him "for the release of the large numbers of the same class" of secessionists "cruelly and outrageously imprisoned" by Federals. (OR, 120, 441)

Even Indiana, far from major battlefields, was the target of an attempt at hostage taking. A party consisting of two officers and 13 men of Col. Adams Johnson's partisan rangers crossed the Ohio River and entered the Hoosier State from Kentucky. Bent upon finding a suitable hostage for a recently captured Rebel surgeon, these raiders were captured and treated as felons by Indiana authorities. (OR, 119, 1)

Natives of Kentucky and newcomers to the state were central to numerous "minor incidents." Ulysses S. Grant authorized the seizure of "two leading secessionists from the neighborhood of Elliott's Mills" in order to use them as hostages for

Gen. William Tecumseh Sherman, who was as fierce as he looked, seems to have considered hostage taking beneath the dignity of an officer and a gentleman.

Unionist William Mercer. In and around Lexington, Union Gen. Alexander S. Asboth, a native of Hungary, made hostages of William T. Collins, John F. Clark, John E. West, George W. Pool, William F. Kiser, Verbin Trico, and William Barnhill. Near Eddyville, men of the 13th U.S. Colored Heavy Artillery took Mrs. Hylan B. Lyon as a hostage, giving them leverage enough to secure the release of captured Federal officers. (OR, 3, 507; OR, 38, 434; OR, 77, 876)

At Feliciana, Kentucky, men led by Union Gen. Henry Prince seized Dr. Robert D. Lockridge as hostage for a captured Unionist identified only as Terrell. An unspecified number of citizens of Lawrence County also became hostages for prisoners confined by the enemy. After the battle of Perryville, three Union surgeons and an assistant surgeon became hostages but were soon released when Grant issued an order to pass Rebel surgeons through the line. Near Louisa, Union Col. John Cranor took seven hostages: G. M. Whitten, S. W. Porter, J. G. Trimble, David D. Sublet, Henry Hager, A. S. Martin, and John M. Burns. Once these men were in custody, Cranor did not know what to do with them in the event Rebels refused to release the prisoners for whom they were seized. (OR, 78, 54; OR, 115, 406; OR, 117, 14–15, 384)

Also in Kentucky, Union Gen. Samuel P. Carter made "a rebel citizen in Laurel County" hostage for captured Unionist Preston Berry. A. H. Townly of Campbell County was taken by men under Confederate Gen. Kirby Smith and held as hostage for imprisoned L. C. Norman of Boone County, a secessionist. Capt. George Austin of the 2nd Kentucky (Union) was made hostage for a Confederate captain whom the enemy refused to exchange. (OR, 117, 411; OR, 118, 3, 648)

Louisiana remembered Union Gen. Benjamin F. Butler's stay in New Orleans for many years. While there, he took A. Deslondes and an undesignated number of other civilians as hostages "for the safety of Mr. Burbank and other peaceable citizens" who had been seized by Rebels. From Vicksburg, Mississippi, General Grant sent raiders into Louisiana, where they discovered that Confederate Gen. "Dick" Taylor, son of former President Zachary Taylor, held a number of males as hostages near Delphi. At Goodrich's Landing, Col. A. Watson Webber of the U.S. 51st Colored took a hostage named Dr. Richardson and held him for the safety of a captive he identified only as "young Webster."

In Louisiana's La Forche Military District, commanded by Union Gen. Robert A. Cameron, Lt. P. J. Maloney held H. Burnley "as a hostage for the further conduct of his son." Taylor, who held hostages of his own, protested to Gen. Nathaniel P. Banks when the Federal commander made hostages of an undesignated number of "non-combatant citizens residing on Bayou Boeuf." Men held by Banks, raged Taylor, were peaceful citizens whose arrest had been arbitrary. "The suffering of these unoffending men for the

Hilton Head, South Carolina, was already a major supply depot when Col. T. W. Higginson brought six hostages to the Federal base.

In New Orleans, where Union Gen. Benjamin F. Butler was portrayed by secessionists as a beast, the man from Massachusetts—central to many later cases—took hostages of his own.

supposed guilt of others has nothing in the rules of civilized warefare to extenuate it," he told Banks. (OR, 21, 554; OR, 36, 110; OR, 83, 294; OR, 78, 102; OR, 119, 309)

A Maryland incident led to a protest directed to Abraham Lincoln. Confederate Gen. Jubal Early took seven residents of Hagerstown as hostages, alleging that he did so to ensure the safety of civilians arrested earlier by Union Gen. David Hunter. There is no record that the president took any action in this case. In a separate incident reported by James G. Wiltshire of Mosby's battalion of partisans, 25 men of this command penetrated Maryland with the goal of making the governor a hostage. Raiders encountered unexpected bodies of soldiers in blue, however, so they never reached the White House at Annapolis where the governor resided. Only eight of the party managed to get back into Virginia and safety. (OR, 120, 576–77; JSHS, 28, 135–45)

In Mississippi, men under Union Gen. Neal Dow seized two hostages at Pass Christian and sent them to Fort Pike "for safe-keeping." Near Grand Gulf, Col. O. C. Risdon of the Union 53rd Colored made a hostage of a Dr. Carroll simply because he admitted that he was not "a Union man." (OR, 21, 112; OR, 103, 85)

Not all such activity was by Federal forces, however. At Vicksburg Confederate Gen. John C. Pemberton, a native of Pennsylvania, held a lottery by which four captives in blue were selected as hostages for Confederates captured in Tennessee. While directing the siege of Vicksburg, Grant received from Maj. N. G. Watts four soldiers who had been held hostage by Rebels for more than six months. Their release came about when men under Watts made hostages of four Rebel fighting men. Also near Vicksburg, correspondents A. D. Richardson and Junius H. Browne of the *New York Tribune* became hostages. Rebels claimed they were seized in retaliation for civilians who had been arrested by Federal forces. At Fort Monroe, William H. Ludlow discounted this explanation and told Edwin M. Stanton that he believed their status as newspaper representatives led Rebels to seize them in order to annoy their foes. (OR, 117, 933; OR, 119, 37, 39, 59)

Missouri's share of small-scale hostage incidents was far less than might have been expected in view of the fact that it saw more clashes between armed forces than any other state in what was then the West. Officials of the village of Bynumville informed Union Gen. Clinton B. Fisk that a Unionist named Clark had been blindfolded before being taken off to serve as a hostage "for one thief at Macon City."

Union Gen. E. B. Brown was stymied when word leaked out that he planned to execute a captive identified only as Erwin. Guerrilla chieftain "Bloody Bill" Anderson seized three residents of Wellington and held them as hostages for the safety of the condemned man. Not to be outdone, Brown had six Wellington civilians arrested and held as hostages for the three Anderson held. Records failed to indicate the winner in this deadly game of "chicken." (OR, 64, 203)

Also in Missouri, Union Gen. Franz Sigel authorized the taking of three civilians as hostages in an attempt to put an end to "thieving and murdering" allegedly committed in the neighborhood of Rolla by unidentified bushwhackers. In Marion County, Confederate Asst. Surgs. Thomas S. Foster and Newton Vowles were seized by Federal forces when they paid a visit to their families. Both captives were sent to Alton Prison and one was reported to be be under sentence of death. An appeal to Richmond led Gen. John H. Winder to order the casting of lots "for two hostages of equal rank" to the Missouri natives then languishing at Alton. (OR, 86, 918; OR, 116, 896)

A few civilians of North Carolina, where most of the fighting took place along the Atlantic Coast, became hostages in contested areas. "Several prominent citizens of Bertie County were brought away" by Federal forces. It was hoped by captors that they would serve as leverage by which to win freedom for Unionists imprisoned in Richmond. At New Bern, men in blue made Joseph G. Godfrey hostage for Baker White, said to be a Rebel deserter who had gone over to the enemy before being captured. The high-profile case in which two Tar Heel females became hostages is discussed in chapter 9. (OR, 60, 24; OR, 117, 951–52)

Pennsylvania was hit very hard by Confederate Gen. J. E. B. Stuart's famous raid into the state. With the express authorization of Robert E. Lee, the cavalrymen took several groups of "public functionaries and prominent citizens" as hostages. A large contingent of these civilians spent a period in the infamous Salisbury, North Carolina, prison. Stuart explained the capture

Guerrilla chieftain "Bloody Bill" Anderson didn't hesitate to kill, but sometimes took hostages he thought might be useful.

of innocent and unoffending nonbelligerents by saying that he hoped their imprisonment would win freedom for some of "our own unoffending citizens whom the enemy has torn from their homes and confined in dungeons in the North." A lengthy protest to Lincoln by Governor Andrew G. Curtin failed to win total protection for the Keystone State or to free its imprisoned civilians. (JSHS, 3, 75; OR, 90, 755)

South Carolina, where the largest single body of hostages of 1861–65 was briefly in a stockade, experienced one incident about which few details were preserved. Confederate Maj. John Jenkins notified Gen. Johnson Hagood, a graduate of The Citadel military academy, that an unspecified number of Rebels captured along the Edisto River were not exchanged. Instead, they were taken to Beaufort and lodged in the local jail. Jenkins speculated that perhaps these hostages were being held "for the safety of officers commanding negro troops and negro troops themselves who may be captured in some of their raids." (OR, 118, 970)

Like Kentucky and Missouri, Tennessee never seceded. But citizens of all three of these states were inextricably divided in their loyalties. Tennessee experienced too many briefly treated hostage incidents to deal with all of them here. For volunteer state cases in addition to those summarized below, see: Neely, *Fate*, 151–52; Foote, 1, 570–71; M, 13, 298; RR, 6, D, 47; OR, 55, 506–7; OR, 56, 366; OR, 117, 477, 491; OR, 118, 16; OR, 119, 139, 1108; OR, 121, 267, 272–73, 425)

Angry at receiving news that a prominent Unionist had been captured by the enemy, Capt. A. T. Snodgrass of the 1st Ohio seized "six of the most prominent citizens" of Whitesides and held them as hostages. None of them denied being secessionists, but Snodgrass released two of them when they solemnly swore to try to secure the release of the imprisoned Unionist. Col. Fielding Hurst of the 6th Tennessee Cavalry (Union) was enraged when told that men under Confederate Gen. Nathan B. Forrest had murdered four Unionists of Weakley and McNairy Counties "in cold blood, without the slightest provocation." He retaliated by making plans to "arrest the fathers, brothers, and sons of these murderers and hold them in prison as hostages." (OR, 77, 494; OR, 78, 56)

Writing to Pemberton from their prison in Oxford, Mississippi, Thomas H. Newbern and G. W. Day described themselves as "representing wealth and influence." They said that along with four other residents of Jackson, Tennessee, they were seized and made hostages for "four Union men arrested by some independent partisans." Preoccupied with the defense of Vicksburg, Pemberton seems to have failed to acknowledge this plea. Almost simultaneously, Union Gen. John C. Vaughn applied to the secretary of war for permission to arrest "a number of prominent men" as hostages for Congressman Joseph B. Heiskell, who had been captured at Rogersville a few months earlier. (OR, 117, 928–29; OR, 120, 1184, 1192)

In McMinn County, three men became hostages in the aftermath of a fracas over swine. Confederate agent John Dunn reportedly showed up at the farm owned by Jesse R. Blackburn and said he had come to impress (that is, seize) all of the hogs on the place. Blackburn stalled for time, permitting his son-in-law to find a couple of his friends and return with their weapons. Dunn fled when the civilians fired at him, but a party of soldiers soon arrested Blackburn as a bushwhacker. Federal authorities retaliated by seizing three hostages for the safety of the imprisoned farmer. The hostages dispatched an urgent appeal to Jefferson Davis to have Blackburn released so that they could be freed, but more than a month passed before their letter reached the president, whose course of action, if any, was not recorded. (OR, 119, 890; OR, 120, 1046, 1126)

Virginia, where more military clashes occurred than in any other state, was the site of numerous large and many relatively small cases in which hostages were involved. A handful of the later are briefly described below. For additional incidents of the same sort see: CV, 25, 349; RR, 5, D, 52; OR, 18, 595; OR, 31, 33; OR, 48, 109; OR, 70, 593; OR, 90, 836; OR, 115, 268, 1509; OR, 117, 28, 276, 777, 840, 879, 947; OR, 118, 817, 822; OR, 119, 27; OR, 120, 7–8, 1066, 1270; OR, 121, 72.

Early in the war, Union Gen. Henry W. Slocum revealed his lack of experience in dealing with civilians whose loyalty was divided. He recommended that two hostages should be held in order to restore quiet in the vicinity of Accotin. Gen. W. B. Franklin, who at that time seems to have been as naive as Slocum, approved the suggestion. Later in the conflict, soldiers in blue took a father and son as hostages. Isaac Motes, all of 15 years old, was held "for the good conduct of his brothers who are now in arms against us."(OR, 115, 90, 1442)

From Fort Wool, four prominent men addressed an 1862 appeal to Gen. George B. McClellan. They told him that "about 100 citizens of Virginia who have in no way been connected with the present war are confined at this place." Continued imprisonment, they urged, would only teach inmates "to hate the Government under which we were born." Forwarded through the headquarters of Gen. John A. Dix, the appeal received a terse reply saying only that "General McClellan does not know for whom you are held as hostages." (OR, 117, 144–45)

Union Secretary of War Edwin M. Stanton, like other top officials on both sides, read newspapers avidly. From the *Richmond Dispatch* he learned that "eleven Yankee ladies captured at Winchester" had been taken to the Rebel capital and imprisoned in Castle Thunder. Consequently he ordered Lt. Col. William H. Ludlow to make an investigation—and simultaneously sent a telegram to Annapolis in which he cited the imprisonment of the women as a basis for taking hostages "for their safe return."

Not one of the scores of instances in which a small number of hostages were taken had any impact upon the course or outcome of the war. Usually reported in as few words as possible, sometimes without indicating numbers or identities of persons seized, these cases are all but sterile when reduced to black marks upon white paper.

Seizure of a civilian who had done nothing to harm the enemy but was nevertheless made hostage for someone of whom he had never heard was indescribably inflammatory. A friend or neighbor or acquaintance arbitrarily seized by the enemy was correctly seen as entirely innocent. Hence even the most insignificant of hostage cases aroused passions of relatives, friends, and acquaintances and frequently led to violent retaliation.

Collectively, these cases—along with others described at greater length—fanned the flames of sectional hatred in a fashion quite different from news about results of clashes between armed forces. Because hostage taking frequently pitted villagers against villagers, this practice played a significant but overlooked role in magnifying the intensity and duration of the struggle between Northerners and Southerners.

12

Indomitable Samuel Price

Protocol, usually but not always embodied in formal cartels concerning exchange of prisoners, dictated that exchanges should be equal. That is, privates should be exchanged for privates, captains for captains, and colonels for colonels. In a few special cases, a negotiator agreed to give a specified number of privates or captains for a colonel or general. Civilians who were held as hostages normally had civilian counterparts but when the pairing was military/civilian, things could become extremely complicated.

On August 11, 1862, Confederate Gen. W. W. Loring sent to the secretary of war in Richmond a dispatch in which he said that

> A letter has been received from Colonel Crook, commanding Federal brigade, by flag of truce informing me that Mr. Samuel Price, of Greenbrier, an unarmed and peaceful citizen, some time since would be dealt with in the same way as Dr. Rucker. May I request that Lieutenant-Colonel [William C.] Starr and the other commissioned officers taken at Summersville be retained as hostages for Mr. Price and that I be advised of the fact. I will send the correspondence to Richmond by mail.

Loring's highly unusual suggestion that Federal officers be designated as hostages for Price hints that he was no commonplace citizen. Union authorities evidently considered him to be of importance, or they would not have made him a hostage for Dr. William P. Rucker, who is treated in chapter 10. Seized by Federals and made hostage for the Confederate-held physician early in August 1862, the influential civilian from Lewisburg was twice warned that he would be "held responsible in his person" for what captors did to his fellow citizen of western Virginia. (OR, 117, 336, 351, 845)

As soon as he knew the facts of the case, Confederate Gen. John S. Williams protested to Federal forces that "The seizure and imprisonment of Price as a hostage for Rucker is manifestly a violation of the usages of civilized warfare and to harm him will be a high crime." Three days later, on August 19, the secretary of war notified the Confederate president that Price had been made a hostage. Col. George Crook, who seems temporarily to have had physical custody of the Lewisburg civilian, refused to discuss the matter with Williams. (OR, 117, 427, 848, 855, 858)

Union Col. S. A. Gilbert, commander in Fayette County, soon took a much more conciliatory course. He notified the commanding officer of Confederate forces in Monroe County that Price had been shipped to Charleston, where he had been "allowed the limits of the town." Having heard rumors that Rucker was kept in close confinement and in irons, Gilbert wanted to know whether or not this was true. If he should get no reply or an affirmative one to his question, the Federal officer warned, Price would be subjected to the treatment Rucker was getting. (OR, 119, 879)

Price came to the attention of Jefferson Davis soon after the Rebel capital was moved from Montgomery to Richmond. In mid-September 1861, the Virginian endorsed and amplified a letter addressed to the Confederate president by Mason Mathews of Lewisburg. Mathews was disturbed and a bit frightened at "the unfriendly relations" between Gens. John B. Floyd and Henry A. Wise. Thinking that he needed a person of influence to support his concern in order to have it addressed, he requested Price to give it an indorsement. In doing so, the future hostage labeled the tension between the former Union secretary of war and Wise as a "dangerous evil." (OR, 5, 864–65)

A friend of Price delivered a letter from him to Judah P. Benjamin, then the secretary of war, in December 1861. As a man of substance in the region west of the Allegheny Mountains, Price expressed indignation that the central Confederate government had not made a strenuous effort to retain control of what became West Virginia. To Benjamin he tossed questions that were difficult to answer, saying in part, that

> Why is the whole of Western Virginia to be given up? Is Virginia too large in this scale of States? Is there any real desire to have Virginia dissevered and the west given over to the Federals? I am pained to think of the treatment which we have received. A small force would have prevented this humiliating result, but now the bloodhounds have fleshed their fangs it will take an army to prevent the recurrence of a like event. We must move away from our homes and give up all we possess, or be subject to the invasions and insults of these robbers. (OR, 5, 1010–11)

Two weeks earlier, the Virginia State Convention had made Price one of nine members of a special committee authorized to consider "the practicability of rescuing from the enemy the waters of this Commonwealth." Clearly, the man for whom Federal officers would later be hostages was heard when he spoke. (OR, 128, 416–17)

Price, who obviously was free before being given this special responsibility, had been exchanged late in August, after Union officials decided to use a Rebel surgeon as hostage for Rucker. Surprisingly, the outspoken Virginia lawmaker was swapped for a mere sutler, R. C. Eveleth of the 17th New York, who had been taken on June 13 near the White House Landing and had spent most of the intervening time in Libby Prison. Concurrently with the exchange, captive sutler S. S. Mann of the 18th Massachusetts, who was held at Frederick, Maryland, was turned loose because of illness. Without explaining their reasoning, Rebel officials said that the Mann release made it possible to effect the Price/Eveleth exchange. (OR, 117, 426–27)

This swap left Rucker in jeopardy and moved Starr from the hostage category to that of prisoner of war. Strangely, Confederate Gen. W. W. Loring had gone on record as saying that an oral statement by Starr constituted the only evidence upon which Rucker could be treated as a prisoner of war. His case was left hanging when he was removed from custody as hostage for Price. (OR, 117, 867)

Issued from the War Department in Washington on August 27, General Order No. 118 constituted a partial list of officers recently exchanged for "prisoners taken in arms against the United States." Union Gen. J. F. Reynolds had been exchanged for Confederate Gen. Lloyd Tilghman and Confederate Gen. Simon Bolivar Buckner had finally been swapped for Union Gen. G. A. McCall. Exchange value of all prisoners delivered at City Point, Virginia, on the James River was calculated to be equivalent to 4,135 privates. (OR, 117, 437–50)

Buckner's imprisonment, much longer than usual, stemmed from the day he surrendered in response to Grant's demand for unconditional surrender. These terms took Buckner by surprise; earlier he had befriended both Grant and his wife, so he expected to be treated as an old friend. Instead, he had to swallow his memories and his pride and sign the surrender before going to prison for many months.

Immediately below the listing of four general officers who were enumerated by the Federal War Department was the name of Col. Michael Corcoran, "Sixty-ninth New York State Militia, for Col. R. W. Hanson." Though he was the first hostage selected in the Ligon Prison lottery held on behalf of Confederate privateers (see chapter 1), Corcoran may have been the last of the 14 to be exchanged. Though the date was not reported, Lt. Colonel Starr of the Ninth West Virginia had been formally exchanged for Lt. Col. A. G. Carden of the Confederate 18th Tennessee regiment. (OR, 117, 438)

Involvement of Price in military matters would seem to end with his exchange, but it did not. On February 3, 1863, Confederate Gen. Samuel Jones notified the resident of Greenbrier County that Union Gen. Eliakim P. Scammon's men had been reported as having committed outrages without orders. Jones asked Price to look into the matter, secure depositions, and forward them to him. Soon afterward, Price sent the Confederate secretary of war a strongly worded protest against removing men in gray from the Greenbrier Valley. (OR, 120, 607; OR, 108, 735)

Union Gen. John F. Reynolds, shown falling from the saddle in the heat of battle, became a prisoner and was exchanged for Confederate Gen. Lloyd Tilghman.

Alfred Waud sketch, Library of Congress

On January 20, 1864, Price was the spokesman for numerous members of the Virginia legislature who requested from Richmond much stronger forces in order to halt Federal invasions of western Virginia. In the Rebel capital, Davis referred the Price letter "for remarks" to Gen. Robert E. Lee. He recommended sending two more regiments to the region, while insisting that he believed it "more important that the troops now in West Virginia should be more thoroughly organized and disciplined than increased." Price must have made a wry grimace when he learned of this recommendation. He undoubtedly had clear memories of the months during which Lee commanded troops in that region and was repeatedly defeated and thwarted by Federals under Gen. George B. McClellan. (OR, 60, 1106–7)

Confederate Gen. Lloyd Tilghman was treated as an equivalent—or "equal"—for Union Gen. J. F. Reynolds in a high-level exchange of prisoners.

Price later heard that Jones had resigned or had been ordered out of what had become West Virginia, so urged "Do not accept of his resignation yet." That was the last military matter upon which the ex-hostage registered an opinion that was preserved in Richmond or Washington. After all, recent elections had forced him to devote most of his time and energy to civil affairs. As the new lieutenant governor of the Old Dominion, he had his hands more than full without continuing to dispense advice to mere colonels. (OR, 108, 736; OR, 119, 934)

Initially a civilian/civilian incident involving Rucker and Price, substitutions of hostages caused both the Starr/Price and the Green/Rucker case to become military/civilian in nature. Though at least two of them were sensational, such arrangements were rare. They seem to have become more frequent soon after the Emancipation Proclamation was issued, however, and continued throughout the conflict. Some reports about hostage taking dangle in the air, since no follow-up records can be found.

At or near Pensacola, Florida, in January, three civilians who refused "to take the oath of allegiance to the Abolition Government" were confined in Fort Pickens. In Mobile, Alabama, Gen. Simon B. Buckner was furious when he learned that Judge B. D. Wright, George W. Wright, and a Mr. Merritt were being treated harshly by the enemy. He therefore issued an order directing that three captured Federal soldiers from the 105th Ohio—officers, not privates—be held as hostage for them. Capt. B. W. Canfield, 1st Lt. A. W. Tourgee, and 2nd Lt. Alonzo Chubb were picked for the civilian/military hostage situation. Since later reports concerning these six men have not been preserved, they were presumably honorably exchanged. (OR, 118, 242)

About two weeks later, at Washington, Gen. E. A. Hitchcock ordered Rebel civilian Fairfax Minor held hostage for Sgt. Michael Mullen. Six weeks after these men were paired at a distance, Col. William H. Ludlow notified Hitchcock that "Mullen in whom you took a personal interest is released and went to Annapolis today." (OR, 118, 268, 437)

Federals apprehended Daniel Dusky and Jacob Varner on charges of having robbed a post office; tried as civilians and found guilty, they were given long sentences. Neither man served his time, however; Rebels contended that both of them were regularly enrolled partisans and by mid-February 1863, were holding Federal officers as hostages for them. (OR, 118, 269)

Three months later Confederate agent of exchange Robert Ould notified his counterpart in Washington that his patience was exhausted. For six months he would have been sending Ludlow lists of captive officers, privates, and civilians, he said. Since only a few of them had been released, he warned that Rebel authorities "will exercise their discretion in selecting such prisoners as they think best, whether officers or privates, in retaliation. He wrote that he was giving Ludlow "an opportunity of saving a resort to so stern a measure." (OR, 118, 690)

Men in blue seized the Reverend G. W. D. Harris of Dyer County, Tennessee, in March 1864. As soon as Rebel Gen. Nathan B. Forrest learned that Harris was confined at Fort Pillow, he addressed a dispatch that, for him, was relatively long. Sent to the commanding officer of Union forces at Memphis, Forrest demanded that the minister be given "a fair trial before a competent tribunal, or else unconditionally and promptly released." To guarantee that his terms would be met, the cavalry leader said he was placing five captured Federal soldiers in close confinement. If Harris died from ill treatment while in the hands of the enemy, warned the Rebel general, "These men shall be duly executed in retaliation." Since nothing more is known of Harris, the five-for-one military/civilian showdown presumably led to his quick release. (OR, 59, 117)

Sgt. James T. Wells of the Confederate 2nd South Carolina was wounded at Gettysburg, then captured. After a hospital stay he was sent to Fort McHenry, where another hostage lottery was conducted. All prisoners from his state were told they could either take an oath of allegiance to the United States "or submit to the drawing of lots." A few men yielded, but Wells later wrote that "the majority remained firm."

When the lottery was held, names of three members of the 2nd South Carolina Cavalry—Williams, McDowell, and Cline—were drawn and they

Confederate Gen. Nathan B. Forrest took five hostages and held them for the safety of a Dyer County, Tennessee, clergyman who had been arrested by the enemy.

were transferred to the old Carroll Prison in Washington D.C. By the time they left Fort McHenry, all captives knew that the trio had become "hostages to be retained by the United States Government for the safe return of three negroes captured by Confederates at Charleston." According to Wells, this military/civilian dilemma was never resolved. He said that he later learned that his comrades "were retained in close confinement during the war." Prison so injured their health, according to Wells, that "two of them died soon after they came home." (JSHS, 7, 324–25)

A potential impasse near Kingston, Georgia, during the fall of 1864 seems to have been solved by Gen. William T. Sherman. Berry Houk, in whose home a wounded soldier in blue lay, was taken prisoner by men of the 74th Indiana. Sherman ordered Houk freed and charged with returning home and taking good care of the wounded man—a service for which he would be paid 75 cents per day in gold. Houk evidently performed his duties faithfully and well, for the wounded man for whom he was responsible was in the Federal military hospital at Chattanooga, Tennessee on November 11. (OR, 79, 744)

Two months later, Union Maj. John McGaughey was captured near Knoxville, presumably by guerrillas. Capt. T. A. Stevenson of the 2nd Ohio Heavy Artillery promptly sent a detachment of the 7th Tennessee into the region of the capture. Their mission was "to arrest three of the most noted rebel sympathizers in the county, to hold as hostages" for McGaughey. This officer, earlier a delegate to East Tennessee conventions of Unionists, did not remain in enemy hands very long; by September 1864, he was a Federal deputy provost marshal. Four months later, the ex-prisoner wore the insignia of a major on his shoulders and was attached to a combat unit. (OR, 78, 384; OR, 94, 616; OR, 103, 13–14; OR, 109, 148, 169, 171)

One of the most complicated and long-drawn of all military/civilian hostage situations revolved about a murder said to have been committed in Mississippi by Federal soldiers. Bucked up the Rebel line of command, a condensed account of the alleged atrocity reached the desk of Jefferson

Davis early in October 1862. Henry C. Daniel of the Rebel president's adopted state informed him that William H. White had been murdered by the Germans of the 6th Illinois Cavalry, whom Daniel termed Dutch. (OR, 117, 923–24)

A resident of DeSoto County, White was said to have been killed near his residence on or about September 11. Capt. John M. Boicourt was accused of having inflicted the first wound upon White on the Hernando and Memphis plank road, about 13 miles from the latter city. Gen. J. C. Pemberton, who feared that every word of the accusation was true, had already taken four hostages.

"Selected by lot," the men whom Pemberton threatened to execute if White's murder could be proved were James E. Gaddy of the 6th Illinois Cavalry, Bernard Collins of the 39th Ohio, A. M. Chipman of the 3rd Ohio, and Nicholas Hot of the 7th Iowa. A blunt accusation and summary by Pemberton was directed to the general officer commanding Union forces in Memphis. Though the Rebel commander undoubtedly knew that officer to be Gen. William T. Sherman, for some reason he did not address him by name. (OR, 117, 702)

Sherman's tart reply began with a charge that though Pemberton was aware of "the most aggravated part of the story," he knew nothing about "the attending circumstances." Men from the 6th Illinois Cavalry were fired upon from ambush near White's residence, the Federal commander pointed out. Two men were killed by parties unknown and one was wounded. Learning of the incident, Boicourt led a detachment to the place in order to investigate.

White's home, said Sherman, was located almost on the Tennessee/Mississippi state line but he was killed in Mississippi. The death of the civilian, he asserted, was an inevitable outcome of guerrilla war then practiced in the region. Boicourt would answer to military authorities and perhaps to civil authorities upon the restoration of peace, he told Pemberton but said the accused man would not answer to "the Confederate Government or its officers." With Grant in command of the department, a final verdict would have to come from him. Meanwhile, Sherman threatened to select four captured Rebel soldiers as hostages for the men Pemberton had chosen. (OR, 117, 724–25)

In a lengthy separate dispatch, Sherman told the story as he knew it to Maj. John A. Rawlins, assistant adjutant general of Grant's forces. Both the mother and the wife of White had asserted that the dead civilian was only 23 years old, "delicate in health and never a guerrilla." White, said Sherman, was seized at his residence and while being led through the yard offered resistance that led to his death, after which "the house of White was burned down."

Stressing that he did not condone the killing of a civilian on suspicion, Sherman nevertheless insisted that White's death was "the natural consequence" of earlier fire upon Federal soldiers by guerrillas. He then added a sentence that went directly to the heart of military/civilian hostage situations. "On what rule General Pemberton or his associates propose to retaliate on the persons of four of our soldiers I do not understand," he wrote. He ended by suggesting that he be permitted to withhold all captured Rebels from exchange until the Pemberton threat was withdrawn. (OR, 117, 729–30)

Clearly furious at being involved in this case, Sherman soon sent a dispatch to the Federal commander of the guard on the steamer *Metropolitan*. After naming the hostages held by Pemberton, he requested that if they were not delivered on demand four Rebel privates selected by lot should be withheld from exchange. "White," he pointed out, "was not a Confederate soldier or even guerrilla, and if the Confederate authorities want to offset the killing of White you can quote plenty of private murders committed by their adherents."

During the period Sherman devoted to composing and writing his dispatches, Confederate Gen. M. L. Smith reported to Vicksburg the names of the four Federals who were being held hostage. (OR, 117, 747–48, 933–34)

Grant's next brief dispatch to Pemberton at Jackson dealt entirely with supplies for wounded men. He made no allusion to the struggle that had ensued from the death of White. His silence was a clear signal that he intended to do nothing to punish the soldiers who killed the young civilian. It also was an unspoken warning that he would accept Sherman's "eye for an eye" proposal concerning eight men in uniform who were taken hostage in the aftermath of the killing near Memphis. Knowing himself to be defeated, Pemberton did not renew his pursuit of what he considered to be justice. (OR, 117, 747)

At least as clearly as any military/civilian hostage situation, the Rebel/Union struggle in the aftermath of the death of White underscores an aspect of the war that is not always seen. Anytime top-level commanders became involved in a situation of this sort, they faced immense difficulties and risked humiliating loss of face.

13

Vague Threats, Grim Warnings

Union Gen. Benjamin F. Butler, who seemed to be almost constantly in a hostage situation of one kind or another, was assigned to Fort Monroe a few weeks after Fort Sumter. Soon he was visited by Maj. J. B. Cary of the Virginia volunteers. Seeking answers to pressing questions, Cary's first concern was the plight of civilians who were caught behind Federal lines that stretched across the state's peninsula. Would Butler permit families who wished to leave the area to go southward or northward, he wondered.

The Federal commander shook his head, explaining that he could not sanction "such removal." Though he did not have to do so, he explained his reasoning to the Virginian. Presence of families of belligerents in a region, he said, "was always the best hostage for the good behavior of the citizens."

Butler's terms specified that the entire population of the lower peninsula would become hostage for actions of other persons at distant point. Cary did not dispute or argue, but passed to another topic. With the fugitive slave law still in effect, he wanted to know what the soldier in blue had in mind "with regard to negroes."

In May 1861, the veteran attorney from Massachusetts had not yet formulated the precedent-setting plan by which he soon began treating runaway slaves as contraband of war—perhaps the first time humans were put into that category. To Cary, he gave a statement that would have been instantly repudiated by Abraham Lincoln, had he known of the interview.

The prewar congressional legislation requiring citizens of all 34 states to return fugitive slaves did not apply in the present situation, Butler said. This law "did not affect a foreign country, which Virginia claimed to be." His reply constituted a legalistic escape from what he saw as a potential verbal trap. The first Democrat to become a general in command of Federal volunteers was keenly aware that Abraham Lincoln had labeled himself president of all of the states, included those claiming to have seceded. Had

104

Contrabands, whose name came from Union Gen. Benjamin F. Butler, were soon put to work as laborers at Fort Monroe and other installations.
The Soldier in Our Civil War

he known of the conversation, the man from Illinois would have emphatically rejected the notion that Virginia could be considered a foreign country. (OR, 2, 650)

Communication being slow and unreliable, there is no reason to believe that Lincoln ever learned about how Butler evaded obedience to a federal law. Neither is it likely that the president was informed that several hundred Virginia families were being treated as hostages simply because they were caught behind Federal lines. Had the commandant of Fort Monroe been anyone other than Butler, this hostage incident could be dismissed as an empty threat.

Whether he arrested and imprisoned persons for the offense of living where they did is unknown. This much is certain, however; grim warnings, usually to civilians, started very early and continued throughout the war. Officers who issued them rarely penned a follow-up report indicating how many hostages were seized or how long they were held. Instead of decreasing as battlefield struggles intensified, incidents of this sort grew more common. Though only Butler's is known to have taken place in 1861, the following year saw at least seven and in 1864 the total jumped to an even dozen.

Early in 1862 Confederate Lt. Col. Reuben Arnold of the 29th Tennessee was forced to deal with an accused bridge burner in East Tennessee. Harold Self had been arrested near the Lick Creek on the East Tennessee and Virginia Railroad. He convinced Arnold that he did not take part in the destruction. Finding that his sons, age 16 and 18, had gone out with a group of conspirators, he followed them to try to keep his boys out of trouble, and wound up with a death sentence. In this situation, Arnold suggested to Richmond that the adolescents "be allowed to volunteer" for military service and that their father be held hostage for their good behavior. If he received a reply from acting Secretary of War Judah P. Benjamin, it was lost. A response to a petition to Jefferson Davis signed by 25 Rebel officers and citizens of the region suffered the same fate. Hence, we do not know whether the father went to the gallows, or his trouble-making sons "volunteered" to fight in gray in order to save his life. (OR, 114, 866–67)

Just two months later, Union Gen. William S. Rosecrans served as a courier of sorts. Briefly stationed in Wheeling, Virginia (now West Virginia), he forwarded to Washington a packet of documents. One piece transmitted in this fashion was a letter from Francis Peirpont, who was called governor of West Virginia by the military commander. According to him, Peirpont's letter declared that "many loyal citizens" of the region not yet recognized as a state had been "dragged off to Richmond." As a result Peirpont suggested "the arrest of hostages." Though logic suggests that he got results, records do not include names of hostages or disposition of them. (OR, 115, 270)

The same fate befell a March proposal advanced by Maj. Joseph Darr, Jr., of the 1st [West] Virginia Cavalry. Concerned about what he described as arrest and imprisonment of Unionists east of the Allegheny Mountains, he suggested that hostages be selected for them. To qualify as a hostage in this instance, Darr suggested, a civilian should be "known to entertain no sentiments of loyalty to the United States." The hostages Darr would have liked to take should in his opinion also "be connected by family ties or other close relationship with the leaders and abettors of the rebellion." (OR, 115, 280–81)

Far to the south in Itawamba County, Mississippi, John Aughey and 39 other men under arrest for "holding Union sentiments" had been "confined in a filthy prison" where they were "famishing from hunger." Addressing their plea to William H. Seward, they proposed that "citizens of avowed secession proclivities" should be arrested and held as hostages "for the safety of Union men." Since a matter such as this was not within the province of the secretary of state, Seward probably passed it along to someone in another department who stuffed it into a drawer without responding. (OR, 118, 128–30)

Union military officers within the state where Jefferson Davis was living when he became provisional president of the infant Confederacy would have supported Aughey's suggestion, had they known about it. Late in July Gen. Grenville M. Dodge issued General Order No. 11. He began by noting that there were numerous "sympathizers with this rebellion" within the region embraced by his command.

Secretary of State William H. Seward probably ignored a plea from a band of 40 civilian hostages; he may have been too busy using his "little bell" to signal arrests, to be bothered.

The American Bastille

These folk, he said, were "aiding in a species of warfare unknown to the laws and customs of war." That is they were sheltering and feeding guerrillas and providing them with information. In addition, Dodge had reason to believe that "returned soldiers" plus deserters from Rebel forces were being encouraged by civilians. Henceforth, said the Federal commander, "the nearest disloyal relative" of a soldier in gray would be arrested and held hostage "till the soldier delivers himself or is delivered up." (OR, 117, 290–91)

Turmoil in what was to become West Virginia increased instead of diminishing. In July Union Col. J. A. J. Lightburn transmitted an urgent appeal for help from a resident of Buffalo. He reported that his town plus Gallipolis and Point Pleasant were threatened by secessionists who were determined that "the Yankees must go." To this troubled citizen, there seemed to be only one way to dampen the ardor of Rebels; the leaders "should be arrested and their property taken as security," he urged. (OR, 18, 513)

Many miles to the south and west, at his lower Rio Grande post Confederate Lt. Col. A. Buchel was furious in December. He had purchased a quantity of corn in Mexico, but provincial Gov. Albino Lopez was refusing to let it pass through the region he controlled. Provided he was authorized to do so by Maj. E. F. Gray, Buchel said he would lead his men into Mexico and return with either the corn or "hostages sufficient to insure its safe arrival" at the headquarters of the 3rd Texas. (OR, 21, 923–24)

On the second day of 1863 the use of hostages was a hot question in what was left of the Old Dominion after its western half had been carved into a new state. Writing to Abraham Lincoln, Gov. John Letcher denounced what he said was the Federal policy of arresting civilians on suspicion. Hoping to end this practice, he said he owed "a duty to the cause of humanity and civilization." That duty consisted of halting arbitrary arrests.

Until this practice stopped, said Letcher, he would hold all prisoners now in the custody of Virginia plus all taken in the future "as hostages for the good treatment of unoffending citizens of Virginia who have been incarcerated for no other cause than being loyal to their own State and the government of their choice." There is no record that he followed through by holding masses of persons as hostages. Yet Letcher did win the release of a pair of Rebels confined in Washington by putting two captured Federal officers in the penitentiary at hard labor. (OR, 119, 148, 266)

At Knoxville, Tennessee, Confederate Gen. D. S. Donelson expressed his considered views in February. The way to put an end to activity of Unionists of the region, he wrote, was to arrest prominent leaders, put them in prison, and hold them as hostages. In the same state and the same month, Union Capt. M. O'Reilly and his command captured a sick Rebel in his own house. While O'Reilly was inside the place, the appearance of a band of about five hundred men caused soldiers in blue to scatter. O'Reilly's riderless horse, "with the bridle-reins hanging about his feet," soon joined the column. Not knowing what had happened to the captain, Col. Thomas J. Jordan of the 9th Pennsylvania Cavalry suggested capturing all male members of the household where his comrade vanished and holding them as hostages for his return. (OR, 34, 59–60; OR, 35, 631)

In March, the man many former citizens of Virginia regarded as their governor got back into negotiating about hostages. Chafing at the slow pace with which noncombatants were being exchanged, Peirpont informed Washington that he was eager to arrest more hostages if he could not get exchanges made. Two months later in Richmond, agent of exchange Robert Ould notified the Federal War Department that he was making a list of officers and men "reserved for retaliation." They would be released, he promised, as soon as "the parties for whom they are held are delivered to us." (OR, 118, 318, 690)

A few days later at Hilton Head, South Carolina, Union Gen. David Hunter suggested that "cadets of the best families in South Carolina" who had been captured by naval forces under Rear Adm. Samuel F. DuPont should be held as hostages for the safety of any of Hunter's men who might be made prisoner by the enemy. Saying that five captives aboard the USS *Vermont* were from "rich, powerful, and malignant" families, Hunter urged holding them as hostages "to be hung man for man with any who may be executed by the rebels." When a force under Col. James Montgomery led

raids into Georgia and Florida, Hunter ordered him to make a hostage of every Rebel male he captured—"citizen or soldier." Sent to Hilton Head in irons, he explained, these captives would guarantee that any of his men who might be captured would get proper treatment. (OR, 118, 698, 712–13, 771)

In November Union Asst. Adj. Gen. T. S. Bowers circulated from Chattanooga General Order No. 4. Striking at Rebel riders who hit Union families at spots where there were no Union troops, it stipulated that a secessionist would become a hostage for "every act of violence to the person of an unarmed Union citizen." In addition, secessionists were warned that they were subject to assessments for the support of Union refugees. (OR, 56, 58; OR, 63, 9)

Union Gen. David Hunter instructed raiders to make hostages of every male captured, in uniform or in civilian clothing.

Action of this sort in 1864 did not start until late in March. At that time, Gen. Franz Sigel directed subordinates to arrest "influential rebel citizens" of Summerville, South Carolina "if there is an opportunity." Such persons could be sent to Charleston "as hostages for some Union citizens taken by rebel guerrillas," he proposed. In Washington 60 days later, Ould seemed eager to accelerate the pace of hostage taking. He "respectfully recommended" two alternatives: (1) stop all arrests of "obnoxious parties" by military authorities, or (2) begin arresting "all persons of standing known to be hostile" so they could be held in retaliation. His personal preference, he emphasized, was for the latter alternative. (OR, 60, 752; OR, 120, 105)

Still bitterly divided, Missouri was in June the scene of a clash in which a Unionist was seized and briefly detained. E. J. Crandall, commander of Linn County's local forces, reported the matter to Gen. Clinton B. Fisk at Saint Joseph. "If any more of our men are molested," he informed Fisk, "I have victims spotted for hostages to retaliate on."

Leaders of the Order of American Knights—a Copperhead body—immediately reacted to Crandall's threat. According to testimony of a defector from the order, plans were made to deal with the arrest of a member by seizing "prominent Union citizens, who will be held as hostages." Also in Missouri during June, a recommendation concerning bushwhackers was made to authorities in St. Louis. Gen. E. B. Brown may have exaggerated, but he said that hundreds of their friends and associates were imprisoned after having received death sentences. He then made the only known recommendation of its sort, saying that inmates of what we now call death row should "be held as hostages for the good conduct of their friends in the brush." (OR, 64, 225, 364; OR, 120, 245)

Well to the east in Ohio, Col. J. P. Sanderson received anonymous word that Copperheads in all Northern states were prepared to deliver an ultimatum to Abraham Lincoln. Leaders in each state, he alleged, would soon warn that they would take hostages if their members now under arrest were not released. Like the Northwest Conspiracy that never got off the ground, this concerted

Union Gen. Franz Sigel wanted residents of Summerville, South Carolina, held as hostages early in 1864.

Union Adm. Samuel F. DuPont was requested to hold as hostages youthful males from "the best families of South Carolina."

Pictorial Field Book

action was not taken. That did not, however, mean that the idea of using hostages was dead. (OR, 120, 719)

In Missouri, late June saw civilian T. J. Stabber pen a lengthy suggestion to Federal authorities in Hannibal. In his view, the least difficult and costly way to deal with guerrillas would be to use 10 to 20 wealthy secessionists from each county as hostages. Three weeks later Virginia state Senator George W. Grouse appealed to William Smith who claimed to be the Unionists' governor of the state concerning the plight of civilians seized by secessionists in North Carolina. He pointed out that lawmakers loyal to the United States had endorsed his proposal that hostages be taken and wanted to know when something would be done. Before the month ended, Confederate Gen. John H. Morgan applied to Richmond for permission to use relatives of "prominent Union men" as hostages for secessionists whom he said "had been sent North." (OR, 64, 589; OR, 78, 732; OR, 120, 779)

Early in August, Confederate soldiers headed toward Cumberland, Virginia, in order to arrest hostages but were stopped by the appearance of three regiments of Federal cavalry. Two weeks later Confederate Gen. Nathan Bedford Forrest was notified that an unspecified number of men would be held as hostages for "violations of civilized warfare"—a term repeatedly used by soldiers and civilians on both sides. Federal leaders played the hostage game about as frequently as did Rebels. Hence Gen. N. J. T. Dana notified secessionists that he would take pleasure in using civilians as hostages for Unionists carried off by their scouts or employees. (OR, 70, 355; OR, 20, 673, 998)

In mid-October Union Col. J. H. Shackling proposed to take civilians as hostages for men who had been carried off by some of Louisiana's many guerrillas. Two months later in the same state Union Gen. R. A. Cameron was briefed concerning depredations of Brattice and Raymond Lake plus their associates. Asst. Adj. Gen. Frederic Speed said that one of the Lakes probably should have been held as a hostage for captured Capt. Columbus Moore of the 16th Indiana. Speed then added that his superiors did not think Moore had "proved himself worthy of taking that trouble in his behalf." (OR, 86, 748; OR, 90, 90)

Moore may have been the only fighting man whose comrades did not think he was worth a hostage. Some of the many surviving vague threats and grim warnings concerning use of hostages almost certainly resulted in action. If so, unreported innocent persons who were seized and imprisoned made talk of "civilized warfare" seem shallow and empty, whether voiced by adherents of the Confederacy or the Union.

14

Hole-in-the-Day and Fellow Tribesmen

In his lengthy handwritten message to Congress of December 1, 1862, Abraham Lincoln dealt specifically with affairs in only one state. He said of it, in part, that

> In the month of August last the Sioux Indians, in Minnesota, attacked the settlements in their vicinity with extreme ferocity, killing, indiscriminately, men, women, and children. It is estimated that not less than eight hundred persons were killed by the Indians, and a large amount of property was destroyed.
>
> I submit for your especial consideration whether our Indian system should not be remodelled. Many wise and good men have impressed me with the belief that this can be profitably done. (AL, 5, 525–26)

His document—which did not prompt legislation—failed to inform congressmen and senators that one of the worst droughts on record occurred during 1862, and that hungry Indians were routinely refused food at trading posts. Neither did he point out to them that withdrawal of Union army units from what was then the western frontier had created a power vacuum in which the Sioux uprising took place.

Neither did the president tell assembled lawmakers that Col. H. H. Sibley of the Minnesota State Militia led a force of volunteers who captured about 1,500 Sioux. Warriors, considered to be the bloodiest among these, were tried by a military court that sentenced 307 of them to die—often upon evidence provided by small children. In Washington, the lengthy list was carefully studied and pared down to 38 names. These convicted men were publicly hanged on the day after Christmas in the largest mass execution in U.S. annals. Meanwhile, a concerted drive to move all native Americans westward was creating new tensions that led Union soldiers to engage in an orgy of hostage taking.

By all odds, one of the shrewdest and persistent warriors with whom fighting men in blue had to deal after 1862 was a Chippewa leader known to

President Grant greets Red Cloud, leader of the great Sioux uprising in Minnesota.

Harper's Weekly

The largest mass execution in American history took place at Mankato, Minnesota, on December 26, when Abraham Lincoln refused to commute the death sentences of 38 Sioux warriors.

white men as Hole-in-the-Day, but called Pug-o-na-ke-schick by fellow tribesmen. When word of impending military clashes between North and South reached him, he responded by sending an offer to Washington on May 1, 1861. From St. Paul, Minnesota he addressed Simon Cameron, through an interpreter.

He and one hundred or more of his headmen and braves were ready "to aid in defending the Government and its institutions" against enemies, Hole-in-the-Day said. Cameron responded promptly, expressing great appreciation but saying that "the nature of our present national troubles forbids the use of savages." He did not anticipate that both the South and the North would soon be using tribesmen as soldiers. (OR, 122, 140, 184)

Military leaders heard no more about the Chippewa leader for more than three years. When his name surfaced again in August 1864, Lt. Miles Hollister of the 8th Minnesota Volunteers registered his doubt that Hole-in-the-Day could persuade "any very great portion of the Chippewa Nation to join him in making war upon the whites." Despite this officer's opinion, Sibley, now a general, was sufficiently concerned to notify Gen. John Pope that a Cass Lake chieftain and a Red Lake brave were warning that Hole-in-the-Day was "engaged in renewed machinations against the peace of the frontier." (OR, 84, 531–32, 578)

Sibley soon received "direct, minute and reliable" information from St. Cloud that the Chippewa chieftain had sent "tobacco tied with red tape to nearly all the chiefs, being desirous of engaging with them in a raid upon the whites." James Tanner, who seems to have been a former trader among Indians of Minnesota, wrote a long letter to Gen. H. Z. Mitchell from Whitewater, Wisconsin, on August 16. Calling the leader who was beginning to attract attention "the scoundrel pet of U. S. Indian agents," Tanner insisted that "he has never once showed the least desire or effort made to get one single family of his band to settle down and become civilized." As evidence of this attitude on the part of the Native American, the trader pointed out that Hole-in-the-Day "never abandoned his narrow breech-cloth" and consistently opposed the work of missionaries. (OR, 84, 126–28, 663)

By the end of the month, Hole-in-the-Day was at the Chippewa agency in Minnesota's Cass County. Indian Agent A. C. Morrill notified Sibley that with a payment due to native Americans from Washington on October 1, the chieftain was less than satisfied with promises made to him in Washington. Merrill warned that a combination of "mixed bloods and whisky" threatened to see numerous Indians taken to St. Paul and there sold as military substitutes. (OR, 84, 949–51)

Like numerous other tribesmen, Hole-in-the-Day made a personal trip to Washington while Civil War was raging among whites. One of his subordinates told Capt. H. S. Howe of the 2nd Minnesota Cavalry that before starting on his journey the chieftain said he planned to launch hostilities as soon as he returned. Back in what was then the Northwest by the spring of

1865, Hole-in-the-Day attended a intertribal council and reportedly threatened to have "all the friendly Indians killed." By this time, Hole-in-the-Day was being called "the chief instigator of all the plots concocted against the white people by the Chippewa." Late in August, Sibley registered grave concern that the Sioux and Chippewa might cooperate in a war "involving the frontier settlements of Minnesota, Iowa, and Wisconsin in one common ruin." (OR, 101, 1265–66; OR, 102, 441)

May 1865 saw Pope twice authorize Gen. S. P. Curtis to seize Hole-in-the-Day and other Chippewa chiefs "and keep them in confinement at Fort Snelling as hostages for the good behavior of their tribes." Hole-in-the-Day and other Chippewa may been confined in a stockade within what is now Minnesota's Twin Cities. Whether such action was taken or not, the long-drawn contest that ended with a threat of such action reveals some aspects of the white man's mid-century struggle to subdue the red man. (OR, 102, 615, 671–72)

On June 6, 1862, Lt. Col. James N. Olney of the 2nd California reported from Fort Humbolt that a five-year-old boy had been carried off by Indians. An unknown number of Indian prisoners were quickly reserved as hostages for the boy's safety. Simultaneously, Lt. William F. Swasey of the 2nd California warned that "Every white man found in arms among the Indians will be hanged on the spot." Whether or not the seizure of hostages resulted in having the boy brought back is unknown. (OR, 105, 67–68, 1131–32)

Just one month later, however, Lt. Col. George S. Evans of the 2nd California Cavalry was authorized to take four or five Indians as hostages and send them to Fort Churchill as a guarantee of good faith on the part of tribesmen. In August, Maj. John M. O'Neill of the 2nd California reported that he held five Indians as hostages; among them were "two of their great chiefs, to wit, Captain George and Te-ni-ma-ha." (OR, 106, 33, 75)

By September, some of the tribesmen who had turned in hostages were complaining to Col. George S. Evans of the 2nd California Cavalry. They had complied with their part of the treaty, they said, by "giving up their arms and their families as hostages, and the whites are 'mucho big lie; no give them nothing.'" In November, Col. P. Edward Connor of the 3rd California sent Maj. Edward McGarry on a hunt for "an emigrant boy about ten years of age, whose parents were murdered last summer by Indians." From Camp Douglas in the Utah Territory, McGarry was ordered to find suspected tribesmen and to take three of their principal men as hostages if the white boy was not produced. (OR, 105, 151–52; OR, 106, 228–29)

After a journey of about one hundred miles, McGarry and his men were met by an uncle of the missing boy. He guided them to an encampment of "Shoshones, Snakes, and Bannocks" who were led by Chief Bear Hunter. After a skirmish between the two forces, Bear Hunter and some of his principal warriors came in under a white flag. Questioned, they said that the white boy had been sent away a few days earlier. McGarry, who believed what they said, held Bear Hunter and four warriors as hostages for the missing boy's safety. Soon three warriors, dispatched by Bear Hunter, disappeared from view. This time, the hostage ploy worked; warriors returned the next day about noon with the boy and McGarry released his hostages. (OR, 105, 182–83)

Compared with 1862, the taking of Indian hostages was at a somewhat slower rate during the following year. Again at Fort Humbolt, Col. Francis J. Lippitt of the 2nd California took several hostages, including "a certain number of Hoopa chiefs", in April. His purpose in seizing these prisoners was "to secure the safety of the whites and their property from the Klamath River to the Van Dusen." (OR, 106, 381)

At Fort Ruby in the Nevada Territory on the following day, Maj. P. A. Gallagher of the 3rd California wrote to Lt. W. L. Ustick, an assistant adjutant general in Utah. Both officers were interested in a band of Indians believed by Gallagher to be encamped close to a mountain 40 or 50 miles from Spring Valley Station. Four warriors who were being held as hostages had offered to guide white men to the encampment, he said. Gallagher said that his motive in holding hostages and sending out raiders was to find and punish "Indians who have been committing depredations on the Overland Mail Line." Whether or not his use of hostages as guides led to a successful expedition is not recorded. (OR, 106, 419–20)

September 19 saw Gen. James H. Carleton issue a decidedly unusual order. He instructed a subordinate to "seize 6 principal men of the Zuni Indians, and hold them as hostages until all Navajoes in and near their village are given up, and all stolen stock surrendered." Carleton had no intention of waiting or wavering. He wanted the Zuni to be told that if they "help or harbor Navajoes" or steal cattle from white settlers or injure a single white man, "I will as certainly destroy their village as the sun shines." Unusual for its severe language, this directive went to a subordinate who was then leading an "expedition against the Navajoes" from Fort Canby, New Mexico. His subordinate was Col. Christopher Carson, who as "Kit" later gained lasting fame as an Indian fighter. (OR, 41, 727–28)

Use of Indian hostages continued in 1864, by which time some tribesmen were beginning to become wise to devices used by soldiers. In July, Capt. Julius C. Snow of the 1st New Mexico Cavalry clashed with a band made up of 76 warriors and four old women. After a parley punctuated by threats from Snow, they agreed to go anywhere he directed if he would give them one month to let their animals feed and recuperate. As a token of good faith they suggested yielding one of their leaders plus 30 warriors as hostages. Snow agreed, and gave them one hour to select their hostages and return to their camp. Soon he noticed some of them gliding away, so he ordered them to halt. When they disobeyed, his men fired a volley and 14 or 15 Indians fell. For the rest of his military career, the New

Mexico officer probably warned anyone who would listen to discount offers of Indians to produce hostages. (OR, 105, 372–74)

Maj. Thomas J. Blakeney of the 1st California Cavalry led his men in a summer hunt for another missing boy. Believing him to have been kidnaped by three Indians, on July 31, 1864, he took six hostages: "two bucks, two boys, and two squaws." As nightfall approached, he directed his men to tie the hostages, and while they were doing so "one of the squaws attempted to run off, and was shot and killed." During the commotion caused by this incident one of the boys who had been made hostage, judged to be about 15 years old, also tried to escape. Reporting to Fort Goodwin in the Arizona Territory, Blakeney said that "about twenty shots were fired at him, and he must have been killed" in brush so thick that his body could not be found.

Men of Company 4, 5th California, were sent over a mountain on the following day with orders to "kill all buck Indians big enough to bear arms and capture all squaws and children they might come upon." That evening, at the suggestion of another officer, Blakeney freed the remaining female hostage but warned her that unless the missing boy was produced he would kill his two remaining male hostages. A very brief notation concerning activities of August 3, 1864 ended with the notation: "Hung the two buck Indian hostages at sundown." (OR, 83, 84–85)

Late in September, General Curtis ordered Col. J. M. Chivington to seize an unspecified number of Indian hostages to guarantee the return of stolen livestock. His dispatch from Fort Leavenworth continued:

> I want no peace till the Indians suffer more. Left Hand is said to be a good chief of the Arapahoes, but Big Mouth is a rascal. I fear agent of Interior Department will be ready to make presents too soon. It is better to chastise before giving anything but a little tobacco to talk over. No peace must be made without my direction. (OR, 85, 462)

Three months later from Fort Riley, Kansas, Maj. B. S. Henning of the 3rd Wisconsin Cavalry directed the taking of hostages in order to try to keep the Arapahoes quiet. Fearful that tribesmen were planning to "cripple the Government by stealing and destroying all the horses and mules possible," he enumerated some of the prisoners whom he wanted to use as hostages. His list included Left Hand, Little Raven, Storms, Nervah, Knock Knee "and other influential members of the Arapahoes Indians." (OR, 90, 796–97)

Though the Civil War in the East was nearly over, to officers stationed in the territories it seemed that Indian hostages and troubles would always be with them. Curtis reported to Gen. Henry W. Halleck concerning a winter expedition led by Chivington that

> Colonel Chivington, after a march of 300 miles in ten days, on the 29 [of December] returned. He came upon a Cheyenne camp of 130 lodges at the south bend of Big Sandy, Cheyenne County Colo. He attacked at daylight, killing over 400 Indians and capturing the same number of

ponies. Among the killed are Chiefs Black Kettle, White Antelope, and Little Raven. Our loss, 9 killed and 38 wounded. Our troops encountered snow two feet deep. (OR, 86, 801)

During the first week of January, Col. R. R. Livingston of the 1st Nebraska Cavalry learned that Chivington's exploit had produced an unexpected effect. Survivors of the band he decimated had sent runners to other tribes, and he had reasons to believe that the warlike Blackfeet would soon take part in an offensive. Chivington, whose fellow officers knew he had engaged in a massacre rather than a battle, resigned and relinquished control of the District of Colorado to Col. Thomas Moonlight of the 11th Kansas Cavalry. (OR, 101, 400, 408, 416)

Repercussions from Chivington's wanton slaughter should have put an end to the use of tribesmen as hostages, but did not. Maj. E. W. Wynkoop, in command of Fort Lyon in the Colorado Territory, had earlier questioned One Eye and two other Cheyennes through interpreter John S. Smith. According to the interpreter, Indians assured Wynkoop that two thousand warriors of the Cheyenne and Arapahoes Nations were ready to release all whites held captive by them. Wynkoop, Smith reported on January 15, personally went to the big Indian camp to talk with warriors—but cautiously took along One Eye as a hostage. (OR, 83, 964–65)

On February 15, Gen. Grenville M. Dodge—for whom Dodge City was later named—sent word from Leavenworth to Omaha that he did not want "any more such outrages as were committed by Chivington." At the same time, he thought it would be a good idea "to hold a lot of Indians as hostages." (OR, 101, 853)

How many Indians it would have taken to constitute a lot of hostages is anybody's guess, and surrender of Confederates in the East brought an end to wartime military records in the West. If Dodge succeeded in putting a large number of tribesmen into a stockade as hostages, the record does not appear in Civil War annals. Yet four native Americans took part in a record-making event—they were the only hostages seized during 1861–65 who are positively known to have been killed by their captor.

Union Gen. Grenville M. Dodge condemned the Chivington massacre, but thought it would be wise to hold many Indians as hostages.

A Sioux warrior attired for battle, as depicted by a white artist.

Harper's Encyclopedia

Part III

Prisons and Prisoners

15

Hostages and Counterparts in Southern Prisons

No prisoners were taken during the April 1861 surrender of Maj. Robert Anderson and his men at Fort Sumter. Members of the fort's garrison were permitted to board Federal vessels that had made a futile attempt to bring supplies and troops to the installation. Once all who were able to travel were aboard, they were taken to New York and given one of the city's earliest public ovations.

Gen. P. G. T. Beauregard, who had been in command at Charleston, adopted a different policy three months later. His officers and men took so many prisoners at Bull Run that officials in Richmond did not know what to do with them. Some were briefly housed in the Henrico County jail, but it was too small to hold more than a fraction of the estimated 1,200 captives.

Gen. John H. Winder, who was responsible for the seemingly endless streams of men in blue, had Ligon's Tobacco Factory confiscated and quickly made an improvised jail of it. In one of the rooms of this three-story building, not yet emptied of tobacco presses, Congressman Ely of New York held the lottery by means of which the first hostages of the war were selected.

Ligon's was soon packed far beyond capacity, so at least two adjoining tobacco factories that belonged to Messrs. Ross and Howard were made into impromptu prisons. Some Federal captives remained in the Rebel capital only a few hours. Squadrons of them were sent to Charleston by train, since the port city was known to have more suitable space than did Richmond. Almost as soon as the first contingent of prisoners reached their South Carolina designation, Jefferson Davis addressed an urgent appeal to governors of seceded states. Citing the probability that far more prisoners would be taken soon, the Rebel chief executive urged governors to report to him concerning existing buildings that could be turned into prisons.

Having had only brief notice that the population of their city would soon increase, municipal officials in Charleston turned first to the city jail.

Charleston city jail held Yankee officers most of the time from August 1861 to the end of the war.

Harper's Weekly

Some of the Yankee officers held at Castle Pinckney in Charleston were members of the famous 11th Fire Zouaves.

Photographic History

By the time an estimated 150 Federal officers and men had been placed in it, more prisoners were on the way. Working around the clock, the dilapidated old fortress known as Castle Pinckney was converted into a prison. This installation, seized a few months earlier from the Union government, soon housed a number of officers who became hostages for the safety of Rebel privateersmen.

Imprisonment at Castle Pinckney constituted a Sunday School picnic by comparison with life in later prisons of the South and the North. Inmates were well fed, and juvenile guards talked and joked freely with them. Arrangements were made for a pioneer photographer to come, and he made a number of images that somehow survived the war.

North Carolina's governor took the Davis appeal seriously and detailed officers of the state militia to search for potential prison facilities. Lt. Col. R. H. Riddick was sent to the state in order to appraise a site at Salisbury. He described the town as "located in the most productive region of the State." To him, that meant locally produced fruits, vegetables, and meat—for which he said there was a very limited market—could be used to feed prisoners at substantially lower cost than "the usual army rations." Almost as significantly, the town was served by major railroads. (OR, 116, 699, 738)

By early November, Col. William Johnston had entered into a contract for the purchase of a factory building at Salisbury so it could be converted into "a prison depot." On November 11 the locally published *Carolina Watchman* newspaper announced to readers that

> The [Confederate] Government has bought the old Salisbury Factory, and is now preparing to fit it up for a prison to accommodate some thousands or more of Yankees who are encumbering the tobacco factories of Richmond. Our citizens don't much like the idea of such accession to their population; nevertheless they have assented to their part of the hardships and disagreeables of war, so bring them along. We will do the best we can with them.

By the time that newspaper announcement was being read in and around Salisbury, Johnston was busy drawing up contracts "for putting the buildings [of the cotton factory] into condition for receiving prisoners of war as well as to furnish quarters for a company of 80 or 100 men as a special guard." Neither Johnston, the editor of the Salisbury newspaper, Jefferson Davis, nor anyone else had the vaguest notion about what the future would bring to the town and its surrounding region.

More than one hundred Yankees who had been captured at Bull Run reached Salisbury in mid-December and a larger contingent followed two weeks later. Until the place held a substantial number of prisoners who were guarded by hastily secured recruits, no one bothered to check about the water supply. A quick investigation showed that the property had only one well, which usually was dry by noon. That meant prisoners under guard would have to be sent to public wells or to a tiny rivulet in order to bring back water in buckets.

Within six months after it was opened, the Salisbury Prison held nearly two thousand men. Capt. A. C. Godwin, commandant, became restless for action. Consequently he recruited enough men to form the 57th North Carolina regiment, was rewarded by a promotion, and marched off to fight the Yankees. He and his men, already weary of war after only a year in the field, got their fill of fighting at Gettysburg. (OR, 28, 694; OR, 31, 540, 622, 1071; OR, 44, 484)

Back in Salisbury, a short-lived agreement concerning prisoner exchange briefly reduced crowding but was followed by the arrival of new contingents of captives. Unlike some prisons whose commandants tried to take only Federal officers or enlisted men or Rebels who faced discipline, Salisbury had a polyglot set of inmates from the first. Before the war ended, it had earned the reputation of having housed about as many if not more hostages than any other comparable facility in the South.

During the summer of 1862 Union Gen. James S. Wadsworth arrested seven civilians living in Virginia's Fairfax and Loudoun Counties. They were taken, he explained to Gen. John A. Dix, as hostages for the release of T. Turner and his four sons who were being held at Salisbury.

Another prisoner lottery was held in December. Richmond's facilities then housed 26 Federal captains, who were assembled and required to draw

Dominated by a tall building that was once a cotton factory, Salisbury Prison was enclosed by a stockade equipped with a palisade along which guards patrolled.

North Carolina Department of History and Archives

lots. Capts. Edward E. Chase of the 1st Rhode Island, Julius B. Litchfield of the 14th Maine, and Charles S. Kendall of the 1st Massachusetts became the unfortunate trio. Sentenced to hard labor for the duration, they were sent to Salisbury and held for the safety of three Confederate officers who were imprisoned at Alton, Illinois. (M, 2, 360; OR, 117, 41; OR, 119, 514, 744)

About the same time, Abraham Lincoln received a newspaper clipping from an unidentified source. It named 11 Richmond Unionists plus 42 other civilians who were said to be held at Salisbury. Many of them were hostages for the safety of secessionist civilians under arrest by Union authorities. Their places of residence reportedly ranged from North Carolina and Virginia to Pennsylvania, New Hampshire, and New York. Since no other record includes this list of names, it is impossible to determine whether or not the report the president asked his secretary of war to preserve is authentic.

There is little question, however, concerning the accuracy of reports that the number of civilian hostages held at Salisbury reached and passed one hundred. At least 26 men from Pennsylvania were included in this number. They may never have known that they were central to a case in which hostages were held for hostages. In Washington, Union Col. William Hoffman had 26 of his "citizen prisoners" sent from the Old Capitol to Fort Delaware. They were to be held there, he informed Grant, as hostages for a like number of "Union citizens held at Salisbury, N.C." (OR, 117, 528; OR, 120, 781; OR, 121, 355)

Hoffman immediately discounted rumors that circulated in Washington early in 1863. According to it, the enemy was so eager to secure the freedom of Zarvona that in addition to turning over the seven hostages designated for him they would free some of the prisoners at Salisbury. Hoffman was right; the rumor had no basis in fact. (OR, 118, 219) By the time Capt. G. W. Shurtleff of the 5th Colored reached Salisbury in May 1864, conditions were almost as bad as at highly publicized Andersonville. He was present at still another prison lottery that involved men whose names he failed to record. A staff officer came into the prison about the first of June, he said, with an order to select two captains as hostages and "treat them in every way like criminals condemned to death." These men were to be executed "in case our government should hang a rebel captain who had been condemned as a spy," according to Shurtleff.

Since 10 Federal captains were in the prison, they decided to number slips of paper from one to ten, drop them into a hat, shake them, and have an imprisoned chaplain draw out the slips—with the understanding that those who received #9 and #10 "should be elected."

It took about 20 minutes to conduct this ceremony, after which two fellow captains whose names Shurtleff did not record became hostages and "were placed in a dungeon, with every prospect of speedy execution." When

At Castle Pinckney in Charleston, guards were youngsters who held
membership in the Charleston Zouave Cadets.

Photographic History

Some of the Federal officers captured at Bull Run were imprisoned for
a time at Castle Pinckney.

Photographic History

Washington learned of events in North Carolina, orders for execution of the Rebel captain were rescinded and "our friends were returned to us, a little paler from the confinement and the starvation." (M, 4, 388–410)

Salisbury proved to be the end of the line for a Federal officer who as a hostage saw from the inside even more prisons than did Confederate Capt. Frank Battle. After being captured at Bull Run, Col. Michael Corcoran of the 69th New York was held briefly in Richmond—probably in the Henrico County jail. Soon the son of a British officer reached Charleston and was placed under guard by the city's Zouave cadets. They escorted the officer destined soon to become the war's first official hostage to the three-story city jail.

He was still there when fire broke out in a factory building located close to the jail. According to the *Charleston Mercury,* municipal authorities became alarmed when flames swept toward the jail because they feared its inmates would escape during the confusion. When their place of confinement seemed certain to burn, Corcoran squeezed through a tiny window and dropped to the cobblestone street below. Other prisoners who followed him formed a tight-knit band that roamed the streets in search of food and shelter.

When captured the next day, the escapees were escorted to Castle Pinckney, the most easy-going Rebel facility in which Corcoran spent time. He was there when a lottery held in Richmond made him hostage for the safety of a Rebel seaman who commanded a privateer. Soon afterward Federal authorities designated noted captive James M. Mason as a hostage for the hostage, but nothing came of this cumbersome arrangement.

Along with other captives, Corcoran probably went into an improvised cell at Roper Hospital when Rebels decided to mount guns at Castle Pinckney. Increasing pressure upon Confederate prisons later caused authorities to send more and more newly captured men to Charleston. This movement led them to dispatch some of Charleston's long-time captives to the state capital, Columbia.

When he reached Columbia, the hostage who was as widely known among Rebels as among Union fighting forces was sent into a hastily erected stockade. Because one of the staples provided to prisoners was syrup made from sorghum cane, the place was informally known as Camp Sorghum. Security was so poor that Rebels hastily threw up a stout stockade fence around part of the property owned by the South Carolina State Hospital. When Corcoran and other men from Camp Sorghum reached the new facility, they facetiously dubbed it Camp Asylum.

From Camp Asylum, Corcoran went to an improvised prison at Florence, South Carolina, and then to Salisbury. He was held in North Carolina until long after the Confederate seaman for whom he was hostage was given a reprieve from his death sentence as a pirate. Exchanged in August 1862, the native of Ireland's County Donegal received a promotion that was retroactive to the day of his capture.

Roper Hospital in Charleston, still a major medical facility, housed prisoners for part of the war years.

Libby Prison, a converted ship chandler's building, as seen from the water at its rear.

Camp Sorghum, a stockade near Columbia, South Carolina, briefly held
Col. Michael Corcoran.

South Carolina Department Archives and History

Camp Asylum at Columbia, South Carolina, represented a step upward
from Camp Sorghum, since most inmates were assigned spaces in tents.

South Carolina Department Archives and History

After fighting at Suffolk and Germantown plus Sangster's Station in Virginia, he was transferred to Washington in order to help defend the capital. By that time he was famous for having survived wretched food, outbreaks of contagious diseases, and rough treatment from brutal guards in one prison after another. In his new post the best-known ex-hostage in a blue uniform bowed to plaudits of crowds in the capital for only a few weeks. Despite Corcoran's record as a survivalist he died as a result of injuries sustained when his horse fell near Fairfax Court House late in 1863. (WWW, 143–44; GB, 93–94; OR, 21, 645; OR, 26, 136, 139, 191, 288; OR, 45, 189; OR, 48, 652, 662, 983; OR, 111, 1111; OR, 116, 132)

Richmond's notorious Libby Prison, where dozens of hostages spent time, is often mistakenly identified as a former tobacco warehouse. Actually a building owned and used by a firm that furnished supplies to ships, it did not house captives until late in the winter of 1861–62. Unlike cadets who served as guards at Castle Pinckney and raw amateurs who filled this role at Salisbury, Libby's guards were veterans in gray. Tradition has it that some of these guards liked nothing better than a chance to shoot at an inmate who appeared to be violating a rule of the prison.

Food at Libby was not as bad as at the worst Confederate prisons but not as good as at the best. Asst. Surg. W. W. Myers, one of about one thousand 1863 inmates, wasted paper and ink by sending to Washington a letter of protest. In it, he alleged that half of the pork and flour consigned to Libby by the Union government was diverted to the Army of Northern Virginia. That charge leveled against Rebels was minor, compared with detailed accusations made by Lt. Col. J. W. Phillips. According to this inmate, a hostage who had attempted to escape was captured and thrown into a tiny dark cell, where his hair turned white within a few days.

Pvt. Michael Hoare of the 5th Michigan Cavalry wrote that Libby's inmates who were in close confinement occupied cells only six by eight feet in size. He said that they received "but four ounces corn bread and from one and a half to two ounces of bacon per man daily, the bacon being maggoty and unfit for use." A lengthy description of life in Libby by Phillips deals with many of the horrors of Civil War prisons. (OR, 119, 571–73; OR, 120, 1190–91; M, 4, 336–37; M, 14, 54–79; M, 28, 248–57)

So many hostages spent weeks or months in Libby that space makes it impossible to deal briefly with more than a fraction of their cases. Lt. Leopold Markbreit, an aide-de-camp to Gen. William W. Averell, had been an inmate for only a short time when he and two comrades became hostages for four Rebels held at Johnson's Island. Maj. Nathan Goff, Jr., had spent about four months in Libby before he became hostage for Confederate Maj. Thomas D. Armesy. This arrangement fell apart when Washington designated Maj. Thomas S. Mills as hostage for Goff. (OR, 20, 197, 422; OR, 48, 39, 932; OR, 120, 149, 626; OR, 121, 30, 211–12, 457, 519, 842)

Ignoring the table of equivalents, Rebels made a captain and two lieutenants in Libby hostages for four privates held in Ohio. Inmate George N. Bliss, a severely wounded captain of the 1st Rhode Island Cavalry, became a hostage but received conflicting reports about his situation. He was initially told that he was being held for an unidentified Rebel who was being held in Tennessee and was awaiting execution. Later, however, he was told that because of the table of equivalents he had become hostage for four Rebel privates at Johnson's Island.

Never grim about his own situation, Bliss soon described retaliation as "one of the longest, ugliest and meanest words in the English language." His reaction to this term stemmed from the fact that his old friend and fellow inmate Capt. Henry S. Burrage was also selected as a hostage for a condemned Confederate. Burrage protested that he had been informed that Confederate Gen. Roger A. Pryor was being held hostage for him, but his words fell upon deaf ears. Bliss, who was held in irons for a time, remained in Libby for at least four months after they were removed. (JSHS, 19, 430; M, 35, 240–45; OR, 120, 1231)

A few hostages spent periods in Richmond's Castle Thunder and other prisons, but the records of Salisbury and Libby as hostage holders were surpassed only by the Federal stockade on Morris Island, South Carolina, that briefly held more than five hundred Rebel hostages.

Sgt. Fred Will of the 20th Massachusetts regiment sketched the main building of Salisbury Prison while he was an inmate.
North Carolina Department of History and Archives

16

Northern Prisons for Hostages and Equivalents

At least 150 facilities, North and South, housed prisoners during the war. Not one of these was built for permanent use of this sort. Relatively small jails and prisons erected by cities and states were crowded to many times their capacity. Many existing structures, in which fortresses predominated, were hastily converted for use as prisons. Camps surrounded by fences and patrolled by armed guards were usually crammed full of flimsy temporary buildings or tents. Open air stockades were used by both sides.

Less than 10 percent of the places used for military and civilian prisoners played a significant role in keeping hostages or prisoners for whom they were being held. Yet these give some insight into the chaos created by a sudden and continuous large-volume flow of captives that neither side was ready to house, feed, clothe, and give medical treatment. The bottom half dozen present-day American prisons are better facilities than the top half dozen improvised ones used during 1861–65.

Fort Delaware, erected on Pea Patch Island, may have been the first Northern installation that was ready to receive prisoners of state, a few of whom reached it about the time Abraham Lincoln delivered his first inaugural address. The site having been selected prior to the War of 1812, a permanent structure was later built by the Corps of Engineers, U.S. Army. Like Fort Sumter and other Atlantic Coast installations, Fort Delaware was intended to serve as a defense from British or European aggression. A handful of Rebels captured in very early skirmishes reached the fort during the summer of 1861 and were shoved into the guardhouse. Within two years the entire structure built under the direction of George B. McClellan was crowded far beyond its capacity and was close to the top of most dreaded Federal military prisons.

Professional soldier Albin F. Schoepf had been exiled for his role in the unsuccessful Hungarian revolution led by Lajos Kossuth in 1848–49. He later came to the United States and as a Federal brigadier was made commandant of the fortress after the October 1862, battle of Perryville. During the Kentucky clash between more than 50,000 men, the Prussian and his men were said to have performed badly. Humiliated and angry, the man who had helped to train the Turkish army gave up field command and was soon put in charge of Fort Delaware. Civilians from the North plus captured Rebels who spent time there characterized it as one of the worst of all permanent structures turned into a Federal prison.

Fort Delaware's largest group of hostages—26 secessionist civilians—arrived from Washington during the summer of 1864. Soon after having been arrested and treated as ordinary prisoners they had been set aside as hostages for a like number of Pennsylvanians believed to be imprisoned at Salisbury, North Carolina. Edwin M. Stanton was in September incensed by a report from an ex-prisoner. Recently released after having been held for 13 months, the resident of Chambersburg, Pennsylvania, said that seven natives of the Keystone State were still languishing in North Carolina.

Without giving specific information, James Hamilton reported that these men were badly underfed. He also declared that at the prison he just left, inmates never received mail. Hence he suggested a resort to the use of hostages. Fourteen to 21 prominent Virginians in Federal prisons, he said, could be made responsible for the welfare of loyal citizens of the Union who were imprisoned in the Tar Heel State. His suggestion about hostages may have stemmed from the fact that Joseph Mead is believed to have been held in Old Capitol Prison as a hostage for him.

Hamilton's plea spurred action; Stanton authorized Col. William Hoffman of the 3rd Infantry, then serving as commissary general of prisoners, to act decisively. As a result he sent Schoepf a directive that the 26 civilians who had recently arrived "shall be treated and fed as far as practicable in the same manner that the [Pennsylvania] prisoners are [at Salisbury].

Harsh retaliatory treatment of hostages was so commonplace that the only unusual aspect of this affair was that 26 men suffered at Fort Delaware because seven were alleged to be suffering in the South. (Neely, *Fate*, 157; OR, 120, 849–50).

Though it did not house Federal prisoners of any kind as early as Fort Delaware, the prison of New York City was the first in the North to hold men for whom hostages were chosen. Capt. T. Harrison Baker and members of the crew of the Rebel privateer *Savannah* were captured two days after the vessel left port. Taken to New York in irons, they were thrust into the forbidding and notorious local facility known as The Tombs. For these men and other privateersmen who were taken very early, a prison lottery was held in Richmond to select 14 captured Federal officers as hostages for the lives of Rebel seamen.

New York City's municipal prison that was known as The Tombs held some of the Confederate privateers for whom hostages were chosen very early.

Fort Delaware as it appeared from outside its walls.

Washington was no less ready to use hostages than Richmond, and was no better prepared to hold them. After much of the city was burned by the British in the War of 1812 lawmakers met in a sturdy brick building until the new capitol was ready for use. After ceasing to be the site at which legislation was enacted, the Old Capitol Building saw no significant use for years. By 1861 it seemed about ready to fall down. Seized for use as a prison, wooden slats that covered windows were soon replaced by iron bars and a high fence was erected around it.

Initially designed to house political prisoners, among whom the famous Rebel spy Rose Greenhow was numbered, it was soon filled to capacity. A March 17, 1862, roster of prisoners listed 107 names of persons who had not been tried but were accused of a wide variety of offenses. Five months later, then Judge Advocate L. C. Turner notified Lafayette C. Baker to "arrest, convey to and detain in the Old Capitol Prison" 14 residents of Fredericksburg, Virginia. Civilians named by Turner were ordered held "in custody as hostages for the safety" of seven enumerated Union citizens who were imprisoned in Richmond. (OR, 115, 271–72; OR, 117, 366)

During the first three years of conflict, numerous hostages were kept for a time in the Old Capitol. Most of them were later moved to other prisons, so by May 1864, the Washington facility was being heavily used for the temporary imprisonment of captured guerrillas and bushwhackers. By that time, most of the many political prisoners it had held were in other places of confinement or had won their release. (OR, 120, 112)

Near Columbus, Ohio, a training camp for state militia became a holding facility for prisoners in the immediate aftermath of Bull Run. Named in

Old Capitol Prison in Washington, D.C., held numerous notables, including some of the conspirators who worked with John Wilkes Booth.
Library of Congress

honor of Salmon P. Chase, a former governor of the Buckeye State, it was long under the control of Ohio officials who unsuccessfully tried to prevent Federal officials from taking it over. The first men and women imprisoned at Camp Chase were political prisoners whose ranks eventually swelled to at least five hundred persons. Most hostages who went there stayed only a few weeks before being sent to Johnson's Island for long periods of imprisonment.

The first hostages sent to Camp Chase were civilians whose homes were in the Kanawha Valley, claimed by both Virginia and the region that later became West Virginia. A party of 23 of these "wealthy and influential secessionists," held as hostages for captured Unionists civilians, arrived under guard on July 5, 1861. Names of these hostages soon appeared in columns of the locally published *Ohio State Journal*, according to which this special band of captives was held only briefly, presumably until release of their equivalents was guaranteed. (CV, 6, 8)

Fort Warren, built of granite on a small island near the entrance of Boston harbor, became a prison at least as early as October 1861. During that month, Gov. John A. Andrew dispatched a contingent of state guardsmen to the fortress and ordered them to keep watch over an expected shipment of about one hundred prisoners of war. When the prisoner-laden vessel reached its destination, it sent into the fortress about seven times the number of men who had been expected. Because no adequate facilities had been prepared, one room approximately 800 square feet in size was crammed with at least 150 men. Numerous Rebels who were considered to be pirates were sent to this facility, and in nearly every instance Confederates designated a specific hostage for each such man.

Though labeled "a Northern keep" in Richmond, Fort Warren was among the best of Northern prisons. Inmates were permitted to hold debates, organize a government of their own, and attend classes in which music, French, and dancing were taught by skilled prisoners. Even numerous Confederate privateersmen at Fort Warren, for whom hostages were held in the South, admitted that they were usually well fed and comfortably housed.

An exploit led by Lt. Joseph W. Alexander of the CSS *Atlanta* became lauded throughout the entire South. Young and slender, Alexander managed to squeeze through a loophole barely more than eight inches wide. He then pulled five other inmates—two of whom had been captured aboard the privateer *Tacony*—through the tiny aperture. Alexander and a comrade were recaptured, but the other five escapees remained at large. Many inmates of Fort Warren were there awaiting trial for piracy despite changes in Federal policy that resulted from Rebel selection of hostages for such men. Some of them did not arrive until after the Lincoln-announced policy of treating captured seamen differently from fighting men captured on land was quietly rescinded. Yet a list of "pirates" held at the Boston prison, for

Flimsy sheds that housed prisoners at Camp Chase in Ohio were built very close together.

Carroll Prison *(four buildings, right forefront)* was constructed as an annex to better-known Old Capitol Prison.

Prison Life in the Old Capitol

whom Rebels swore to provide man-for-man hostages, was provided to Richmond late in 1862. (PH, 7, 123, 133, 135, 139)

St. Louis, through which large numbers of POWs and hostages were funneled into eastern facilities, had no large prison in 1861. Hence Provost Marshal George E. Leighton looked about for a facility that could be made into a detention center. He learned that secessionist Joseph N. McDowell owned a big stone building—known as McDowell's Medical College—that was situated on Gratiot Street. Seized within days after secessionists tried to take over Camp Jackson in the city's suburbs, it was put to a variety of uses before becoming a Federal prison in December.

Gratiot Street Prison received its first contingent of inmates a few days before Christmas. One of the most conspicuous of these was Col. Ebenezer Magoffin, whose brother Beriah was the Kentucky governor who moved heaven and earth in a futile attempt to keep the state of Abraham Lincoln's birth neutral. No large group of hostages is known to have passed through the St. Louis facility, but numerous individual hostages were processed there before being shipped to Alton, Illinois, and other facilities. Brief accounts concerning some of these men appear elsewhere in this volume.

Illinois included numerous Copperheads but was never so badly divided as Missouri. The two states were alike however, in their lack of a facility in which substantial numbers of Rebels and their sympathizers could be securely imprisoned. In desperation, Gov. Richard Yates turned to the long-abandoned Alton State Prison—empty since a crusade led by Dorothea Dix caused it to be closed when a new prison was erected at Joliet. Prodded by Gen. Henry W. Halleck, Illinois leaders adopted the Yates suggestion that Alton be reopened for military use. A few prisoners reached it early in 1862 and by the end of February it was badly overcrowded.

Some hostages were sent to Alton from Gratiot Street Prison and others went directly there after having been arrested and selected as equivalents for men held in Rebel institutions. By November it held an undesignated number of civilians who were being held as hostages in a bid to force Rebels to parole a group of captives who had been taken in a Fayetteville, Arkansas, hospital by men under the command of Gen. John S. Marmaduke.

Within a year after receiving its first contingent of prisoners, Alton had the deserved reputation of being one of the worst pest holes in the North. Nuns who belonged to the order of Sisters of Charity were used as nurses, but they could do little more than give comfort to dying men. In St. Louis, Lt. Col. F. A. Dick promised soon to secure for Washington a full and accurate list of men plus women who were imprisoned at Alton, but seems never to have produced it. (OR, 117, 949; OR, 118, 245; OR, 120, 221, 373)

Maj. Thomas Hendrickson became commandant early in 1863 and made valiant efforts to clean up the prison. Pleading for funds with which to make essential repairs, he was informed by Washington that Alton was

Gratiot Street Prison in St. Louis was a converted medical school.

An unidentified member of the 3rd Ohio regiment made this sketch of Fort Delaware early in 1863.

the property of the state of Illinois, so repairs should be made from the woefully inadequate prison fund allocated to the facility. Despite his efforts, spoiled and rotten food plus putrid water continued to be given to inmates, who experienced waves of dysentery and typhoid fever but received little or no medical treatment. Hoffman's hard work had led to no noticeable improvement when a shipment of 768 prisoners, among whom numerous hostages were included, arrived on July 26. Two weeks later, he happily relinquished command to Col. G. W. Kincaid of the 37th Iowa regiment—whose men were already on duty at Alton as guards. (OR, 118, 338, 369, 396, 484; OR, 119, 195; OR, 120, 81–83, 221, 373)

J. S. Riley, who was imprisoned at Alton in 1864, escaped and joined the band led by John Y. Beall that made a futile effort to free an estimated seven hundred Confederate officers who were imprisoned on Johnson's Island, near Sandusky, Ohio. Before being tried and executed as a spy, Riley's leader was central to a long and complicated hostage case that grew out of charges that he and his men were pirates. (CV, 9, 3–4)

Partly because its location in Lake Erie, approximately one mile from the mainland, promised to make escape difficult, Johnson's Island was personally selected as a prison site by Col. William Hoffman. As soon as a stockade was built to enclose barracks hastily thrown together by use of green lumber, Mayor William S. Piersen of Sandusky was given a commission as major and put in command. Reserved exclusively for captured Rebel officers, its initial population of about six hundred soon soared past two thousand. Many of the hostages who were sent to Charleston in 1864 to be put on Morris Island under the fire of Rebel guns were shipped to the port city from Johnson's Island.

Though perfunctory inspections took place at frequent intervals, inadequate shelter from severe winter weather plus an irregular flow of substandard food were seldom mentioned in reports. Like many other Northern installations whose inmates had spent their earlier lives in the Cotton Belt, the prison had periodic outbreaks of pneumonia and tuberculosis. Guards, some of whom were untrained and some of whom were malicious, took periodic shots at prisoners without provocation.

Capts. John S. Spriggs and Marshall Triplett of Virginia's Partisan Rangers were sent to Johnson's Island in 1862. Their imprisonment at the Lake Erie site led the Confederate Senate to pass a resolution condemning the enemy's "many and most flagrant acts violative of the usages of war, of the rights of humanity and even of common decency." Since the legislative measure had no effect whatever upon Federal policies concerning treatment of prisoners, two Federal officers were selected as hostages for their safety.

By 1864 an unspecified number of Rebels held in Ohio were designated as "hostages for Union men imprisoned by rebels." Records fail to

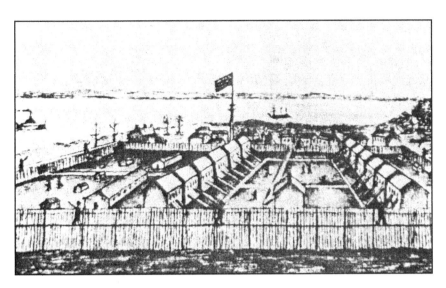

Inmate James Andrews made this sketch of the Johnson's Island Prison for the *Confederate Veteran* magazine.

Escapee Joseph W. Alexander *(rear, extreme right)* and some of his fellow prisoners at Fort Warren.

Photographic History

indicate how many scores of hostages and equivalents were involved with Johnson's Island, but the number is known to have been large. In December 1864, Washington requested Col. C. W. Hill, who was then the commandant of the prison, to provide information about the total number of men who had been confined on the island and the total number who had died there. He reported that 7,377 men had been received "at this depot," and that only 198 had died from pneumonia, typhoid, camp fevers, and chronic dysentery. If his data were accurate, the death rate was far below that at Alton and other wretched prisons but the relatively low mortality meant little or nothing to hostages and other prisoners who were barely clinging to life. (OR, 117, 907; OR, 120, 122, 228, 428–29, 468–70, 484–88, 809, 853, 1084, 1207–9, 1235, 1241, 1257)

Numerous hostages who were sent from one prison to another spent only a few weeks or months in any of them. One such person was Capt. Frank Battle, chosen by Federal authorities as the equivalent for Capt. Shad Harris—captured by Rebels after having allegedly deserted and being pardoned by Jefferson Davis. Their intertwinement, with which neither had anything to do, generated at least 24 dispatches, letters, and reports.

Battle fought with the 20th Tennessee and after his alleged desertion from Rebel forces Harris was a member of the 3rd East Tennessee Cavalry. Both were captured and Rebels threatened Harris with execution; in retaliation, his captors made a hostage of Battle. Clapped in irons, he was briefly imprisoned at the Nashville, Tennessee, penitentiary. Robert Ould, the Confederate agent of exchange, was in April 1864 under the impression that the hostage had been sent to Johnson's Island. Three days later, however, Col. William Hoffman had firm information that the Rebel captain was at Fort Warren in irons.

Soon Union Gen. S. P. Carter and Rebel Gen. J. C. Vaughn entered into an agreement that had not been officially sanctioned by their respective government. Vaughn "bound himself" to get Harris released and to deliver him at Union lines in East Tennessee. Carter took the same solemn pledge to secure Battle and deliver him to Rebel lines so that an exchange could be effected. Union Gen. E. A. Hitchcock made an informal pledge to oversee the projected exchange.

By this time, however, Battle was being held in close confinement at Fort Warren for having been involved in an attempt at a mass escape. Carter, who was already beginning to have cold feet about his role in the exchange, had information that Battle had been moved to Fort Delaware. Hence he suggested that the Rebel officer should be "continued in close confinement and in irons" at that point until the enemy agreed to turn over Harris—last heard from about December 1 from Columbia, South Carolina. Hitchcock, who admitted that he was having trouble keeping the papers relating to the

Battle/Harris matter together, put pressure on Washington to expedite the release of Battle.

Before the end of January 1865, Gen. John H. Winder requested from Gen. Samuel Cooper specific instructions about how to deal with Harris. Thirty days later, Battle had left Fort Warren and was en route to Fort Monroe. Confederate agent of exchange Robert Ould did not know where Harris was confined, but noted that he had been "sentenced to hard labor for [the duration of] the war." A circular dispatched from the Richmond headquarters of Confederate military prisons soon asked for any available information about Harris.

Late in February Lt. Col. L. S. Trowbridge of the 10th Michigan Cavalry notified Hoffman that Lincoln had become involved. The chief executive had directed that Capt. Thomas W. Elliott, who was being held at Nashville under sentence of death, should be exchanged for Harris. Meanwhile, Battle continued to be the designated hostage for Harris at Fort Delaware. Harris was released early in March and was delivered to Federal forces near Wilmington.

Having heard nothing from or about Battle for six weeks, in early April Ould asked Federal authorities for a report concerning his whereabouts. He apparently never received word that six months earlier, Hoffman had given subordinates two options concerning the Rebel captain. He was (1) to be released from close confinement, or (2) sent home to wait for exchange by an equivalent. Since he was listed as being at Fort Delaware in January 1865, and at Fort Monroe the following month, Federal officers must have chosen Hoffman's first alternative.

After being reported at Fort Monroe, no other mention of Battle was preserved in the *Official Records*. Hence the last few months of the war found the hostage who had seen numerous prisons from the inside on the way home to wait for an exchange, or vanishing into thin air, never to be heard of again. (OR, 119, 476; OR, 120, 23, 1175, 1229, 1265; OR, 121, 26, 53, 71, 159, 196, 208, 225, 230, 307–8, 364)

Part IV

Selected for Special Risks

17

Charleston, 1864 –50/50

General officers sent tens of thousands of dispatches, letters, orders, and telegrams. Yet comparatively few were signed by two men, and documents penned by three or more wearers of stars are rare. During 1861–65 five general officers signed a single document—and the quintet was made up entirely of hostages. Sent by way of Hilton Head, South Carolina, to Gen. Lorenzo Thomas the dispatch that originated in Charleston on July 1, 1864, included carefully worded language but was an urgent plea that read in part:

GENERAL: We desire respectfully to represent through you to our authorities our firm belief that a prompt exchange of prisoners of war in the hands of the Southern Confederacy, if exchanges are to be made, is called for by every consideration of humanity.

While we cheerfully submit to any policy that may be decided upon by our Government, we would urge that the great evils that result from any delay that is not desired should be obviated by the designation of some point in this vicinity at which exchanges could be made—a course we are induced to believe, that would be acceded to by the Confederate authorities.

And we are, general, very respectfully, your obedient servants,

H. W. WESSELLS, *Brigadier-General, U.S. Volunteers,*
T. SEYMOUR, *Brigadier-General, U.S. Volunteers,*
E. P. SCAMMON, *Brigadier-General, U.S. Volunteers,*
C. A. HECKMAN, *Brigadier-General, U.S. Volunteers,*
ALEXANDER SHALER, *Brigadier-General, U.S. Volunteers,*
Prisoners of War (OR, 66, 162)

On the same day, another five-signature message went to Gen. John G. Foster who was in command of Federal forces at Hilton Head. It called to his attention that "5 general officers of the Confederate service have arrived at

Many of Charleston's fine old mansions were built very close to the water along the seawall known as "the battery."

Hilton Head, with a view to their being subjected to the same treatment we are receiving here." Since Union officers said they were "as pleasantly and comfortably situated as is possible for prisoners of war," they hoped that the same courtesies would be accorded to their counterparts in gray. Confederate Gen. Samuel Jones, in command at Charleston, transmitted both letters and expressed to Foster his fervent hope that "there should be an exchange of prisoners of war." (OR, 66, 161, 163)

Union Gen. George Stoneman, celebrated for his leadership of cavalry raids, may unwittingly have accelerated the train of events that led to appeals by Union soldiers held in the port city at which the war started. As commander of the Cavalry Corps, Army of the Ohio, Stoneman had planned and directed an expedition designed to free some or all of the many prisoners of war at Andersonville. Headed for the site of the Georgia prison that lay close to the Florida state line, Stoneman did not get far. Attacked on July 31 near Macon by a superior force of Confederates, he and about two hundred members of the 5th Indiana Cavalry were captured. Since Rebels were already in the process of trying to move some prisoners from badly overcrowded Andersonville, Stoneman and most of his men were sent to the jail in Charleston. (OR, 73, 914)

Maj. O. R. McNary of the 103rd Pennsylvania, who was quartered in the same facility as Stoneman, doubted that there was any "Rebel prison where there was more consolidated misery to the square inch." One of six hundred fellow inmates told him that "it was the nastiest, dirtiest, filthiest, lousiest place he was ever in." To make things much worse, Federal warships of the blockading squadron under the command of Rear Adm. John A. B. Dahlgren were regularly dropping shells upon Charleston and no one knew when one would land in the middle of the jail yard. (M, 15, 36-37)

Military and civilian Confederates were furious that their enemies whose avowed goal was the reduction of Fort Sumter had started to let missiles hit the city. Many that accidentally or deliberately missed Fort Sumter screamed past their target and hit in the city. Some downtown streets had become so deserted that they were described as being grass-covered.

There is some evidence that Rebels packed as many captured Federals into the local jail as possible, hoping that gunners would be ordered to stop firing upon the city in which many of their own men were held. Calculated and deliberate steps designed to put officers in blue under the fire of guns on warships and Morris Island might save Charleston, they reasoned. So they had requested from their comrades in Virginia a shipment of 50 Federal officers who would be placed under the fire of their own guns.

Stoneman, who knew nothing of this plan, sent to Abraham Lincoln a long and argumentative letter about prisoners of war—whose exchange had been halted upon orders of Grant. Making light of conditions in which he and 1,800 other officers were living, the cavalry leader based his appeal upon the condition of "35,000 suffering, starving, and dying enlisted men" who were being held by Rebels. (JSHS, 11, 86; OR, 30, 77–104; OR, 40, 279–81; OR, 50, 277–78; OR, 120, 616–18, 874–75, 1129–30; CM, 6/18/64)

Though he emphasized the plight of enlisted men and said nothing to the president about his own situation, Stoneman pulled every possible string in order to get himself exchanged. As a result of his appeals, even his old foe Gen. John B. Hood penned a request that the rules be bent in order to get the Federal raider out of jail and out from under the fire of big Federal guns. (OR, 120, 837, 846, 878)

Confederates, who knew little or nothing about the loud noises being made by Stoneman, were optimistic that the hostage ploy would put an end to the bombardment of Charleston. Residents indulged in an orgy of rejoicing when they learned that 50 Federal officers had reached the city. As reported in local newspapers, the body of men "brought hither to share the pleasures of the bombardment" consisted of the five generals who soon wrote to Thomas, plus 11 colonels, 25 lieutenant colonels, and nine majors. One editor chortled that ordinary and incendiary shells thrown into the city would now "risk the death of a Yankee officer every time a gun is fired." Jones sent a brief notice to Foster that these prisoners of war were in Charleston "for safekeeping" and did not designate them as hostages who were designed to end the bombardment of the city. (OR, 66, 132; NOR, 15, 528; CM, 6/14/64; CDC, 6/14/64)

Far to the north, the Federal commissary general of prisoners responded to a request from Hilton Head. Foster said he needed 5 Rebel generals, 15 colonels, 15 lieutenant colonels, and 15 majors as soon as they could be selected. Col. William Hoffman detailed Maj. E. N. Strong to take charge of conducting Rebel officers to Hilton Head so that they could be put under fire of the guns of Fort Sumter. Prisoners selected to go to Charleston were assembled at Fort Delaware and listed by rank in descending order. Maj. Gens. Edward Johnson and Franklin Gardner headed the list; their names were followed by those of 3 brigadiers, 15 colonels, 13 lieutenant colonels, and 17 majors. Each officer's unit was listed, along with the place and date of his capture. Though ranks did not correspond as neatly as Foster wished, this arrangement resulted in plans for a 50/50 split of hostages under fire at Charleston. (OR, 66, 147–48)

Two of the Federal hostages, Seymour of Vermont and Shaler of Connecticut, had been taken in The Wilderness; two Rebels, Johnson of Virginia and Steuart of Maryland, had been captured at Spotsylvania. One Confederate general, Gardner, was a native of New York City who had been forced to surrender at Port Hudson on May 12, 1864. Federals Henry W. Wessels and Charles A. Heckman, from Connecticut and Pennsylvania, were captured at Plymouth, North Carolina, and Drewry's Bluff, Virginia, within a period of 30 days. Scammon, who hailed from Maine, had been taken by men in gray during a February foray into West Virginia. That meant no

At Spotsylvania, men in blue were confronted by an officer and two Rebels of high rank who were captured and later sent to Charleston.

A. R. Waud in *Harper's Weekly*

other Federal general, now a hostage in Charleston, had been in prison as long as he had. His capture was, however, antedated by that of the Maryland-born James Jay Archer, a Rebel who was taken at Gettysburg.

Confederate Meriwether J. Thompson was in a class all by himself; if captors had known the details of his background, he probably would not have been among the 50/50 in Charleston. A staunch secessionist who was born and reared in Virginia, he was rebuffed when he offered his services to Stonewall Jackson. Nursing anger he never got over, Thompson led the battalion he had raised and organized into Missouri, where its members operated as partisans. Having proclaimed himself to be a general who eventually headed a body of about five thousand men, Thompson had no formal military title. Yet the use of one bestowed upon himself caused him to be close to the top of the list of 50 men selected to go to the South from Fort Delaware.

Military experiences of the 10 general officers whose rank made them the most important of the one hundred men in Charleston or on the way to the port city were as varied as their places of birth and capture. Wessels, who was cited for gallantry at Contreras and Churubusco during the Mexican War, was on the Kansas border when war broke out. After suffering a slight wound at Seven Pines, he was sent south and soon became commander of the Military District of the Albemarle in North Carolina.

While at the head of the Federal garrison in Plymouth, he was attacked by Rebels under Robert F. Hoke and was forced to surrender—as a result of which Hoke was promoted and became a Confederate major general not much younger than Rooney Lee at the time of his jump in rank while held hostage. Possibly because he was viewed as exceptionally experienced, soon after having shaken the dust of Charleston off his feet Washington made Wessels commissary general of prisoners for all states east of the Mississippi River. (OR, 120, 1117, 1128)

Born at Baltimore, Steuart went to West Point more than three decades before his state became bitterly divided by the Civil War. He graduated at age 19, then was shifted from one dreary and desolate frontier post to another for 30 years. Despite his long career in the Union army, he was given only a captain's commission when he resigned on April 22, 1861, and offered his services to the Confederacy-in-the-making. After becoming a brigadier he served under Richard S. Ewell in the Shenandoah Valley and took a serious hit at Cross Keys. At Gettysburg, he was captured inside the Mule Shoe; imprisoned, he had the bad luck to be picked to go to Charleston as a counterhostage.

Gardner was one of thousands of Rebels who were born in the North. His parents having moved from New York City to Iowa, he went to West Point from what was then the far West. One of his classmates, Lyss Grant, ranked 21st in the 1843 class of 39 men, but Gardner was #17. He, too, fought in the Mexican War and remained in the Union army until March 1861. Apparently without bothering to turn in his commission as captain, he put on a gray uniform and jumped two grades.

His performance at Shiloh brought a second two-level promotion and before 1862 ended he was a major general and was soon put in command in the Mississippi Valley. The New Yorker held Port Hudson, Louisiana, against Federal forces for seven weeks and when he finally capitulated was made a prisoner of war on July 8, 1864. When he agreed to surrender terms, he had no idea that he would soon be on the way to Charleston as a counter-hostage whom men in blue planned to put under Rebel fire.

Some of his fellow Federal hostages knew that Heckman had no military training or experience before the war. He quit his job as conductor on the New Jersey Central Railroad in order to become lieutenant colonel of the 9th New Jersey. While in North Carolina as a member of the early Burnside expedition the Pennsylvania native won two promotions in 1862. Top leaders, aware of his lack of experience, steered him into noncombat posts that included command of the garrisons at Portsmouth, Virginia, and all-important Norfolk.

Since Drewry's Bluff on the James River was conveniently close to his post, Heckman was sent into Gen. Benjamin F. Butler's Army of the James when operations against Rebel posts in the region were launched in May 1864. At the head of his brigade, Heckman led a May 6 scout in the direction of Petersburg but failed to learn that Confederate-held Fort Darling at Drewry's Bluff was being heavily reinforced. Two days later Butler launched a major offensive, one of whose objectives was the James River site famous for being the place at which Rebels had seen a gunboat with Lincoln aboard come under fire from other Federal vessels. Expecting a counterattack, Federal units stretched spare telegraph wire between stumps to form the war's first defensive work of its sort. The supply of wire ran out before Heckman's position was reached, so a May 16 attack under cover of dense fog by four brigades of Rebels led to a breakthrough. Along with about four hundred of his men, the former railroad conductor was taken and within weeks found himself in Charleston as a hostage for the safety of the city.

Maryland attorney Archer had no military training, but learned a lot during the Mexican War. Memory of a citation for gallantry at Chapultepec may have played a role in his 1855 decision to enter the Union army as a captain. Like Steuart, who was admiringly dubbed "Maryland," his secessionist views were strong and pronounced; without a change in rank he was wearing a gray uniform two days after leaving Federal ranks.

Archer fought under former U.S. Sen. Louis T. Wigfall and in Hood's Texas Brigade before being made a brigadier in June 1862. He led five regiments at Cedar Mountain and Second Bull Run before arriving at Antietam a few hours before fighting stopped on September 17, 1862. Suffering from an undiagnosed illness that would have sent most men to a hospital, the

Rebel general officer's command post at Antietam was the ambulance in which he rode there. A few months later at Fredericksburg, still not fully recovered from his bout with an unknown malady, the man not among the ranks of West Pointers fought stubbornly and well. His performance at Chancellorsville caused fellow brigadiers to predict that he would soon be promoted. That jump in rank was in the works when his decimated brigade fought at Gettysburg under Gen. Henry Heth. On July 1 the Marylander became the first general officer to be captured since Robert E. Lee took command of the Army of Northern Virginia. Though his health was permanently impaired by having spent many months at Johnson's Island, his rank led Federals to select him to go to Charleston as a counterhostage.

Instead of bringing the shelling of Charleston to an end by putting 50 Federal hostages under the fire of their own guns, the pace of the bombardment increased dramatically after they arrived. During a period of a single week, nearly six thousand balls and shells were directed at Fort Sumter, which remained the primary target. Union Gen. Quincy A. Gillmore, who commanded military forces in the region, issued an ultimatum that Rebels ignored. Hence an immense gun in the Marsh Battery on Morris Island was aimed at the heart of the city during the night of August 21.

Confederate Gen. P. G. T. Beauregard, in command at Sumter, denounced the deliberate shelling of the city as "an act of inexcusable barbarity," but it continued day and night until the eight-inch Parrot rifle that was dubbed the Swamp Angel burst. Located in a bog on Morris Island, the Federal piece could throw a 150-pound projectile about five miles and its shells dropped upon what newspapers called "sleeping women and children" until it burst on August 24. (CDC, 8/26/64)

Rebel civilians and military leaders were less than satisfied with results achieved by use of hostages, but Federals who had sent for counterhostages were positively mortified before they arrived. They had failed to take into account the fact that Sumter's guns were trained largely upon the new Battery Wagner, whose location was such that there was no place to put 50 Confederate officers so that they would be under fire from the fort. In this dilemma, the counterhostages remained aboard a Federal vessel and Washington was besieged with pleas for a "special hostage exchange."

Soon the Union secretary of war agreed to the special exchange, "rank for rank, or their equivalents." Foster, who was pleased that the ugly business was about over, made plans for Dahlgren to send exchanged Federal officers to Hilton Head aboard the USS *Cosmopolitan*. (OR, 66, 161–63, 170, 378; JSHS, 3, 77–81; NOR, 15, 644)

On August 3, the exchange took place in Charleston harbor. Foster's wishes having been ignored, the freed Federal officers boarded the steamer *Fulton* and headed north toward Norfolk. Rebels who escorted the freed hostages to their steamer expressed their wonder that not a man among them had been hit, despite the fact that shells from their own guns fell upon

Charleston during every day they were there. Since all of the one hundred officers involved in this high-stakes contest were formally exchanged and were not under parole, Confederate counterhostages immediately reported for duty.

18

Searchers for "Infernal Devices"

Gen. George B. McClellan got one of the biggest surprises of his military career before midnight on May 3, 1862. A dispatch from one of his subordinates revealed that Rebel forces had pulled out of Yorktown, Virginia, a few hours earlier. Federal intelligence had indicated that the strategic town, famous for its decisive role in the American Revolution 80 years earlier, was defended by at least 100,000 Rebels. Since McClellan reckoned his own force at only 105,000, he had decided upon a siege rather than a frontal assault.

Confederate Gen. John B. Magruder, whose 10,000 men had been stretched very thin during a late winter bid to prevent Federals from moving up the Virginia peninsula, knew that he faced a vastly superior enemy. Delaying tactics north of the Warwick River but south of Yorktown had slowed McClellan considerably, but had failed to stop him. Alarmed that their capital might be in danger, Confederates had sent Gen. Joseph E. Johnston to assess the situation at Yorktown.

Johnston, who returned to Richmond in mid-April, was less than optimistic about stopping McClellan's vastly superior forces. An extremely long conference was held, with Jefferson Davis presiding and the secretary of war plus Robert E. Lee participating. Fearing that Virginia might lose Gosport Navy Yard, where the CSS *Virginia* was based, Davis eventually ruled that Yorktown must be held at all costs. Hence Johnston soon made preparations to take his 45,000 men there.

An early and forceful Federal probe near Lee's Mill on April 16 had been a near disaster. Men of a Vermont brigade led by Gen. W. T. H. Brooks successfully forded a stream swollen by spring rains, but were turned back by Confederates under the command of Gen. Howell Cobb. Delegating to Gen. F. J. Porter on-the-spot direction of the operation, McClellan decided upon a siege that began about the time Johnston left Yorktown after

Vermont forces waded an overflowing stream to make a futile assault upon Rebel positions at Yorktown.

Harper's Weekly

having inspected its defenses. Hence 13-inch guns began dropping shells upon the town on or about April 28. (OR, 12, 351–52)

Defenders put up stout resistance, despite the fact that enlistments of many men in gray were about to expire. In the Rebel capital that was McClellan's goal from the start of the Peninsula Campaign, frightened law-makers took a step that was both innovative and potentially dangerous. The first conscription act designed to bring Americans into uniform or to keep them there became law on April 16. Though this brought about new elections of officers, it enabled Johnston to keep most of his men.

By the end of April, Federal commanders had an estimated one hundred siege guns in position. Many of the Federal pieces that made up 14 batteries were 100- and 200-pounder Parrott rifles which opened fire on May 1. When their huge projectiles began falling on defensive works, Johnston began making plans for an immediate evacuation. McClellan, one of only a handful of general officers who made balloon ascensions during the war, went up on the afternoon of May 3 and returned to the ground supremely confident. He planned to keep up a steady barrage of artillery and to start moving his troops toward the besieged stronghold on May 6. He expected to proceed cautiously despite the fact that his army was im-mensely larger than the combined strength of Colonials, French, and Brit-ish who fought at Yorktown much earlier. (OR, 12, 338–49)

Three days before the scheduled start of the Federal advance it be-came clear that there would be no battle in 1862; during a steady downpour of rain, Johnston had withdrawn in order to seek a better defensive posi-tion. Jubilant men in blue poured into their objective on May 4; knowing that the place had been abandoned by the enemy, discipline was so lax that many troops fanned out to seek souvenirs and to inspect the famous town. For a few of them, these activities proved to be disastrous. Devices that we today would call "anti-personnel land mines" exploded from the ground plus a few flour barrels that appeared to be nearly empty.

Union Gen. William F. Barry reported that when his men entered the town, a few were killed and several were injured by explosions unlike any that fighting men of 1861–65 had encountered earlier. Barry, who was chief of artillery in the Army of the Potomac, described lethal events, in which he saw two men die, due to loaded shells buried in the ground. He wrote that

These shells were the ordinary 8 or 10 inch mortar or columbiad shells, filled with powder, buried a few inches below the surface of the ground, and so arranged with some fulminate, or with the ordinary artillery fric-tion primer, that they exploded by being trod upon or otherwise disturbed. In some cases articles of common use, and which would be most likely to be picked up, such as engineers' wheelbarrows, or pickaxes, or shovels, were laid upon the spot with apparent carelessness. Concealed strings or wire leading from the friction primer of the shell to the superincumbent articles were so arranged that the slightest disturbance would occasion the explosion.

These shells were not thus placed on the glacis at the bottom of the ditch, &c., which, in view of an anticipated assault, might possibly be considered a legitimate use of them, but they were placed by an enemy who was secretly abandoning his post on common roads, at springs of water, in the shade of trees, at the foot of telegraph poles, and, lastly, quite within the defenses of the place in the very streets of the town.

A soldier believed to have been a member of a New York regiment saw a pocket knife lying near a spring. He picked it up without noticing that a string was tied to it "and the next instant was torn into fragments, since the cord had been fastened to the machinery of a concealed torpedo." (OR, 12, 349; Lord, *They Fought*, 272b)

McClellan, who rode triumphantly into Yorktown in an ambulance, never forgot the use by Rebels of "infernal devices" that soon came to be widely known as torpedoes. In his autobiography he suggested that placement of such explosives at points where an enemy assault was expected could be "admissible under the customs of war." Their use at Yorktown he branded, however, as "barbarous in the extreme."

The Union commander reacted by ordering the first use of hostages who were deliberately commanded to do work that could have brought about their death. Recalling the event years afterward, he wrote that "I at once ordered that they [the land mines] should be discovered and removed by the Confederate prisoners" taken during the Federal advance. He added that "They objected very strenuously, but were forced to do the work." If a hostage ordered into a mine field at Yorktown was killed or injured, no report was made about this matter. (McClellan, *McClellan's Own Story*, 326–27)

Newspapers of the Cotton Belt denounced McClellan's novel employment of hostages as "cruel, barbarous, and not warranted by the usages of war." Gen. James Longstreet condemned such use of torpedoes and military leaders on both sides called for an investigation. Inquiry initially suggested, erroneously, that the explosives had been manufactured by Gen. George W. Rains. His brother having been briefly in command at Yorktown, Rains was said by Barry to have been responsible for "this dastardly business." According to the Federal general officer, many of his former comrades knew that George W. Rains had used similar devices "while disgracing the uniform of the American Army during the Seminole War in Florida." (Lord, *They Fought*, 272b; D, 470b; OR, 12, 350)

Barry's harsh words failed accurately to distinguish between brothers who were natives of North Carolina. Gabriel James Rains graduated from West Point in 1827 and spent 34 years in the U.S. Army before resigning in order to fight for the Confederacy. He became interested in explosives

before age 20, and was sometimes described by acquaintances as being ob-
sessed with them. He, rather than his brother who was 14 years his junior,
fought in the Seminole War.

His use of antipersonnel land mines during that conflict backfired;
when Rains and his men arrived at the spot where a Seminole had been
killed by a buried explosive, they found that they had ridden into an ambush. Men not familiar with the Florida record of the professional soldier
mistakenly described his use of land mines at Yorktown as "a hitherto unknown mode of warfare." (GG, 250)

George Washington Rains, who graduated from the U.S. Military Academy in 1842, also had strong and long-lasting interest in explosives. He left
the U.S. Army after 39 years in order to take charge of an iron works in New
York state, but donned a gray uniform in 1861 with the rank of major. Though
he never became a general officer, in the aftermath of Bull Run he was named
to head the mammoth task of procuring gunpowder for Rebels. After a quick
tour of the South, he selected Augusta, Georgia, as the ideal spot at which
to build an immense powder factory. Before the conflict ended he was credited with having produced nearly three million pounds of "the most de-
pendable powder made in the Confederacy." (Ency., 611a)

Confederate Gen. Gabriel J. Rains
was the innovative genius who put
torpedoes to work on land and in
the water.

Union Gen. William F. Barry believed that explosions in which some
of his men died were due to "subterranean shells," which actually
were among the earliest land mines.

The manufacturer of powder strongly defended his brother's novel use of explosives. At least as early as the 16th century, devices of the same general type were occasionally employed for demolition purposes. Though they had been called torpedoes for more than three hundred years before Gabriel Rains put them to new use, all such devices were immobile. World War I saw the rise of the torpedo as a projectile, and in World War II John F. Kennedy achieved fame in the specialized naval service to which self-propelled torpedoes were central.

Improving upon the improvised antipersonnel land mines he left behind at Yorktown, Gabriel Rains produced a percussion-type torpedo that could be triggered by a trip wire or a pressure-sensitive fuse. His invention was widely used by Rebels, who produced increasingly sophisticated versions. At Virginia's Fort Gilder in 1864, seven of them were placed in front of the installation for defensive purposes. All of them were under a single plank, and it was said that less than 10 pounds of weight at any point on the plank would cause all of them to explode.

During the long and bloody struggle over Morris Island, near Charleston, immense numbers of torpedoes were used by Rebels in the defense of Fort Wagner. As a result of one dramatic explosion, a corporal of the 3rd Colored Troops was thrown 25 yards. The dead soldier landed "entirely naked, with his arm resting on the plunger of another torpedo." This bizarre episode led to a yarn according to which the corpse was attached to an explosive as a decoy to draw Rebels to it. (OR, 46, 26, 204–5, 296; OR, 89, 613)

Torpedoes "came of age," not on land, but in naval warfare. Never remotely competitive with the Union in terms of powerful warships, Rebels used explosive devices freely. Hence at least three-fourths of the more than 450 references to torpedoes in the *Official Records* deal with naval incidents. Before the conflict ended, new and more sophisticated explosives were to the earliest percussion torpedoes what the computer is to the typewriter. Many underwater torpedoes were wired so that they could be set off from shore by electricity from batteries when enemy vessels approached their location. Others, commonly called spar torpedoes, were attached to the ends of poles so that even a large vessel could be sent to the bottom by a very small one. Horological torpedoes included clockwork mechanisms by which they could be set to detonate at a given time in the future.

Rains, who became a brigadier in September 1861, saw relatively little combat. He opposed McClellan at Yorktown and led a brigade at Seven Pines before being named to head the Rebel bureau responsible for securing volunteers and conscripts. In May 1863, he was detailed for special duty "in connection with torpedoes and subterranean shells." Just a year later he was assigned to superintend "all duties of torpedoes" among Rebel forces despite the fact that devices made by competitors were in common use. (OR, 38, 919; OR, 69, 883)

Artist's conception of the explosion of a very early torpedo, which today would be called an antipersonnel land mine.

Harper's Weekly

Long before the Rebel explosives expert began devoting full time to his inventions and their use, Federal commanders had adopted the torpedo—with reservations. At Charleston, Gens. J. G. Foster and Alexander Schimmelfennig turned to Adm. John A. Dahlgren for advice on their use on land and at sea. Most torpedoes that were put into service by Union forces were designed, however, for use as portable explosives with which to blow up bridges and similar structures. Famous bridge builder Herman Haupt secured one hundred of them in 1862, then designed and reproduced a diagram showing the vulnerable points of bridge trusses. Some Federal demolition parties were given boxes of 14 torpedoes, "loaded, with fuse inserted" with Haupt's set of instructions on how best to use them. (OR, 31, 827; OR, 39, 1070; OR, 60, 220–21; OR, 6, 190, 206)

At New Bern, North Carolina, Union Gen. I. N. Palmer became furious because a number of men who were handling torpedoes were killed and wounded. He raged that rumor said "these torpedoes were placed in an open wagon with no one but the driver." Were these lethal devices actually "exposed at the depot the same as barrels of provisions?" he demanded. "Was it true that at their destination they were turned over to a party of negroes to trundle into the commissary store-house, with no one to watch them?" There is no record that Palmer's questions were ever answered to his satisfaction, but he indulged in hope that torpedoes devised by a Mr. King "will do service." (OR, 52, 375; OR, 69, 245, 267, 453)

Rebels used immense quantities of the Rains's percussion torpedo in naval warfare plus the defense of military installations. Smaller but still significant numbers of these "infernal devices" were planted in roads. Though believed by many Federals, the widespread rumor that all approaches to Richmond had been heavily mined was false. Torpedoes made portions of numerous railroads dangerous during a period of more than two years. They were used on the Orange and Alexandria Railroad in Virginia, Alabama's Memphis and Charleston Railroad, the South Edisto Railroad Bridge in South Carolina, Georgia's Western and Atlantic Railroad and numerous other points. (OR, 49, 653; OR, 56, 579; OR, 65, 14; OR, 66, 447; OR, 75, 634; OR, 76, 64–65; OR, 88, 116; OR, 89, 281)

A member of the 100th Indiana accused Sherman of having set booby traps for the enemy, but his account cannot be substantiated. No official document details the use of antipersonnel land mines by a Federal commander. It follows that there is no reliable account of a Rebel commander having used hostages to locate and/or detonate "infernal machines." (Lord, *They Fought,* 273a)

Gen. Philip Sheridan may have been the first man wearing blue to imitate McClellan's actions at Yorktown. In the aftermath of his show of great strength at Yellow Tavern, he was convinced that Richmond lay within his grasp. Moving rapidly toward the Meadow Bridge crossing of the

Chickahominy River during May 11–12, 1864, Sheridan found that Rebels had anticipated that he might follow this route. After torpedoes had killed several horses and wounded a number of his men, the Federal commander ordered 25 captured Rebels to a dangerous area. These prisoners, now hostages for the safety of their enemies, were forced to "get down on their knees, feel for the wires in the darkness, follow them up and unearth the shells." (OR, 67; OR, 791; ACW, 5/94, 40)

Though almost certainly ignorant of events near the Chickahominy River far to the north, in early June 1864, Sherman also began following the example of McClellan at Yorktown. According to a Rebel witness, the man from Ohio gave strict orders to Gen. J. B. Steedman on June 3. This date is contradicted by an official dispatch of June 23, in which part of the message reads:

> I now decide that the use of the torpedo is justifiable in war in advance of an army, so as to make his advance up a river or over a road more dangerous and difficult. But after the adversary has gained the country by fair warlike means, then the case entirely changes. The use of torpedoes in blowing up our cars and the [rail]road after they are in our possession, is simply malicious. It cannot alter the great problem, but simply makes trouble.
>
> Now, if torpedoes are found in the possession of an enemy to our rear, you may cause them to be put on the ground and tested by wagonloads of prisoners, or, if need be, citizens implicated in their use. In like manner, if a torpedo is suspected on any part of the [rail] road, order the point to be tested by a car-load of prisoners, or citizens implicated, drawn by a long rope. Of course an enemy cannot complain of his own traps.
> (OR, 75, 579; JSHS, 13, 442–43)

A few weeks later in Charleston, a conference of Rebel leaders led to the conclusion that Sherman's path toward the sea could be accurately predicted. That being the case, some of them argued, the route he would follow as he came close to Savannah should be heavily mined. On November 21, Gen. Samuel Jones requested that torpedo expert J. R. Tucker be attached to supervising the mining of Sherman's expected itinerary. Gen. P. G. T. Beauregard followed by suggesting that all roads between the Savannah River ferry and Port Royal, South Carolina, should be mined. (OR, 92, 880, 941)

When blue-clad marchers and their bevy of attendant foragers came close to Savannah, Rebel planning paid off on December 8. According to Col. Charles H. Howard, who was there, the foot of a staff officer's horse hit a buried torpedo. The animal was killed and his rider's foot was "blown to pieces in such a way as to necessitate amputation." Furious, Sherman denounced the incident as murder rather than war. Hence he immediately sent for an unspecified number of prisoners and made them hostages for the safety of his men. Provided with picks and spades, these

At Fort McAllister, Confederate hostages were forced to dig for buried torpedoes.

Rebels were forced to "march in close order along the road, so as to explode their own torpedoes, or to discover and dig them up." (M, 13, 443; Miers, *The General*, 258–60)

Applying the formula he had passed along to Steedman, Sherman did not use hostages to search for torpedoes as he approached Fort McAllister. When approximately one hundred of his men became casualties in the attack—most of them having been mangled or killed by torpedoes—he made no recorded attempt at retaliation for battle losses. After the fort fell, however, he put captured Confederates to work digging up torpedoes that had been sown by order of high-ranking officers. (OR, 92, 79, 88–89, 111, 790)

Use of hostages to try to shield Federal personnel from the effects of Rebel land mines seems to have ended at Fort McAllister in December 1864. Torpedoes continued to be employed until the unconditional surrender of Confederates, however. Gabriel Rains was feted everywhere in the South for having devised a way to use his explosives against enemy personnel.

Neither his admirers in the South or his detractors in the North then imagined that use of land mines would proliferate more than a century later. A variety of sophisticated infernal devices descended from the Rains percussion torpedo have made large areas of some nations all but uninhabitable today.

19

Transportation and Communication

Use of hostages to guard transportation and communication was an idea so novel that it seems to have been first employed in August 1862. Gen. Lovell H. Rousseau, in command of occupied Huntsville, Alabama, became irked at the number of instances in which railroad trains were hit by shots from woods and thickets. Determined to put a stop to this practice, he issued Special Order No. 54 on August 8. The directive from the commander of the Third Division, Army of the Ohio, said that

> Almost every day murders are committed by lawless bands of robbers and murderers firing into the railroad trains.
>
> To prevent this, or to let the guilty suffer with the innocent, it is ordered that the preachers and leading men of the churches, (not exceeding twelve in number,) in and about Huntsville, who have been active secessionists, be arrested and kept in custody, and that one of them be detailed each day and placed on board the train on the road running by way of Athens, and taken to Elk River and back, and that a like detail be made and taken to Stevenson and back. Each detail shall be in charge of a trusty soldier, who shall be armed, and not allow him to communicate with any person. (RR, 5, D, 56)

Apparently no other commander in blue or in gray used clergymen and "leading men of the churches" to protect railroad trains. Rousseau's novel special order did not get into the *Official Records*, probably because of the turmoil caused by Federal evacuation of Huntsville on August 31.

Moore's *Rebellion Record* might be believed to have made an error concerning this special use of special hostages, were it not for independent testimony from Capt. Frank J. Jones of the 13th Ohio. An acting assistant adjutant general at the time, Jones must have considered Rousseau's order remarkable or humorous. He remembered the matter for years, and when given an opportunity to speak to Ohio veterans recalled it vividly. Though the hostage ploy could not have been used for more than three weeks, Jones labeled it as a success. "It was not very long before the guerrillas put a stop to their practice," Jones recalled, "fearing lest they would miss a loyal soldier and injure one of their spiritual advisers." (M, 6, 124; cf. DxD, 249)

Six months after the Huntsville caper, Gen. Alexander S. Asboth faced a problem much like that Rousseau seems to have solved. From his base at Columbus, Kentucky, the native of Hungary issued General Order No. 11, on February 28, 1863. He decried the actions of "lawless bands of guerrillas" who had given a great deal of trouble to the Mobile and Ohio Railroad. Citing Articles of War 56 and 57 from Union army regulations, he warned that anyone giving aid to "these lawless bands" was subject to court-martial and a possible death sentence.

Probably fully aware that his threat would mean little to some of the many secessionists in the region, he gave notice that he would resort to use of hostages in order to keep trains running. The final paragraph of his special orders informed the general public that

> For every raid or attempted raid by guerrillas upon the railroad, and for every attack upon the steamboats or Government transports on the river, the families living in closest proximity to the scene of the outrage will be arrested and held as hostages for the delivery of the real perpetrators. The civil law re-established in Kentucky for the benefit of the loyal shall never shield the traitor from his doom. (OR, 38, 74)

Several accounts by Federals of Sherman's Atlanta Campaign fail to indicate their author. Writing from "In Front of Kenesaw Mountain, Georgia" on June 24, 1864, one record described the action in detail before turning to the subject of guerrillas. Decrying their incessant attacks on "railway trains, etc.," the writer suggested that most attempts to control them had failed. He then credited Sherman with having "unravelled the knotty problem of suppressing guerrilla depredations."

Sherman, he says, was determined to put an end to the use of torpedoes on railroad tracks by guerrillas. Not content with having issued threats, the man whose father named him for the great Indian warrior, Tecumseh, on June 24, 1864:

> arrested a number of prominent secession sympathizers along the route [of the single-track Western & Atlantic Railroad that linked Atlanta with Chattanooga], whom he placed in an old box-car, and daily ran them over those portions of the road where torpedoes are supposed to have been placed. These old traitor rapscallions do not enjoy the boon of free railway transit, but the medicine administered has cured guerrillaism effectually. (RR, 11, Doc. #39, p. 223)

Subordinates of Union Gen. Philip H. Sheridan reputedly tried the same "medicine," but in Virginia failed to effect a cure. Oral tradition has it that in the aftermath of Cedar Creek, Federals felt that it was essential to get the Manassas Gap Railroad operable. By means of it, transportation of

Sheridan's troops to the Richmond theater would be relatively easy and rapid.

Partisan Rangers led by Lt. Col. John S. Mosby were determined to prevent the railroad from aiding the enemy by stopping one train after another. Trees were cut down along both sides of the rail line in order to deprive Mosby's men of cover, but they continued to hit trains. When Union officers gained nothing by moving civilians away from the railroad, they resorted to the Rousseau/Asboth/Sherman technique and put secessionists aboard every train.

Partisan Rangers, unlike the guerrillas of other regions, were not stopped by the use of civilians as hostages. When attacks on trains continued, word was sent to Mosby that women and children would be put aboard trains. This time, breath used in voicing warnings was wasted. Instead of bowing to the pressure created by threatened use of these special hostages, Mosby sent word to Federals that "I do not understand that it hurts women and children to be killed any more than it hurts men."

Hostages took center stage in another form of transportation a few weeks before Mosby refused to quit delaying and stopping trains. On the James River not far from Drewry's Bluff, Benjamin F. Butler had decided to cut a canal at an extremely sharp bend in the river where the channel was about 20 feet deep and 50 feet wide. Use of it, he was convinced,

"Blowing out the bulkhead" of the Dutch Gap Canal that was cut between two points on the James River.

J. E. Taylor in *The Soldier in Our Civil War*

On the James River above Bermuda Hundred, a Confederate battery was so positioned that its gunners could give serious trouble to men directing the building of Butler's canal.

A. McCallum, *The Soldier in Our Civil War*

would enable gunboats to use the James without coming under fire of a formidable battery on the bluff. When Robert E. Lee learned of the Federal plan, he warned that men in blue at that point, whom he assumed to be marines, would soon have the place fortified. Two days later, he said that if work could not be stopped batteries should be erected at points where guns could reach the Federal project. (JSHS, 14, 573; OR, 16, 261)

Soon Rebels began making things hot for men working to get the canal ready for use. Enraged, Butler notified his foes that he would put Rebel prisoners of war into work details. For this purpose, he used 42 men who were captured at Charles City Road early in October 1864, by forces under Gen. Edward O. C. Ord. Most of these men who became hostages to a canal belonged to what was once the Texas Brigade under the command of John B. Hood. After Gen. Maxcy Gregg became the leader of this body, Federals took many of its members prisoners during and after the clash at Charles City Road.

Notice of his plan to intermingle these Rebels with workmen digging his canal was sent to Confederate authorities at three new batteries located on the south side of the river. Leaders at all three points responded by a cease fire that lasted about 24 hours, after which the bombardment from Rebel mortars was resumed. B. L. Alcock, who was one of the hostages, later said that shells were directed toward intermingled workmen, hostages, and their guards at the rate of several times an hour. After more than a week during which Rebel projectiles continued to fall, Butler sent his hostages—none of whom had been injured—to City Point, Virginia. "Butler's ditch" was eventually finished, and in postwar years was described as being "of inestimable value to the commerce of the James." (CV, 7, 25; JSHS, 24, 40; OR, 28, 288; OR, 38, 21)

About the same time that Butler tried to shield his workmen with hostages, others were used in Missouri in an effort to protect—of all things—a stage line. A guerrilla leader known only as Poole, but mentioned as though he were ranked with William Quantrell, headed a band of about 60 ruthless cutthroats. Some of them were killed in brushes with Federal soldiers, so they apparently retaliated by trying to stop the stage from running between Lexington and Warrensburg.

According to Union Gen. Alfred Pleasonton, Col. Basel F. Lazear promptly struck back—very hard. Throughout the region he controlled, the Federal officer "ordered the arrest of a number of Poole's friends, intending to hold them as hostages for the security of the stage and telegraph line." (OR, 83, 254–58)

Since communication was almost as vital as transportation, bushwhackers who did not dare meet Federal troops in open combat targeted telegraph lines during the summer of 1864. Benjamin F. Butler seemed to get involved in about as many complex situations as any general officer in blue. As head of the Military Department of Virginia and North Carolina, he came to despise wire cutters almost as much as bridge burners.

With the sun about to set on July 21, he gave a terse order to Col. Gustavus S. Innis: "Unless the citizens give you some information before the act, who it is and where they are that are engaged in cutting the telegraph, burn their buildings, and catch and hold some of the principal ones as hostages to be hanged if the outrage is repeated. (OR, 82, 284)

Innis, who had a penchant for firing questions to headquarters about seemingly trivial matters, reported two days later that he had completed the work of repairing the military telegraph line between Fort Powhatan and Swan Point, Virginia. He had seized four civilians as hostages and had notified persons living along the line that they would be held responsible for its safety. Evidently disturbed by having learned that one of his hostages was a clergyman who had "relieved and dressed the wounds of one of our soldiers," he wanted to know what to do with the four he had in custody. (OR, 82, 421)

Without having received orders from Butler, which presumably would have come over a contested telegraph line, mercy prevailed over justice in the mind of Innis. On July 28 he said nothing to his chief about having released two hostages, but merely noted that he held a pair of them. Both had assured him that they were eager to take the oath of allegiance to the United States. Both had given a pledge to "do all in their power to prevent the telegraph line from being cut" again. Both had promised him that they

This station of the Union military telegraph is typical of many; though vital to Federal forces, it was isolated and poorly protected, providing an invitation to wire cutters.

Frank Leslie's Illustrated History of the Civil War

would "become answerable with their lives for the faithful performance of their obligations."

In this difficult situation, Innis was willing to give them a chance to live up to their words but was reluctant to release his remaining hostages without Butler's approval. Hence he inquired, "Shall I try them?" Butler seems to have been so out of patience with his chicken-hearted subordinate that he did not bother to answer his question.

Innis dutifully notified him that he was daily sending work details of 50 to 100 men to repair a telegraph line. Then on July 29 the colonel triumphantly reported that he thought he had discovered the hiding place of wire-cutting guerrillas. But he said that in order to catch them, he needed three or four squadrons of cavalry. Col. J. W. Shaffer notified him to expect cavalry "in a couple of days," and no more was heard of wire cutters, hostages for them—or Innis. (OR, 82, 499–500, 590, 635)

20

One Clipping, Six Hundred Hostages!

Henry W. Halleck, who read every issue of the *Richmond Examiner*, noticed in the issue of August 9, 1864, a terse summary of an account said to have been originally published in Charleston. It was a common practice for editors to borrow from other papers, condensing and sometimes modifying news stories found in them. Halleck probably personally took the brief item purporting to have come from the port city to Edwin M. Stanton. At Stanton's direction, he sent a copy of the newspaper clipping to Gen. John G. Foster who was at Hilton Head, South Carolina, in command of the Department of the South. The brief account that caused a stir in Washington read:

> CHARLESTON
> It is also reported that the rebel officers who were recently exchanged in Charleston Harbor [that is the 50 Federals and 50 Confederates who went there as hostages] were never placed under fire by General Foster, and that Gen. Sam Jones, the rebel commander in Charleston, has now a large number of newly arrived Federal officers under the fire of Foster's guns.

Foster was given a terse order to "report whether this statement is true; if so, why the order [to place 50 Rebel officers under fire] was not executed." (OR, 120, 607–8)

The commander of the Department of the South knew the importance of newspapers; located about 25 miles from Rebel-held Savannah, he depended upon its *Morning News* for information about activities in the river port. He knew that in addition to the secretary of war, the Union quartermaster general and numerous other officials in Washington regularly read Rebel papers. For many months officials had pled with editors not to publish military news that could aid the enemy, because Rebel leaders such as Gens. P. G. T. Beauregard and Braxton Bragg had standing orders for Northern newspapers. (OR, 120, 1122)

176

Though Union Gen. John G. Foster is widely blamed for having brought Rebel officers to face their own fire on Morris Island, he probably acted on orders from Gen. Henry W. Halleck.

Harper's Pictorial History of the Great Rebellion

Foster disposed of Stanton's first question by explaining that the 50 Rebel counterhostages were kept on a ship while waiting for suitable jails to be built at Hilton Head and transported to Charleston. Jails for the counterhostages were completed "the day before instructions were received" concerning a special one-time prisoner exchange, he explained. That was why the 50 Confederates never came under fire from their own guns, he pointed out. Believing that he had given a full explanation, he expected to hear no more about the brief newspaper story that carried no date line. (OR, 120, 709–10)

The Hilton Head commander soon found that he was badly mistaken. Stanton wanted to know exactly how many "newly arrived Federal officers" in Charleston were there as hostages in a new bid to shield the city from guns of warships and Union batteries.

Queried about this matter on August 15, Gen. Samuel Jones sent a decidedly testy reply.

No prisoners presently in the city were there "for the purpose of being placed in positions where they may be reached by your shot," he wrote. All Federal officers in Charleston were ordinary prisoners of war, not hostages, and they had come simply "because it is found more convenient at present to confine them here than elsewhere." Probably knowing that his offer would not receive a reply, he suggested an immediate wholesale exchange of prisoners, "man for man, rank for rank." He said nothing about the fact that Foster had ordered the pace at which Charleston was being shelled to be increased as soon as the 50 Federal hostages left. (OR, 65, 21; OR, 120, 624–25)

In Washington, Halleck was far from satisfied with the statement from Jones that was relayed to him by Foster. He put more stock in his newspaper clipping than in a dispatch from a Rebel commander, and became convinced that many prisoners had been "requisitioned from Andersonville" in order to become hostages for the safety of Charleston. He was not alone in clinging to this point of view; it was also held by numerous Confederates who knew a bit about what was taking place in the city where the shooting war was launched. (JSHS, 22, 132, 139; CV, 9, 391)

Foster did not tell him for some weeks that an estimated 1,800 Federal officers and six thousand privates were still imprisoned in Charleston and that an entire car load of the latter had arrived naked and ravenously hungry. Foster wrote that more officers were held at Columbia, while an estimated 16,000 privates were "in a stockade at Florence, S.C." These bits of news simply strengthened the general in chief's belief that Charleston's places of detention were crammed full and that many prisoners were there as hostages.

He was not surprised to learn from Foster on September 5 that two captains from the command of Gen. George H. Thomas were held in the port city under special conditions. These men, captured during Sherman's march through the Carolinas, were in close confinement and were being fed mush and water while they waited to be tried as spies. (OR, 66, 317–18; OR, 120, 769, 874–75)

For decades following this tense period, there was widespread belief in the South that Foster—who had been scolded for his role in the 50/50 affair—reacted by ordering Confederate officers to be placed under their own fire at Charleston. Prevalent as it was for many years, this view seems to have been mistaken. All signs point to Halleck as the moving spirit in the new and much larger P.O.W incident that was staged at the port city. Furious at allegations made in a newspaper and not satisfactorily explained by Foster, Lincoln's general in chief seems to have demanded that a new set of hostages be sent to Charleston—precisely six hundred this time, no more and no less.

An estimated 1,500 Rebel officers were then confined in Fort Delaware, located about 40 miles from Philadelphia on Pea Patch Island in the Delaware River. Late in August slightly less than half of them were selected to be sent to Charleston in order to try to silence guns from installations that ringed the vast harbor. One count reported that 6 colonels, 6 lieutenant colonels, 16 majors, 176 captains, 175 first lieutenants, and 220 second lieutenants were told they would soon be boarding a vessel headed to the South. Many of the men selected had just

Georgia-born W. H. Chew, a lieutenant when made a hostage, spent much of his time compiling lists of men who were sailing southward toward an unknown destination.
Georgia Department of Archives and History

come from Johnson's Island. Lt. Peru H. Benson, who was one of this number, said that when they heard of their impending voyage they were overjoyed because they thought this meant they were about to be exchanged. (CV, 9, 271, 391; JSHS, 22, 572)

Their crowded little transport, the *Crescent City,* was a converted Gulf of Mexico steamer that had not been built for Atlantic Ocean travel. Lt. Richard H. Adams said that prisoners were packed in the hold "a la sardine." Capt. F. N. Graves was more explicit. He said that their quarters were arranged "four on the floor," surmounted by two tiers of bunks. If his calculations were accurate, every six cubic yards in the hold held 12 prisoners. (NOR, 15, 637; CV, 2, 6; OR, 29, 178)

Partly to relieve boredom, Adams and Lt. Peter B. Akers devoted much of their time to compiling an alphabetical list of their comrades from all nine seceded states plus divided Kentucky, Maryland, and Tennessee. Each man's rank and military unit went into the record, along with the place and date at which he was taken prisoner. The list put together by Adams and Akers later proved to be extremely useful, since the *Official Records* do not include the data they gathered. Though they are not identical, lists may be found in both the *Confederate Veteran* and the *Journal of the Southern Historical Society.* According to Adams, "intense and continuous suffering and privations" caused the six hundred to become closely knit together before the voyage ended. (CV, 2, 90; OR, 7, 313–23; JSHS, 17, 34–46)

Long after having survived the ordeal on Morris Island, Col. J. E. Cantwell of North Carolina said he "could hear the shells screaming overhead every night."
North Carolina Department of Archives and History

Confined below deck, many of the prisoners soon suffered acute seasickness. Having been without water for 40 hours on one occasion, one account says that "strong men broke down under this privation and wept, begging like little children for a drink of water." Intense summer heat was augmented by steam from the ship's engine and made more excruciatingly painful by the constant odor of grease and tar. (CV, 27, 68)

Gales combined with heavy seas forced the *Crescent City* into Georgetown, South Carolina. When the weather improved, the little vessel limped to Hilton Head. By the time that port was reached more

On Morris Island, a stockade fence encircled an area of two acres, more or less, in which more than five hundred hostages lived, ate, and slept under the fire of comrades.

South Carolina Department of Archives and History

than two dozen men were so ill that they were taken from the ship and put into a military hospital. From the base where Foster's headquarters were located, the transport steamed for Charleston.

Though her voyage from Fort Delaware had taken about three weeks, she arrived at the besieged port before the stockade designed for her passengers had been completed. Hence Rear Adm. John A. Dahlgren, commander of the South Atlantic Blockading Squadron, detailed the USS *Ottawa* to guard the *Crescent City* and about 570 prisoners until men ashore were ready to receive them. (NOR, 15, 655; CV, 5, 119)

Designed to shield Battery Wagner (formerly Confederate Fort Wagner) on Morris Island from the fire of Confederate guns, the stockade about two acres in size was placed squarely in front of the Federal installation. Hostages were taken ashore on August 31, and told they would have to wait under heavy guard until the place of their confinement was completed. As an extra precaution, Foster arranged to have some schooners anchor near Morris Island under the guns of the blockading fleet. If at any time the captives showed "indications of an attempt at escape or rescue," he ordered, they were to go aboard the waiting vessels to be guarded by warships. (OR, 66, 242; OR, 120, 712, 818)

No untoward incidents having taken place, the Rebel officers were herded into their stockade made from palmetto logs during the first week of September. A hemp rope that constituted a deadline just inside the fence was pointed out to them, and they were warned that any man who touched it would probably be instantly shot by guards. To the captives, it seemed that insult had been added to injury when they learned that their guards were survivors of the 54th Massachusetts regiment of black soldiers who lost scores of comrades in an assault upon Confederate-held Fort Wagner. (CV, 5, 119; JSHS, 22, 130)

Benson later reported that captives received their food in tin cups. He wrote that

> We received twice a day one-half pint of mush well seasoned with worms, and about two ounces of bacon. One of our party, being of an inquiring turn of mind, counted the worms in his half pint of mush. He said he got seventy-two, and seeing that he was losing too much of his grub, quit and ate the balance. (CV, 9, 271, 391)

Water was so scarce that some of the captives arranged their tents in such fashion that little troughs were formed. They put cups underneath these improvised conduits and happily drank the "drippings" that accumulated. (CV, 7, 425; OR, 9, 271, 386, 391; OR, 29, 179; JSHS, 35, 274)

Only two men—Lts. J. C. C. Cooper and W. P. Calahan—constantly exposed to torturous summer heat and forced to eat whatever their captors provided are known to have died while in the stockade. Seven others became too weak to walk, so they were removed and taken to a hospital. Their illness reduced the number of hostages to about 560.

During their first morning in the prison pen, some hostages decided that their captors were making a determined effort to get them killed. Most of the guns on warships and on Morris Island began firing almost simultaneously. Confederates fired back from batteries on nearby James and Sullivan's Islands plus Forts Sumter, Moultrie, Johnson, and Beauregard on the rim of Charleston harbor. So many shells screamed immediately over the heads of captives that near-panic developed. Within less than an hour, however, men who had been brought from Fort Delaware decided that Confederate gunners were shooting high and that their missiles would not land in the stockade.

This verdict was correct; though an estimated four thousand projectiles were fired against Battery Wagner while it was protected by captives, only 17 fell among the Confederate officers and all of them were duds. Rebel gunners cut their fuses a trifle too long for Battery Wagner since a difference of one-tenth of a second in a trajectory could be crucial. Whatever else might be said of it, clearly the experiment of putting hostages under the fire of their own guns was effective this time. (JSHS, 22, 139; OR, 5, 275; CV, 7, 415; OR, 24, 80; OR, 29, 178–79; OR, 36, 425, 468)

Despite the fact that the only deaths among captives were caused by sickness and lack of sanitation, a few men wilted under pressure and let it be known that they would do whatever it might take to be freed. Before their first day in the stockade, three officers whose names Foster did not mention "asked permission to take the oath of allegiance and avail themselves of the President's amnesty proclamation." Halleck, who was notified of this turn of events, replied that the secretary of war would not act upon the applications until he was informed of the names, rank, and states from which the trio came. His verdict was probably influenced by the fact that at

Capt. J. L. Hempstead of Virginia attended numerous reunions of former hostages who were numbered among "The Immortal 600."
Virginia Department of Archives and History

Grant's directive he had informed Foster that he was not to exchange prisoners of war under any circumstances. (OR, 66, 254)

Not yet having provided the information demanded from Washington, on September 22 Foster notified his chief that Lt. J. J. Maddox of the 38th Georgia wished to have his name added to the list of those willing to the the oath of allegiance in order to gain their freedom. By October 4 the number of men ready to take this step had increased to six, but Foster had not acted since he wondered whether they were worthy of such treatment. (OR, 65, 24; OR, 120, 711, 774, 860)

It is doubtful that the half dozen gained their freedom before Halleck finally decided that the *Richmond Examiner* had been in error and consented for hostages to leave their stockade after 40 days and nights. Soon after some of them returned to Hilton Head, a careful count revealed that 17 officers "could stand the suffering no longer, so took the oath of allegiance, and thus surrendering their manhood, were freed from the prison miseries."

At the Federal base where they were being held, a body of six captives headed by Col. Vannoy H. Manning of Arkansas decided to punish one man who had taken the oath. They ripped off his insignia of rank, turned his coat wrongside out to identify him as a turncoat, and told him that his comrades would ostracize him. The Federal provost marshal learned what had happened, so punished Manning and his five young followers by confining all of them in a single cell for seven days and nights. (CV, 27, 70)

With their number now reduced to about 540, former hostages who had reverted to the status of prisoners of war were in for much more suffering. Many of them had gone from the stockade directly to Fort Pulaski near Savannah, where they were confined in casements of the fortress. Soon their hunger became so acute that they roasted all the rats they could catch. During severely cold weather, a daily issue of two pieces of pine went to each squad of 28 men.

Special inmates of Pulaski eventually joined their comrades who were still being held at Hilton Head. This placed so many Rebel officers from Fort

Matters became so bad at Andersonville that self-appointed "Regulators"
convicted and hanged some of their fellow prisoners.

Urban, *Battlefield and Prison Pen*

Delaware at Foster's headquarters that some were put into buildings much
like livery stables. Each cell, or stall, had been equipped with two bunks that
accommodated four men. Guards informed the captives that Federal prisoners were being starved at Andersonville, so men who had been under fire at
Morris Island would also be starved. Benson, whose account of their tribula-
tions is among the most detailed that has survived, wrote that

> Our rations were then issued, each man drawing ten days' rations at one
> time. When divided into ten parts it consisted of about ten ounces of
> corn-meal, fully one-half of which could crawl, four ounces of flour, three
> cucumber pickles, and a tablespoonful of salt.
>
> Those who could live on this diet were kept on it for forty days. About
> twenty-five percent were crippled from black scurvy, and after the forty
> days were out they added to our rations four ounces of pork and four
> ounces of Irish potatoes, and we lived on this twenty-seven days. (CV, 9,
> 391)

With the unconditional surrender of all Confederate armies only weeks
away, survivors of the eight-month ordeal were put aboard the USS *Illinois*
and sent back to Fort Delaware. Grant, however, issued a terse special order
forbidding the exchange of any who had been sent to Morris Island. So the
remnant of the band of six hundred that had been sent to Charleston as hostages for the safety of Battery Wagner did not take the required oath of allegiance until mid-June 1865. Only then were they freed from the long ordeal
that was triggered by an erroneous newspaper story. (CV, 27, 70)

Part V

Regulars and Irregulars

21

Morgan, Streight, and Other Hostages in Uniform

Confederate Gen. John Hunt Morgan and Union Col. Abel Streight had a lot in common. Both were experienced and skilled leaders of cavalry. Both were so imaginative that comrades who heard of some of their schemes dismissed them as too fantastic to undertake. Both ignored skeptics and critics and led men deep into enemy territory. Both were captured and imprisoned. Most remarkable of all, both escaped from high-security prisons—Morgan from the Ohio State Penitentiary and Streight from Libby Prison. A final aspect of their careers that they shared is not widely known; they were hostages for one another until they broke out of their respective prisons.

Morgan's Ohio raid was launched in disobedience to orders; Gen. Braxton Bragg had told him bluntly to stay south of the Ohio River. Persuaded that a raid into Ohio would boost Confederate morale and attract the open support of Copperheads in the Buckeye State, Morgan acted as though he was unaware of Bragg's order. On July 5, 1863, he and his band of picked men crossed the Ohio River expecting to "bring terror into the hearts of Yankees everywhere."

Their arrival in the outskirts of Cincinnati ended the longest continuous troop movement of the war; stopping only to destroy commercial buildings plus bridges and to empty the treasuries of towns, they covered 90 miles in 35 hours while capturing and paroling hundreds of prisoners. Morgan's luck ran out on July 19 when troops under Gen. Edward H. Hobson trounced the Rebel raiders at Buffington Island. Pursued for a week after their defeat, the majority of the Confederate riders—Morgan included—were captured. He and a few of his officers were sent to the Ohio State Penitentiary; his men were widely scattered, with more going to Camp Douglas at Chicago than any other installation. August 1863 saw an estimated six hundred of them in prisons located in several Northern states.

Streight's raid into Rebel country was, if possible, more daring than Morgan's into staunchly Union territory. Three months before Ohio was

Confederate Gen. John Hunt Morgan, for whom Col. A. D. Streight was held hostage, escaped form the Ohio State Penitentiary.

invaded, on April 11, 1863, Streight and his command struck out from a Mississippi River port toward Rome, Georgia. They hoped both to cut a major railroad and to destroy iron works located in the city to which they headed.

Since the long trek through hills and low mountains was more than horses could possibly endure, Streight mounted his men on mules. He seemingly did not give a thought to the fact that constant braying of these animals would keep pursuing forces under Nathan B. Forrest aware of his exact location at all hours of the day and night. Pushing through heavily Unionist northern Alabama, Streight and his aides enlisted scores of the region's natives and made soldiers out of them despite being unable to provide them with uniforms. Both Streight and Forrest were of the opinion that Federals greatly outnumbered pursuing Rebels.

Within a short distance of his objective, Streight was deceived by Forrest into thinking himself to be surrounded and outnumbered. He surrendered his entire command, bringing an end to the only significant Civil War raid conducted by men mounted on mules. Streight and some of his officers were soon inside Libby Prison; some of his men went to the open stockade in Richmond—Belle Isle—whose name every inmate cursed as a misnomer. Numerous other members of Streight's command were dispersed into the prisons of several states, since Rebels did not want too many of them to be held at any one spot.

Morgan's famous escape took place on November 26, 1863. Though Streight had been captured earlier, he did not break out of Libby Prison until February 9, 1864. That night, he and 108 other officers—for no privates were held at Libby—completed a long tunnel and broke through the surface during darkness. Two escapees drowned and 48 were recaptured, but Streight safely made it to Union lines.

There is no certainty that either of these commanders knew what took place while they were in confinement.

In the immediate aftermath of the disastrous raid led by Streight, Gov. Oliver P. Morton of Indiana directed the attention of the War Department in Washington to a newspaper notice. Clipped from an unidentified Rebel publication, it dealt with about four hundred Alabama natives "enlisted by

Colonel Streight and regularly mustered into the Fifty-first Regiment Indiana Volunteers." According to the newspaper, these men who were captured near Rome had been refused paroles and sent to prison. Hence Morton demanded that Washington select eight hundred prisoners "from those now in our possession and hold [them] as hostages for the safety of these loyal Alabamans." His request concerning a two-for-one hostage deal was referred to Gen. Ethan A. Hitchcock, commissioner for exchange of prisoners. (OR, 118, 590, 626–27)

Mortified, on May 21 Hitchcock told Morton the truth—"rebel authorities now hold Union prisoners considerably in excess over rebels held as prisoners by the Government." This unhappy situation made it impossible for him promptly to act on the request from Indiana's chief executive.

Capture of the raiders who had penetrated deep into Ohio seems to have tipped the scales, for just 60 days later Gen. Henry W. Halleck ordered that "General John H. Morgan and his officers will be placed in close confinement and held as hostages for the members of Colonel's Streight's command who have not been delivered in compliance with the conditions of the cartel [concerning prisoner exchange]" which Union Gen. John A. Dix and Confederate Gen. Daniel H. Hill had signed for their respective governments. (OR, 118, 153, 590)

Union Col. Abel D. Streight, later a brigadier, helped to plan and execute the escape of more than one hundred men from Libby Prison.
Photographic History

By the time that message was on the way to Indianapolis, Gen. Ambrose Burnside had entered the increasingly complex situation. One of Morgan's officers, Lt. Col. R. A. Alston, was the accuser in an upcoming court-martial of Confederate Col. Charles S. Hanson, who was to be tried for cruelty to prisoners. Burnside, who wanted to nail Hanson's hide to the wall, was unwilling for Alston to go to jail in Ohio and had enough influence to get his way. (OR, 121, 154, 186–87)

The situation with respect to Morgan was complicated even more by a factor that played a major role in the long detention of Dr. William P. Rucker. In the latter instance, Confederate and Virginia state officials both wanted the physician, so they quarreled over him. Civil authorities in Ohio refused to yield to Federal military leaders and insisted upon treating Morgan as a wanton breaker of the state's laws rather than as a prisoner of war. This position on the part of state authorities was abruptly and almost rudely repudiated by Judge Advocate General Joseph Holt. (OR, 119, 160–61)

Robert Ould, the Rebel agent of exchange, typically signed dispatches to his Federal counterpart "Respectfully, your obedient servant." Yet some of his messages were anything but respectful or obedient. Replying to accusations from Washington, in September he retorted that

> Colonel Streight can at least congratulate himself in one respect—he has not been shaved and dressed in convict's clothes. The Federals have so treated General Morgan and his officers, who are alleged to be held as hostages for Colonel Streight and his command. . . . As to the refusal to allow Colonel Streight to appropriate money for purchases, I beg leave to state that a recent order emanating from Federal authority prevents our prisoners from receiving food or clothing from their friends. (OR, 119, 267–68, 338)

Argumentative exchanges between agents of exchange aside, it appears that no one knew precisely where all of the Federals captured in Alabama and the Rebels taken in Ohio were imprisoned. Escape from two of the strongest prisons in North America by both Morgan and Streight seems to have made moot the entire issue of treating their captured officers and men as hostages.

Nothing more concerning hostages was heard from either cavalry commander until July 22, 1864. That day Morgan directed a brief inquiry to Gen. Samuel Cooper in Richmond:

> Will the Government sustain me in arresting the families of prominent Union men in East Tennessee and holding them as hostages for the families of Southern men who have been sent North? Answer. (OR, 120, 483)

Cooper undoubtedly replied immediately, but his answer seems to have been among the many Confederate records that were destroyed.

In addition to men in the commands of Streight and Morgan who were hostages for a period, numerous Rebel and Yankee fighting men were used in the same fashion. Union Capt. William Gramm and Lt. Isaac A. Wade were held by Richmond as hostages for Confederate Capt. Daniel Dusky and Lt. Jacob Varner, who were initially imprisoned in Washington and then sentenced to hard labor at Albany. Labeled by Union Lt. Col. George Sangster as "bushwhackers or mail robbers," health of the two Rebels who seem to have been bona fide Confederate officers was seriously impaired by long confinement. An exchange was effected in July 1863. (OR, 118, 268, 323, 359, 610–11; OR, 119, 1–2, 86, 222; OR, 120, 267–68)

Confederate Gen. Daniel Ruggles became involved when John Kesterton and Alexander Robinson were accused of having murdered prisoners of war. Union Gen. William S. Smith threatened to shoot four prisoners unless the accused were delivered to him. Ruggles responded by informing the Federal general officer that four recently captured men of his command would be held as hostages for "the four men you have placed in irons." At Fort Monroe, Benjamin F. Butler made hostages of Cpl. R. H. Curry and Pvt. W. J. Neeley when Rebels captured two Federal scouts— Cpl. James Pike and Pvt. Charles R. Gray. (OR, 118, 752; OR, 120, 1043, 1174, 1206)

Union Capt. Richard Blazer having taken a man led by Confederate Capt. Philip J. Thurmond in 1864, Rebels made hostages of F. C. Rode, James Palmer, W. H. Salisbury, James Cassidy, and C. Horsfield. All of the hostages were soon treated as ordinary prisoners of war, possibly because Blazer and 30 of his men were captured near Snicker's Gap by John S. Mosby and his partisan rangers. (OR, 120, 1268–69)

Col. William Hoffman, who had a captured Rebel in his charge, had difficulty deciding whether he was Maj. Thomas D. Armesy (his actual name) or Ormsley. Tried on a charge of having recruited men "for the so-called Confederate Army" within Union lines, Armesy was convicted and sentenced to hard labor at Fort Warren. In some subsequent correspondence, his captors labeled him as a spy and put him on trial. It is not certain that the trial was ever held; if he had been convicted on this charge he would have received an automatic death sentence.

Earlier, Rebels had retaliated by making Libby Prison inmate Maj. Nathan Goff, Jr., hostage for Armesy's safety. Officials wrangled over the two men for months, and the Confederate Congress became actively involved. On August 18, 1864, Abraham Lincoln made one of his "suggestions" that amounted to an order:

> If General Hitchcock can effect a special exchange of Thomas D. Armesy, now under conviction as a spy, or something of the sort, and in prison at ——, for Maj. Nathan Goff, made a prisoner of war, and now in prison at Richmond, let it be done. A LINCOLN

The president's intervention broke the impasse and the hostage was soon exchanged for the Rebel whose life was on the line. (OR, 39, 90; OR, 88, 542; OR, 95, 1312–14; OR, 118, 522; OR, 119, 135, 164, 708, 714; OR, 120, 84, 148–49, 222, 390, 522–23, 615, 672, 683, 1139–40)

In numerous cases, officers or officials were so busy or so unconcerned that they did not bother to list names of soldiers whom they held as hostages. A few of many such incidents took place at: Malvern Hill, Virginia, where the only identified Yankee hostage among 39 was Gen. Henry Prince; Murfreesborough, Tennessee, in December 1862; nine hostages held at Wheeling, Virginia, the following February; "a few officers confined in cells as hostages" at Richmond in June 1864; and Rebel officers held as hostages in North Carolina the following February. (OR, 117, 843; OR, 118, 271, 801; OR, 119, 994–95; OR, 120, 205)

With Rebel hopes still soaring late in 1862, Gen. Braxton Bragg was temporarily absent from his headquarters. Hence one of his aides, W. K. Beard, dispatched a memorandum to Col. B. S. Ewell from Murfreesborough, Tennessee. With the message he sent to Ewell an unspecified number of Federal prisoners, whose names he did not mention.

Union Gen. William Rosecrans had "declined to receive them through his lines," he explained. Hence Ewell was directed to dispose of these men in blue by sending them to Atlanta "to be held as hostages until further orders." (OR, 118, 800)

During Sherman's March to the Sea, a number of men in blue were taken by their enemies. Howell Cobb, then heading what Gov. Joe E. Brown called his "Georgia Reserves," heard rumors that an exchange was about to take place. Soon he sent a dispatch to the secretary of war in Richmond endorsing an immediate exchange but suggesting that

> With proper efforts the right kind of prisoners could be selected. Only be sure to let no more officers be exchanged. They should be held as hostages for the good treatment of our prisoners. I write in haste to send by private hands, but will add that the feeling in the army and country is improving.

Referred to Ould by Seddon, the Cobb communication evoked a response that helps to show why Grant put a halt to prisoner exchange:

> ... we had better send off disabled men and those whose terms of service have expired to the extent of the remaining unexchanged Vicksburg men [where more than 20,000 Rebels were paroled]. I Doubt the policy of going further. The Yankees will force the men whose term of service has expired into the field, regardless of any parole they may give. ... I fully agree as to the policy of retaining officers (except disabled). Very much depends upon our holding on to this policy. (OR, 120, 796)

Records that have been preserved suggest that despite the fact that numerous good soldiers became hostages for enemies they had never seen, their total was only a fraction as large as the number of civilians who were forced into this special role.

At Malvern Hill, numerous Yankees were taken hostage, but only Gen. Henry Prince was listed by name.

Harper's Weekly

22

Fresh and Saltwater Cases

Federal records indicate that 97 prisoners of war left Fort Monroe at 1:30 P.M. on June 10, 1863. A lieutenant and 24 guards were aboard the *Maple Leaf* with its crew of 50—an army transport about which the Union navy kept few records. Knowing themselves headed for Fort Delaware, captives—all of whom were officers with combat experience—began whispering among themselves about an escape before Fort Monroe faded from sight in the distance.

Since guards rotated during three shifts, only eight were on duty at any time. Though they were heavily armed, Rebel officers were sure they could be overpowered. If guards could be seized, they would have to deal with only a few members of the crew—the pilot, helmsman, and some engineers who were on duty. A prearranged signal was given at about 10:00 A.M. on June 11; guards plus members of the crew were quickly overpowered at a point not far from the mouth of Chesapeake Bay. (OR, 43, 1; OR, 44, 786; CV, 19, 220; OR, 29, 375)

Fearful that a change of course might betray them, the conspirators moved steadily toward Fort Delaware until darkness fell. They then forced the steamer to turn to the south. Soon the vessel ran aground in shoal water, leaving her stranded about two hundred yards from the shore. A skiff aboard the *Maple Leaf* was the only means of reaching land. Many of the prisoners aboard were so severely wounded that they shook their heads at the prospect of a long and dangerous trip over land. Hence only about 74 or 75 men were ready to leave their ship. (CV, 6, 529)

Having paused to elect officers and make the son of Raphael Semmes their captain, they held a brief strategy session. Most members of the ship's crew were blacks who did not have access to arms. Though not considered to be a source of serious threat, these men would have to be restrained during several trips of the skiff between ship and shore. Possibly at the suggestion of Col. J. U. Green, it was decided to take the Federal lieutenant as well as the ship's officers, pilots, and engineers to land. Before the skiff pulled away from the *Maple Leaf* with these men aboard, members of the crew were warned that Federals who were going to shore would be held as hostages. Green may have been the only escaping officer who kept a diary. According to him, use of hostages was designed to prevent members of the crew from making trouble during the landing of escapees. (JSHS, 24, 166–67)

Rebels who got ashore that night were a diverse lot. Capt. John B. Wolf had been captured at Port Hudson, Louisiana. Shipped first to New Orleans, he had reached Fort Monroe aboard the *Catawba*. Taken in Missouri, Col. A. Edgar Asbury's initial strict captivity was in Gratiot Prison, St. Louis. Green had surrendered in Tennessee. After going to Memphis by rail, he was also briefly at Gratiot. Then he and Asbury went through Indianapolis, Cincinnati, Baltimore, and Norfolk before reaching Fort Monroe. They had expected to be paroled or exchanged at the huge old fortress, so were disappointed and angry at the prospect of spending more months at Fort Delaware. (CV, 6, 58–59; OR, 20, 242; OR, 29, 374)

Hostages, who were guarded on shore with weapons seized from the transport, were fearful of being shot. Consequently they remained docile while the skiff made slow and awkward trips between the *Maple Leaf* and the unidentified point of land near Cape Henry where it was grounded. Once all Confederate officers physically able to walk a considerable distance were ashore, the hostages were forced to take an oath. Their captors had talked in the hearing of hostages about burning the transport, but never seriously considered this option because numerous wounded comrades were still aboard. Hostages swore that they would look after Rebels who had not left it and would continue on their voyage to Fort Delaware. Then they were told to climb into the skiff and return to their vessel. No other group of hostages is known to have been released so soon after having been taken. (CV, 6, 529)

Escapees held a brief council session and decided that there were too many to travel together; hence they split into two bands. Members of one group soon seized a small boat from salt makers, so they made their way across Currituck Sound. Though Capt. Edward S. Parker had been captured in North Carolina, he was not familiar with this section of the state's coast. Believing that Rebel guerrillas known to be in the Great Dismal Swamp would help them, they soon reached it. With four regiments of Federal cavalry said to be in pursuit of them, these men traveled by night with guerrillas as guides and most or all of them reached Richmond safely. (JSHS, 24, 168–71; CV, 13, 41)

After wandering about in North Carolina for a few days, the other band of escapees turned into Princess Anne County, Virginia. There, they encountered guerrilla leader W. B. Sandlin, who escorted them to the Rebel capital.

Members of the crew of the *Maple Leaf* plus the unidentified Federal lieutenant who headed guards aboard it had one of the briefest and least uncomfortable of recorded periods as hostages. In spite of this factor, once aboard their vessel they repudiated their oaths and turned back to Fort Monroe. There Capt. John W. Fuller of the *Star of the West* was heavily ironed before being shipped to Johnson's Island, where he died in captivity. Before many months the *Maple Leaf* was in Florida waters in which about a dozen torpedoes designed by Gabriel Rains were floating beneath the surface. On April 1, the big double-stack side-wheeler steamer—described as one of the largest of its kind in Federal service—hit a torpedo and went down in the Saint John's River about 15 miles from Jacksonville. (JSHS, 29, 374–76; OR, 47, 57; OR, 65, 1, 370, 380, 387–88, 476; NOR, 15, 307, 315)

The hostage incident in which men aboard the *Maple Leaf* were central lasted only a few hours. Not so a drama that revolved about one seaman who was for a period an officer aboard Comdr. W. D. Porter's USS *Essex*. Early in the conflict, Porter divorced his pro-Southern wife and saw two of his sons don gray uniforms. Fiercely combative by temperament, he described Spencer Kellogg as a fourth master and said he had been taken at Port Hudson by guerrillas. Soon he requested Gen. Henry W. Halleck to select a captured Rebel officer and confine him "as a hostage for the safety of Mr. Kellogg." (OR, 119, 174–75)

Union Gen. E. A. Hutchinson learned from a member of the U.S. Sanitary Commission that Kellogg was believed to be in Richmond, facing a death sentence. He reported about this to Gen. S. A. Meredith, but the combined influence of the two commanders had little or no effect. Robert Ould, the Rebel commissioner in charge of prisoner exchange, several times informed Washington that he had no record of Kellogg or his whereabouts. (OR, 119, 381)

Ould eventually discovered that Kellogg was in Castle Thunder, so he quickly notified his Federal counterpart of this fact. It was unusual for a military prisoner to be in this place, hence he did not make an early inquiry there, Ould explained. Using informal language, the Rebel commissioner hastily summarized the case against the prisoner, saying that

Union Comdr. W. D. Porter clearly knew that Spencer Kellogg was a deserter and a spy when he protested about Rebel treatment of his case.

Harper's Weekly

The USS *Essex* from which Spencer Kellogg was captured at Port
Hudson, Louisiana.

U.S. Army Military History Institute

He is charged with being spy and deserter. The specification states that
about the latter part of January, 1862, he appeared in front of Columbus, Ky., on the Mississippi, in a small boat, representing himself as a
deserter from the Federal service and desirous of joining the Confederate Army; that he was placed first on the floating battery and afterward
transferred to the gun-boat General Polk, and then again at his own
request transferred to the engineer corps on duty at Island No. 10, that
whilst at the latter place he made sketches and drawings of the fortifications and defenses, that he was arrested and made his way to the
Federal authorities. (OR, 119, 161)

Despite Porter's considerable influence and his close connection with men
even more powerful than himself, there is no certainty that his request for a
hostage was granted. Washington probably already had reason to think that
Kellogg had a shady past and knew that his execution by Rebels was scheduled. Edwin M. Stanton tried on September 26 to secure a stay of execution, but failed to get it.

On September 26 Ould informed William Ludlow that Porter's fourth
master had been tried by a general court-martial "composed of intelligent
and honorable officers." Found guilty both of being a deserter from the Confederate service and a spy at Island No. 10, he had been executed at Camp
Lee three days earlier. According to Ould, the condemned man "openly confessed that he had been employed by the Federal authorities as a spy and
acknowledged the justice of his sentence." (OR, 52, 925; OR, 119, 321, 325)

Not knowing that the central figure of this drama was dead, Halleck
appealed to Francis Lieber in New York. To the scholar who had drafted
general instructions for the Union army, he pointed out that Kellogg was

an ex-spy rather than a spy when captured in Louisiana. Unaware of "a case exactly parallel," he wanted to know from Lieber whether or not it was legal to condemn a man who was not actively spying at the time he was captured. If Lieber was able to give him guidance about a possible procedure designed to save Kellogg's life, his reply came too late to have any effect. (OR, 119, 328)

Early in October, Union Gen. George A. Hitchcock notified Meredith that Rebel summaries of the case seemed largely satisfactory. Perhaps he had read and reread the dispatch in which Porter requested that a hostage be set aside for Kellogg. In it, the naval officer said that his fourth master had earlier performed "valuable services for the Government of a character which it would not be proper for me to state in a written communication."

Carefully framed as that sentence was, it reveals that Porter knew Kellogg had been a spy when he took him aboard the *Essex*. The deserter from Confederate forces had been made fourth master of the warship before he prepared an April 8, 1862, detailed report concerning Confederate installations on Island No. 10 that is preserved in Union naval records. (NOR, 22, 767–68)

Porter could not have failed to know about the past of the man whose life he tried to save. Spencer Kellogg may have been the only Civil War spy for whom an officer of high rank requested a hostage—fully aware that on both sides the penalty for espionage was death. Probably knowing when he framed his appeal for a hostage that it was futile, Porter reported to Gen. Benjamin F. Butler the capture of his fourth master and four seamen from the *Essex*. Guerrillas who made the capture were initially believed to have hanged all five Federals. Consequently Porter's first request was for Butler's approval of his retribution proposal—that "for each seaman of mine hanged one guerrilla be shot, and for my officer ten." (OR, 21, 567; OR, 119, 175, 337; NOR, 19, 187; OR, 22, 689–767)

Few commanders on land or on the water were as rough and stern as Porter; few seamen had so checkered a past as Kellogg. Hence the majority of hostage incidents involving ships and their personnel were resolved fairly simply. The first of these involved the burning of the guano carrier *Alleghanian* in Chesapeake Bay. A band of Rebels led by Lt. John Taylor Wood of the fledgling Confederate navy pulled off the job in October 1862. Using four boats, a party of 25 men fired the London-bound cargo vessel between 10:00 P.M. and midnight. When flames died out, nothing was left above the water but part of the hull. To Union Gen. John Dix, the affair seemed so serious that he reported about it to the president. (OR, 26, 555)

Acting Master Nelson Provost of the mortar schooner *T. A. Ward* became suspicious that there had been collusion between seamen and Confederates. To him, it seemed that members of the crew of the burned 1,400-ton commercial carrier were "entirely too well dressed." Consequently, he arrested all of them and sent them to the capital. He initially

Confederate Lt. John Taylor Wood led a party of 25 sea-men who set a London-bound cargo ship afire in Chesapeake Bay.

U.S. Naval History Center

believed the fire itself to have been the work of civilians alone, but in Washington it was known very early that an enemy naval officer had been involved. (NOR, 5, 137–39)

Peter Smith, soon charged with having helped to destroy the ship and its cargo, was arrested by Federals early in November. John H. Winder promptly asked Capt. Thomas P. Turner, an official in the Confederate prison system, if a man was available to use as a hostage for Smith. Turner replied that he considered any of three captives to be suitable—the paymaster of the steamer *Daylight* plus two ensigns. In a postscript he added that he also had on hand 18 sailors who had been captured in North Carolina a week earlier. (OR, 117, 942)

Warner T. Jones, who represented Gloucester County in Virginia's House of Delegates, was incensed that Smith had been taken. A reference to use of double-irons in a Federal dispatch led him to believe that the civilian would be treated as a pirate—meaning he would be executed if found guilty. Jones may have had considerable influence, for if a hostage was formally selected an exchange evidently took place very soon. For his role in burning the guano-carrier and other exploits, Wood—by then a commander—was voted the formal Thanks of the Confederate Congress in August 1863. (NOR, 5, 141)

January saw the capture of three black seamen who were members of the crew of the USS *Isaac Smith*. When the vessel was taken by Rebels in the Stone River, captors threw the three seamen into the Charleston jail. These men must have held citizens somewhere in the islands, for when they penned an appeal it went to the U.S. consul at Nassau, Bahamas. If he did anything in their behalf, it must have been through aides of Edwin M. Stanton.

Enumerating the captives as Odin H. Brown, William H. Johnson and William Wilson, the secretary of war ordered that three prisoners who were natives of South Carolina should be selected as hostages for them. His directive produced action, for on February 1, 1864, C. J. McDowell of the 2nd South Carolina Cavalry dispatched an inquiry to

Richmond. Writing from Carroll Prison in Washington, he said he and two friends were hostages "for three negroes captured in South Carolina." McDowell wanted to know when and where the men held at Charleston had been captured and whether their release could lead to freedom of the trio held in the Union capital. If Richmond answered his questions, the reply was lost. (OR, 119, 172, 188, 904)

Late in the spring of 1863 Rear Adm. Samuel F. DuPont had a group of prisoners from the enemy's *Isaac Smith* on his hands. Following instructions from Washington he prepared to ship them to Fort Monroe, but postponed their voyage. At Port Royal, South Carolina, Gen. David Hunter wanted the men from the Confederate vessel to be held as hostages aboard the USS *Vermont*. Though Hunter did not specify the reasons for that request, DuPont agreed to keep them. Since some of them are known to have been held earlier in Columbia, an exchange of these hostages may have already been under way. (OR, 118, 708–9)

Six months after this incident, Surg. R. J. Freeman of the CSS *Atlanta* was being held at Fort Monroe as hostage for Asst. Surg. W. W. Myers of the Union navy. The two must have been exchanged promptly, however. On November 24 Myers sent to the Navy Department an account of what he considered to be irregular or illegal handling of pork destined for Libby Prison while he was an inmate there. His letter written in the aftermath of having been a hostage may have influenced Confederate officials to act. Meredith soon notified Hitchcock that "several officers in charge of our prisoners at Richmond have been cashiered." (OR, 119, 570–71, 624)

Rebel John Y. Beall, whose exploits are described elsewhere in this volume, was at Fort McHenry in December 1863. Along with 16 of his men he was awaiting trial on a charge of piracy. Robert Ould, the Confederate agent of exchange, felt it his duty to try to see that the captured seamen got fair treatment. Hence he put Lt. Comdr. Edward P. Williams, Ens. Benjamin H. Porter, and 15 seamen of the U.S. Navy in irons and close confinement. All of them, he notified Washington, were being held as hostages for the proper treatment of Beall and his men. (OR, 119, 705)

Two naval incidents involving hostages took place in 1864, but only brief mention of them has been preserved. Rebels having learned that the *Jane Duffield* was in the Warwick River in mid-September, a party boarded the vessel and captured her without resistance. Captors readily went through the process of bonding the vessel to guarantee that she would report to a prize court, but her captain could offer no cash security. Instead, he told Rebels to take a member of his crew as a hostage. They did so and the seaman who was a pawn in the North/South power struggle on water was in December still being held as a prisoner in Richmond. (OR, 87, 954)

Slightly earlier, Benjamin F. Butler played a decisive role in one of the many hostage situations in which he was involved. Angry that J. R. McDonald and seven of his men had been seized from a Federal light-ship,

The *Star of the West*, whose Rebel captain was made a hostage and did not survive captivity.

he authorized Gen. Charles K. Graham to arrest "eight or ten of the most respectable citizens" of the area close to the point where the seizure took place and bring them to him as hostages. (OR, 89, 174)

The *Official Records* include a brief account of only one naval hostage incident in 1865 that has not been treated elsewhere in this volume. At Grand Gulf, Mississippi, Col. O. C. Risdon arrested two residents in March. One of them, a Mr. Sanders, had reputedly been involved in sending the steamer *Monroe* on a false mission during which the vessel was "pillaged and robbed."

Risdon's second arrest was of a citizen identified only as Dr. Carroll. This captive admitted that he was not a Unionist and that he had earlier been connected with Confederate armed forces. "In accordance with instructions," the Federal officer therefore sent Carroll to Vicksburg as a hostage and the naval aspect of this special treatment of prisoners came to an end.

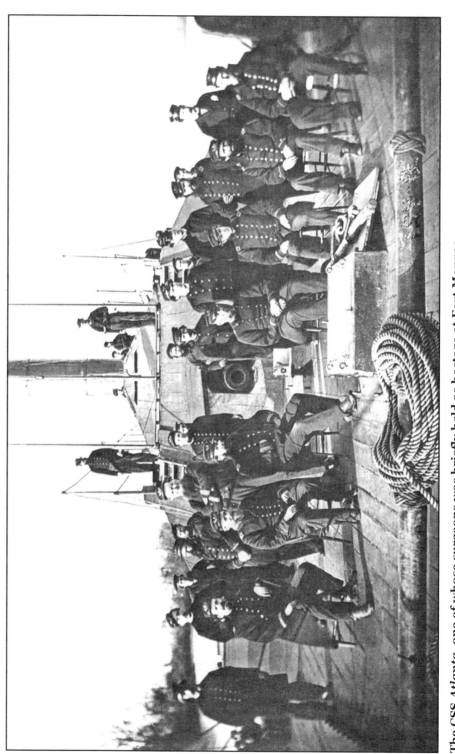

The CSS *Atlanta*, one of whose surgeons was briefly held as hostage at Fort Monroe.

23

Ragged Ratios

"An eye for an eye and a tooth for a tooth" expressed the Old Testament concept of just reconciliation. That principle, embodied in military traditions and codes of the Western world, was taken for granted at the beginning of the Civil War. Exchange of prisoners and selection of hostages was theoretically on the basis of "service for service and grade for grade." That is, a Federal assistant surgeon was supposed to be exchanged for a Rebel assistant surgeon—or held by Confederates as hostage for a similar captive considered to be in special danger. A captured Rebel civilian was supposed to be exchanged for a Federal civilian, or held by Union authorities as hostage for an equivalent captive whom the enemy was reluctant to exchange.

A formal set of "equivalents" was drawn up and accepted by both sides. It stipulated that

one commanding general is equivalent to 60 privates
one lieutenant general is equivalent to 40 privates
one major general is equivalent to 30 privates
one brigadier general is equivalent to 20 privates
one colonel is equivalent to 15 privates
one lieutenant colonel is equivalent to 10 privates
one major is equivalent to 8 privates
one captain is equivalent to 6 privates
one first lieutenant is equivalent to 4 privates
one second lieutenant is equivalent to 3 privates
one noncommissioned officer is equivalent to 2 privates

Difficult situations and especially valued prisoners sometimes led authorities to disregard equivalents. During one period seven Federal hostages were held by the governor of Virginia for Richard Thomas, a swashbuckling Rebel who called himself Zarvona and was successively a colonel and a naval lieutenant. Commandant Justin E. Dimick of Fort Warren Prison

paid no attention to tables of equivalents. Instead, he calculated that a brigadier was worth 480 privates—an appraisal that was more realistic than the
20:1 ratio that was widely observed.

All civilians were theoretically on the same level, so that one Rebel
used as a hostage was judged equivalent to one captive, or vice versa. In the
case of military hostages, the formal set of equivalents was considered to be
standard. This held true even when guerrillas, bushwhackers, state guardsmen, and partisan rangers were involved—for the most part.

Late in the summer of 1864, Confederate Gen. John H. Morgan's men
captured Capt. Benjamin Rogers of the Tennessee Union Guard, who was
said to have been recruiting within Rebel lines. He knew that Capt. J. T.
Reynolds of the 64th North Carolina was held at Knoxville for the same
offense. According to a report that reached Richmond, the Rebel officer
was "closely confined in a cage eight feet square" at Knoxville. Another account said only that he was "confined at Knoxville in irons." Hence Morgan
set up a 1:1 hostage situation, asking Union Gen. S. P. Carter to "inform him
as to what disposition has been made of Captain Reynolds." The famous
Rebel raider said that as soon as he learned the fate of Reynolds, he intended to "act understandingly with Captain Rogers." (OR, 120, 209, 561,
929, 1112)

When the 1:1 ratio was not scrupulously observed, the number of hostages involved was not always specified. That was the case in May 1864,
when guerrillas captured 10 members of a Federal picket guard near
Mayfield, Kentucky. Furious over this incident, Union Gen. Henry Prince
ordered the colonel in command at Paducah to even the score. He was told

**Located on the Neuse River, New Bern, North Carolina, was a center
upon which military forces and civilians converged.**

The Soldier in Our Civil War

immediately to detach a mounted force "with orders to arrest some influential rebel sympathizers in the neighborhood in which these guerrillas are maintained and hold them as hostages for the safe return" of captured pickets. To assist Col. S. G. Hicks in selecting an undesignated number of hostages, Prince sent him a list of leading citizens and wrote that some of them "will be sufficient, in all probability." (OR, 78, 24)

Nearly two years later, Confederate Gen. George E. Pickett took stern measures with deserters plus Unionists of eastern North Carolina. By doing so, he stirred up a hornet's nest. Operating around New Berne, Pickett had 53 men seized and soon oversaw the execution of 22 of them at Kingston. Union Gen. John J. Peck insisted that all of the men severely punished by Pickett were duly enlisted members of the 2nd North Carolina regiment. Two of them who were executed, he charged, were deserters from forces in blue. In a desperate bid to put an end to hanging, the Union general told his enemy that

> Having reported this matter to higher authority, I am instructed to notify you that if the members of the North Carolina regiment who have been captured are not treated as prisoners of war the strictest retaliation will be enforced. Two colonels, 2 lieutenant-colonels, 2 majors, and 2 captains are held at Fort Monroe as hostages for their safety.

Ranks of the 53 captives whom Peck described as recently recruited Union soldiers were not indicated in exchanges between the two leaders. If the table of equivalents was scrupulously observed, however, the Rebel officers who became hostages were equivalent to 72 privates.

Probably without having inquired into specific details of the incident, Benjamin F. Butler honored Peck's request for hostages. In a wholly uncharacteristic moment, however, the man who earlier became known as "Beast" while in New Orleans said he had not yet put the hostages in irons. This gesture was made, he said, because "I do not believe the story that any harm is intended to the officers and men of the Second North Carolina Regiment." (OR, 60, 569; OR, 869)

Confederate Maj. Thomas P. Turner, who was in command of Richmond's military prisons in December 1864, communicated directly with two of his inmates. Ignoring the rank-for-rank custom, he wrote:

> Capt. D. R. Boyce and
> Lieut. W. D. Hoff, Fifteenth West Virginia Infantry
> GENTLEMEN: This is to inform you that you are held in close confinement in retaliation for Lieutenant Gandy and Private George Dusky, who are now in close confinement and in irons at Wheeling, W. Va. The latter-named parties are held by the bogus government of West Virginia.
> P.S.—You can inform your Government and friends.

Boyce, who was a member of the 3rd New Jersey Cavalry, soon notified Washington that he had no idea why Gandy and Dusky were being held.

Castle Thunder, named because prisoners heard the thunder of big guns so often, was one of several Richmond prisons under the control of Maj. Thomas P. Turner.

He and Hoff, he wrote, had been "general prisoners of war for several months." Their selection as hostages meant solitary confinement, which he said their physical debilitation made unbearable. He wrote that he and Hoff prayed that "our Government will not leave us now in our new and greater peril, as our physical energies must soon be destroyed." Since there is no subsequent mention of either Boyce or Hoff in the *Official Records*, these hostages for acts of civil authorities may have been in solitary when the war ended. (OR, 120, 1228)

Members of two bodies whose roots were far apart clashed on October 4, 1862. On that day, Virginia Partisan Rangers led by John D. Imboden soundly defeated the 54th Pennsylvania Volunteers. Lt. Harry G. Baer of the Keystone State soon dispatched to Gov. Andrew G. Curtin a summary of events and an urgent plea. Writing from Libby Prison, he copied a memo received the previous day from the commander of military prisons in the Rebel capital.

Capt. T. P. Turner had wasted no words; he simply sent to prisoners a note saying that "All prisoners taken by our partisan rangers are held as hostages for our rangers, who are held by the Northern Government not as prisoners of war but outlaws." Baer, who had no hard data, was of the opinion that Rebel rangers held by Washington were not nearly so numerous as men in blue who had become hostages for them. Hence he hoped that the governor of his state could induce Federal authorities to release captive rangers so that their hostages "may be exchanged and be made useful to our country." In addition to the 152 officers and men captured by Imboden's rangers, he said that 40 more "Pennsylvanians captured by rangers" reached Libby Prison on November 19. Records fail to indicate how many Rebel rangers were then held by Washington or how many men made prisoner by rangers were hostages.

Like Boyce and Hoff, Baer seems to have been left in limbo. He probably would not have addressed an appeal to Harrisburg had he known that Col. J. M. Campbell had penned a report to Union Gen. William B. Franklin before the prisoners reached Richmond. Campbell recommended that Baer, Hite, and Lt. John Cole be dismissed from the service for cowardice in the face of the enemy. He reduced the estimated number of captives from the 54th Pennsylvania to 93, but castigated the three imprisoned officers for having surrendered without firing a gun. (OR, 28, 21; OR, 117, 741)

Especially when troops not under the direct control of their central governments were involved, prisoner/hostage ratios that were specified were often extremely ragged.

Both Col. R. V. Richardson, commander of the 1st Tennessee Partisan Rangers (Confederate), and Union Col. J. K. Mizner rejected the 1:1 formula out of hand.

In January 1863, the Rebel ranger learned that Union Col. J. K. Mizner had issued a proclamation at Brownsville. Addressed to 14 civilians, Mizner's mandate said that the men he named would be held responsible for guerrilla molestation of loyalists within the military district of Jackson, Tennessee. He then warned that if any loyal citizens should be arrested, twice as many secessionists would be arrested and held as hostages. What's more, he said that the 14 prominent men he named would be held responsible for twice the property seized or damaged by secessionists.

Terming his foe's mandate "a paper bullet fired across the Hatchie River at unoffending non-combatants," Richardson made public his plans for counteraction. For each secessionist arrested by order of Mizner, said the partisan ranger, "I will have shot twice the number of Yankee soldiers taken in battle or on duty." He promised also to take or destroy two dollars' worth of property for each dollar's worth seized by the Yankee colonel. Richardson's third threat constituted an impromptu addition to the table of equivalents. He warned that for every house burned by men in blue "I will shoot five Union soldiers on duty or taken in battle."

Earlier, the Tennessee partisan sent to his foe under a flag of truce a warning in which he said that

I have now in my possession Second Lieut. Robert Hill, Company D, and Adj. James E. Philpott, of the Eightieth Ohio Regiment Volunteers, also Surg. Joseph S. Martin of Seventh Kansas Regiment U. S. Volunteers, whom I intend to hold as hostages for the violations of civilized usages of war.

The burning of houses infuriated Confederate partisan ranger Col. R. V. Richardson, who promised to shoot five captives in blue for every house burned in the Hatchie River region.

In the event foes were willing to exchange his surgeon and forage master, wrote the head of the irregular body of fighting men, he would parole the three officers named. (OR, 118, 155–56, 821–22)

Having been reared in the Duchy of Brunswick, Baron Adolph Wilhelm August Friedrich Steinwehr—a Union brigadier—may have considered the American table of equivalents to be "provincial." Whether that was the case or not, he raised the ante from 1:1 to 5:1 on July 13, 1862, when he issued a formal order to one of his cavalry officers immediately to arrest "five of the most prominent citizens of Page County, Va." These men were to be held as hostages, he directed, and would suffer death if any soldier in Steinwehr's command should be shot by bushwhackers. Stern warnings by the native of a German principality must have pleased his commander. Ten days later, Gen. John Pope's General Order No. 11 dictated the arrest of all "disloyal male citizens" within Federal lines. Any of them who refused to take an oath of allegiance to the Union government must be escorted to the south, he stipulated. A citizen who took an oath and violated it would be shot "and his property seized and applied to the public use," said the commander of the Army of the Potomac.

Few other Federal edicts except from Abraham Lincoln and Benjamin F. Butler plus Ulysses S. Grant's order expelling Jews created an instant and immense storm of indignation. Jefferson Davis consulted Robert E. Lee and then promptly issued General Order No. 54. In this document the Confederate president said he took it that "bushwhackers" was a term by which was meant "the citizens of this Confederacy who have taken up arms to defend their homes and families."

Transmitted to Rebel forces everywhere by Gen. Samuel Cooper, paragraph 7 of this set of general orders stipulated that Pope, Steinwehr, and all commissioned officers under them were "not entitled to be considered as soldiers." Confederates were notified that if Pope or Steinwehr or their officers should be captured, they would not receive the benefits of the cartel then prevailing concerning exchange of prisoners. (GG, 530; JSHS, 29, 104; OR, 329–30, 830–31, 836–37)

One sensational case in which a ratio of 10:1 was central was widely commented upon in European newspapers. Trouble started when partisan Joseph C. Porter and his men captured the village of Palmyra, Missouri, early in 1862. One resident, Andrew Allsman, was particularly hated by them because he was a former member of the 3rd Missouri Cavalry and often acted as a guide to bodies of soldiers in blue. Seized by members of this irregular body, Allsman was spirited away to a place of captivity not known to Federals in the region.

On October 8 the provost marshal general for the military district of Northeast Missouri issued a warning that had been framed by Gen. John McNeil. Among other things, W. R. Strachan said that

this is to notify you that unless said Andrew Allsman is returned unharmed
to his family within ten days from date, ten men who have belonged to

your band, and unlawfully sworn by you to carry arms against the Government of the United States, and who are now in custody, will be shot as a meet reward for their crimes, among which is the illegal restraining of said Allsman of his liberty.

Many secessionists discounted the McNeil threat, saying that "the whole thing was simply intended as a scare." But on the tenth day, Friday, October 17, ten hostages were selected "to pay with their lives the penalty demanded." These men were notified that unless Allsman was returned to his family by 1:00 P.M. on Saturday, they would all be shot at that time.

According to the *Courier*, which listed the names of the 10 fighting men who were held for the return of one civilian who was described as "aged," most were composed or indifferent. That night the Rev. James S. Green of Palmyra "remained with them, endeavoring to prepare them for their sudden entrance into the presence of their maker." The newspaper account continued by saying that

A little after 11 a.m. the next day, three Government wagons drove to the jail; one contained four and each of the others three rough board coffins. The condemned men were conducted from the prison and seated in the wagons, one upon each coffin. . . .

[Upon arrival at the fair grounds] the ten coffins were removed from the wagons and placed in a row 6 or 8 feet apart, forming a line north and south with each coffin having its foot to the west and its head to the east. . . .

Thirty soldiers of the Second Missouri State Militia were drawn up in a single line, extending north and south, facing the row of coffins [at a distance of about 25 feet from them]. Each prisoner took his seat upon the foot of his coffin, and only two or three showed signs of trepidation.

With about one hundred spectators watching intently, untrained executioners failed to fire simultaneously. "Two men fell backward upon their coffins and died instantly." Capt. Thomas A. Sidner of Monroe County sprang forward and falling with his face upward died at once. The remaining seven were hit but did not die immediately; hence "a reserve squadron was called in and its members used their revolvers." Reprinted in the *Memphis Daily Appeal* of November 3, the account of how 10 hostages died for one man quickly made the rounds in the South and attracted the keen attention of foreign journalists.

A blistering editorial in the *New York Times*, accompanied by extracts from foreign newspapers, prompted Strachan to write to the editor a lengthy letter of explanation for the Federal action. He ended by saying that the event, called a butchery by the New York newspaper, was actually "the just punishing of guerrillas, assassins, and violators of paroles"—and had resulted in "finally restoring safety" to the Unionists of Missouri. "A wise punishment has once more enabled the dove of peace to hover over our households, unterrified," he wrote—having no idea that Missouri's special version of civil strife would continue for two more years.

Jefferson Davis seems earlier to have believed that hostage taking would always lead to negotiations by which the lives of principals would be spared. About a year older and wiser than when he ordered the Richmond lottery that saved condemned Rebel privateersmen, he condemned actions of McNeil as murder. Sending the Memphis newspaper's account to Gen. T. H. Holmes, he directed that if the account was true, Holmes should demand "the immediate surrender of General McNeil to the Confederate authorities."

Should that demand not be met, Davis continued, "You are ordered to execute the first ten United States officers who may be captured and fall into your hands." There is no record that this directive of the Confederate president was carried out. Yet were there no other documented cases, the 10:1 spur-of-the-moment ratio established by McNeil demolishes the myth that no Civil War hostage was executed by his captors. (OR, 32, 817–18, 861; *Palmyra Courier*, October 1862; *New York Times*, December 1862; RR, 6, Doc. #10)

Executions took many forms, but it was not unusual for a condemned man to face a firing squad while seated upon his own flimsy coffin.

24

Trouble in Loudoun County

John S. Mosby, a prewar attorney who read law while jailed for the shooting of a fellow student at the University of Virginia, entered the war as a private. While a 1st lieutenant he largely guided men in gray under J. E. B. Stuart who rode around the Army of the Potomac in June 1862. Rebel authorities yielded to his pleas and early in 1863 gave him permission to organize a body of partisan rangers.

He and his approximately two hundred men were formally mustered into Confederate forces about a year after Stuart's famous ride. They continued to be a source of continuous major trouble to Federals, so their leader received a series of promotions by which he became a colonel late in 1864. For two years or more Mosby and his men so dominated Virginia's Loudoun Valley that it came to be widely known as "Mosby's Confederacy."

After he relinquished independent command in order to lead what became the 43rd Battalion of Virginia Cavalry in the Army of Northern Virginia, Mosby encouraged and advised leaders of small bands of Rebels. Though all of them called themselves rangers, some of these bodies were made up of guerrillas who did not take orders from any man in uniform. One of these forces, Means' Loudoun Rangers, was organized at Waterford, Virginia, plus Point of Rocks, Maryland, and fought continuously until May 31, 1865. Other men who called themselves rangers belonged to loosely organized groups whose personnel was continually changing. (D, 2, 671)

Small wonder, therefore, that Union authorities initially believed a not-yet-identified body of rangers was responsible for an affair that became highly publicized. With western Maryland firmly in Federal hands, picket posts of soldiers in blue were extended to the bank of the Potomac River at points that included Edwards Ferry. Late in May or early in June 1864, three men showed up on the Virginia side of the crossing point and attracted the attention of pickets across the river.

According to extensive testimony that did not get into the *Official Records*, the trio who seemed to be civilians waved an improvised white flag and shouted that they wanted to come into Union lines. Exchanges between the banks of the river convinced Federal pickets that the strangers were refugees who had been driven from their homes because they opposed secession and the Confederacy.

Once this matter seemed to be settled, a pair of soldiers in blue crawled into a rowboat in order to bring the refugees across the river. As they approached the Virginia side of the Potomac, the men with whom they had exchanged shouts dropped their white flag and picked up muskets. Simultaneously, another band of men concealed in thick underbrush near the river's edge opened fire upon the pair of men from the 2nd Massachusetts Cavalry.

Both Federals surrendered after one of them took a direct hit from a marksman he had not seen. Records concerning this incident and its aftermath are preserved in the National Archives and at least one scholar has made a careful investigation of what he called "The White Flag Affair." (Case No. 3, 198, microfilm section, Turner-Baker Papers, National Archives; Neely, *Fate*, 152–55)

Surviving records suggest but do not prove that exultant Rebels paraded their captives at gunpoint through the streets of nearby Leesburg, Virginia. One citizen whose name was not preserved seems to have told Federal authorities that nearly everyone in the village turned out to see the show. According to this source, civilians applauded the eight captors and taunted their two prisoners, one of whom limped badly because he had been hit in the thigh.

News of the affair traveled quickly and soon reached Union Gen. Christopher C. Augur, who was in command at Point Lookout, Maryland. He initially believed that an unidentified body of rangers was responsible for the kidnapping. From the first, however, he expressed doubts that it would be easy to identify and arrest the perpetrators of what he termed "the outrageous affair at the ferry." In the light of this difficult situation Augur decided to have hostages picked up.

Intelligence suggested that two of the men who helped pull off the ambush were Leesburg residents Henry Clay Ryan and Noble Rinker. Hence Augur's men seized George W. Ryan, believed to be the father of the leading bushwhacker, plus the elder Ryan's younger son and namesake. Joseph Rinker, allegedly the father of the other leader of the ambush, was arrested along with the two Ryans.

Three decoys and five marksmen were said by men of the 2nd Massachusetts Cavalry to have been involved in the kidnapping at Edwards Ferry. Though he was in custody, adolescent George W. Ryan, Jr., hardly counted as a hostage. Therefore soldiers under the command of Augur picked up eight other males whom they considered to be among the most prominent citizens

Union Gen. Christopher C. Augur,
whose men picked up eight hostages
from the civilians of Leesburg.
Pictorial Field Book

of Leesburg. Along with young Ryan, they were shipped to Washington and consigned to the Old Capitol Prison.

Joseph Holt, the Union judge advocate general, immediately received a summary of events that had taken place. He denounced actions of the pretended refugees in the strongest possible language. Having characterized their deed as a crime "of unspeakable baseness & atrocity," he voiced a solemn warning. "The [Union] government," he said, "may well resort to all means known to civilized warfare to compel a surrender of the criminals." He then released two of the hostages on June 13, saying that they had no previous record of opposition to the Federal cause. Holt's actions had the additional appeal of reducing the number of adult male hostages to eight—making them numerically equivalent to the eight bushwhackers who pulled off the Edwards Ferry seizure. (Turner-Baker Papers, Case No. 3, 198)

John P. Smart's age may have affected Holt's actions. At 69, he was too old to fight and could hardly be considered a menace to Federal forces across the river from his residence. Possibly because many leaders still tried to treat surgeons with some degree of civility, the other hostage who was freed by Holt was Dr. Armstead Mott. Actions of the judge advocate general left eight adults and one adolescent in jail. There, they were grilled repeatedly until one or more of them deliberately or accidentally revealed names of some who had taken part in the ambush in addition to Rinker and Ryan.

When the Union secretary of war became apprized of "the Leesburg affair" and its aftermath, he issued an order to Col. William Hoffman. Following that directive, the commissary general of prisoners sent a formal notice to Gen. Albin F. Schoepf. A native of Hungary, Schoepf was at the time in command at Fort Delaware, Delaware. On the day two hostages were turned loose, Schoepf was notified that he was to receive the remaining eight: Charles F. Faidley, Thomas Edwards, Joseph Rinker, W. S. Prickett, George W. Ryan, Dr. William Cross, E. L. Bentley, and William H. Gray. Though nothing was said about George W. Ryan, Jr., he must have been included in the prisoner transfer since he eventually reached Fort Warren and was held there until December 24.

With eight mature males and an adolescent still held as hostages for a crime with which they had nothing to do, an impartial observer might have wondered what Holt meant by invoking the principles of civilized warfare. No one in authority questioned his actions, however, and no one is known to have called his attention to one of the most solemn directives issued from Washington during the year that preceded the Leesburg incident.

At the request of the War Department, scholar Francis Lieber prepared the rough draft of a lengthy set of instructions for Federal armies and their commanders. After Lieber's draft had been revised by Gen. E. A. Hitchcock's board of distinguished officers and approved by Abraham Lincoln, it was issued as General Order No. 100.

Of the document's 157 articles, two of the shortest dealt with hostages. Men in blue who received the lengthy general orders were told that

> 54. A hostage is a person accepted as a pledge for the fulfillment of an agreement concluded between belligerents during the war, or in consequence of a war. Hostages are rare in the present age.
>
> 55. If a hostage is accepted, he is treated like a prisoner of war, according to rank and condition, as circumstances may admit. (OR, 118, 671–74)

If Benjamin F. Butler perused the document that had been approved at the highest level, he must have chuckled at the naive views of Lieber, Hitchcock, and their associates who thought that "hostages are rare in the present age."

Gen. Ethan Allen Hitchcock headed a board of distinguished officers who said, among other things, that hostages were rarely taken in the Civil War.

National Archives

Citizens of Leesburg who were still imprisoned but were not being treated as prisoners of war would have had no opportunity to see General Order No. 100, or to be apprized of its contents.

Aided by information secured from hostages, search parties discovered and arrested George Ryan's older brother and Noble Rinker; consequently, their fathers were released in December. Records fail to indicate whether or not their six accomplices were apprehended. Ryan and Rinker were presumably executed, but there is no documentary evidence that they paid the ultimate penalty for having used a white flag to lure men in blue within easy range of concealed marksmen.

How and why George W. Ryan, Jr., wound up at Fort Warren remains an unsolved mystery. Most or

At Fort Warren, prisoners who were photographed may have included an adolescent hostage who was released during the Christmas season.
U.S. Army Military History Institute

all of the remaining hostages who were seized in Leesburg probably remained at Fort Delaware for six months or more, with extra precautions taken to prevent their escape. Release of the adolescent a few hours before the beginning of Christmas Day suggests—but does not prove—that he might have been turned loose when Federal authorities had an uncontrollable burst of the holiday spirit.

No one knows how Augur, Hoffman, Schoepf, Holt, and Stanton reacted to articles #54 and #55 of General Order No. 100—if, indeed, they bothered to read the document that stipulated why hostages might be selected and how they should be treated.

Christmas celebrations may have prompted the release of hostages from Fort Warren at the beginning of the holiday season.

Thomas Nast in *Harper's Weekly*

25

Approval at the Top

Many policies practiced by men on both sides, general officers included, were improvised in the field and were never approved by top military or civilian leaders. That was not the case with the use of hostages in attempts to gain leverage or make retaliatory moves. From the beginning to the end of the war this policy was approved and used by top soldiers and elected officials. Ulysses S. Grant, the first Union lieutenant general since George Washington, was also the first general office to resort to the use of hostages.

Though it escaped the compilers of the *Official Records*, this matter was first mentioned in a late August 1861 order to a Captain Chitwood. Headed on a scouting mission, he was told by Grant to take "a few leading and prominent secessionists" as hostages, then to carry them along with his party for protection. Concurrently, Grant sent another officer to seize the printing equipment of the *Booneville Patriot* and arrest its editor.

Testifying at the February 1862 court-martial of Col. Ebenezer Magoffin, Lt. Col. H. M. Day amplified sparse information about the earliest instances in which hostages were used in the field. Commanded by Col. Thomas A. Marshall, the 1st Illinois Cavalry left Jefferson City, Missouri, on or about August 24. A list "of what was supposed to be the principal rebels or secessionists on our line of march to Lexington" had been given to Day.

He was instructed to take two hundred to four hundred men ahead of the main body in order to surround and picket each town on the route. This was done, Day swore under oath, so that "the principal secessionists" could be arrested and "held for the good behavior of the citizens of the place." Day's deliberate use of the term "supposed to be" supports the conclusion that few, if any, Federal officials had firm knowledge about views of leading citizens of the towns in which he took an unspecified number of hostages. (Grant, *Papers*, 2, 136–7; OR, 114, 217, 292, 320)

An order directed by Grant to Col. E. P. Wood at Fort Holt, Kentucky, was brief but specific. Wood was told to "take two leading secessionists from the neighborhood of Elliott's Mills" and imprison them "as hostages for the safety of William Mercer, a Union man." (OR, 114, 511)

Grant's most sweeping attempt to exploit hostages came nearly 18 months later. Aggravated beyond measure by the way rangers under John S. Mosby annoyed his forces, from his City Point, Virginia, headquarters he sent an August 16, 1864, dispatch to Philip H. Sheridan at Winchester. In it he said that

> If you can possibly spare a division of cavalry, send them through Loudoun County, to destroy and carry off the crops, animals, negroes, and all men under fifty years of age capable of bearing arms. In this way you will get many of Mosby's men. All male citizens under fifty can fairly be held as prisoners of war, and not as Citizen prisoners, if not already soldiers, they will be made so the moment the rebel army gets hold of them.

Though he did not mention hostage taking in this dispatch, earlier the same day he had said to Sheridan that

> The families of most of Mosby's men are known, and can be collected. I think they should be collected and kept at Fort McHenry, or some secure place, as hostages for the good conduct of Mosby and his men. Where any of Mosby's men are caught hang them without trial. (OR, 90, 811; Ency., 514b)

This program seems to have little or no effect. Late in November Gen. Wesley Merritt was informed through Sheridan that he and his men had been selected to operate "against the guerrillas" in the region where Mosby's influence was greatest. Described as "a hot-bed of lawless bands," the Loudoun Valley was widely known by men in blue as well as in gray to have resisted all efforts at Federal control. Since hostage taking had not been effective, Merritt was instructed to: ". . . consume and destroy all forage and subsistence, burn all barns and mills and their contents, and drive off all stock in the region."

Almost as an afterthought, Merritt was offered justification for the retaliation he was about to work upon civilians whose only offense was that they lived in "Mosby's Confederacy." He was told that

> This destruction may as well commence at once, and the responsibility for it must rest upon the authorities in Richmond, who have acknowledged the legitimacy of guerrilla bands. The injury done this army by them is very slight. The injury they have inflicted upon the people and the rebel army, may be counted by millions [of dollars]. (OR, 90, 55–56)

Biographer Douglas Southall Freeman has insisted that the commander of the Army of Northern Virginia "never believed in retaliation."

To buttress that contention, he cited comments by Robert E. Lee that may be found in manuscript collections. (Freeman, *Lee*, 3, 210)

The scholar who idolized Lee failed to investigate his actions relative to hostages or overlooked them in the light of what the Rebel commander said. Several times the man who left the Union army as a newly promoted colonel approved or personally ordered hostage taking and retaliation.

On August 2, 1862, he directed an inquiry to Washington concerning newspaper reports that William B. Mumford had been murdered at New Orleans and that Col. John L. Owen had been murdered in Missouri by order of Gen. John Pope. Acting on behalf of the president of the Confederacy, Lee said that unless his inquiry was answered within 15 days he would presume the newspaper reports to be true. "In such event," he concluded, the responsibility for "retaliatory measures which shall be adopted" will be the responsibility of the Union government. (OR, 117, 328–29)

Shortly afterward J. E. B. Stuart briefed his commander in some detail concerning what he initially called "an expedition into Maryland." On October 8, 1862, the cavalryman received specific instructions about the expedition that became famous as "Stuart's post-Antietam ride." Lee said that if the movement could be successfully executed it was desirable. Hence he authorized the formation of a detachment of 1,200 to 1,500 men whose objective would be a railroad bridge near Chambersburg, Pennsylvania.

Any and all civilians likely to give information to the enemy must be arrested, Lee wrote. He then added that

> should you meet with citizens of Pennsylvania holding State or Government offices, it will be desirable, if convenient, to bring them with you, that they may be used as hostages, or the means of exchanges, for our own citizens that have been carried off by the enemy.

Without specifying how many hostages he took, upon his return to Virginia, Stuart reported that "A number of public functionaries and prominent citizens were taken captives and brought over as hostages." Some of these men ultimately reached the notorious Confederate prison at Salisbury, North Carolina, where they figured in acrimonious debates about the place. (OR, 28, 53–55; JSHS, 14, 478)

Ninety days after having approved of hostage taking in Pennsylvania, Lee concluded that Union Gen. Robert H. Milroy and subordinates were oppressing civilians in the region they occupied. Consequently, he recommended to the secretary of war that the parole planned for an unnamed major of the Union 10th Virginia be withdrawn so that he could be "detained as a hostage." (OR, 31, 1079, 1086; OR, 118, 807; OR, 124, 11)

When the Army of Northern Virginia was within two months of its humiliating surrender at Appomattox Court House, Grant showed great interest in a newspaper clipping. He probably did not know that a similar snippet earlier led Halleck to use nearly six hundred Rebel officers as hostages on

Morris Island, near Charleston. A December 8 story in the *Richmond Examiner* did not reach Grant until February 1865.

According to the newspaper, Rebels had put 37 Unionists into Richmond's Castle Thunder to hold them "for the good treatment and return of Confederate citizens alleged to have been captured by us." Upon seeing the published account but without inquiring into its accuracy he fired off a dispatch to Lee. In it Grant demanded to know the names of the Rebels held by Federal forces for whom the unnamed citizens loyal to the Union "were seized and held as hostages."

Lee, who was battle weary, bone tired, and more than a little dejected, took only two days to respond to Grant's inquiry of February 16. He had referred his foe's letter to the Confederate secretary of war, he indicated. Disclaiming having ordered the arrest of antisecession Virginians, he gave a casual reply to Grant's central question. "If it be true that those mentioned were taken by any of our forces," he said, "I presume they are held as hostages generally for persons of the same class in the custody of the Federal authorities and not for particular individuals." (OR, 121, 261)

Despite his cavalier attitude toward the hostage question in 1865, he earlier felt very strongly about it—when his brother was taken at Hickory Hill. According to Lee, the captive was "driven away, a soldier on the box [of the carriage] and a mounted guard surrounding him." Transported to White House on the Pamunkey River, he was "then sent by water to Fortress Monroe." There, fumed the commander of the Army of Northern Virginia, his own flesh and blood "was held as a hostage for the safety of some Federal officers we had captured for nine long, weary months." (OR, 31, 99–100)

Abraham Lincoln's second vice president, destined to succeed him and become the 17th chief executive of the United States, zealously espoused the use of hostages quite early. Soon after being made military governor of Tennessee, Andrew Johnson told soldiers to hold a dozen Rutherford County citizens as hostages "to secure the safety of Murfreesboro."

His stratagem must have proved effective, for a few weeks later he brought the president into a much bigger hostage situation. In a June 5, 1862, dispatch from Nashville, he informed Lincoln that 70 eastern Tennesseans were "lying in prison at Mobile" for the offense of being Union men. Johnson alleged that "They are treated with more cruelty than wild beasts of the forest."

In a bid to halt this treatment or to gain their freedom, reported the future president, he had that day arrested "seventy vile secessionists" whom he expected to offer in exchange for the captives. Should that proposal be rejected, Johnson planned to send his 70 hostages beyond Federal lines with the threat that if they should "recross or come again within said lines during the existing rebellion" they could be expected to be treated as spies. That is, one and all would face the death penalty. Having reported about events already in the process or decisions announced, he tossed a five-word question to Lincoln: "Does this meet your approval?"

In Washington, the man from Springfield weighed his words carefully and employed a double negative to indicate an affirmative reply. His June 9 two-sentence response to Johnson's question concerning civilians who had been accused of no wrongdoing read simply: "Your dispatch about seizing seventy rebels to exchange for a like number of Union men, was duly received. I certainly do not disapprove the proposition." (OR, 116, 643, 666; AL, 7, 264)

Soon Lincoln and his chief aides were forced to deal with a much more complex hostage issue. Fort Pillow, not far from Jackson, Tennessee, was in Federal hands during the spring of 1864. Maj. Lionel F. Booth, commander of the post, had less than six hundred men plus the gunboat *New Era* with which to defend it. Early in April Confederate Gen. Nathan B. Forrest dispatched Gen. James R. Chalmers and about 1,500 men to the installation with orders to "attend to it."

Rebels launched a probe at dawn on April 12, and by the time Forrest arrived at 10:00 A.M. they had the fort surrounded. The only man who entered the war as a private and rose to the rank of lieutenant general took his time in deciding how best to assault the Federal position. With the sun well past its zenith, he decided that Rebels could take paths along which neither the guns of the fort or of the little warship could reach them. When the enemy refused his surrender demand, Forrest signaled for his men to swarm upon the fort from several points at once.

Andrew Johnson, who became president after the assassination of Abraham Lincoln, made early and extensive use of hostages.

War weariness clearly showing in his face, the man from Springfield who is often best remembered for his humor considered taking hostages for Fort Pillow.

Before the shooting and the use of bayonets came to an end, more than half of Pillow's defenders had become casualties and the attackers had lost only one hundred men. Almost half of the Federal force was made up of black soldiers—only about 60 of whom were taken alive. It was therefore logical and inevitable that abolitionists and other zealots in the North should label the affair as an atrocity rather than a battle. An inquiry by the anti-Lincoln Joint Congressional Committee on the Conduct of the War resulted in a scathing report that said Rebels went into the fight determined to take few black prisoners.

Six days after Fort Pillow, Lincoln addressed a Sanitary Fair gathering at Baltimore. Knowing that the Tennessee matter was on the minds of most listeners, the president said that three hundred "colored soldiers and their white officers" had reportedly been victims of a massacre. Stressing that rumor was a long way from established fact, the chief executive told his Maryland audience that if atrocities had been committed, Federal retribution would follow. He implied that he was reluctant to lead an investigation, but said that "it must come." (AL, 7, 302–3)

Before speaking in Baltimore, he had read and pondered a long May 5 dispatch from Grant, whose opinion concerning Pillow he had solicited. Grant wrote what for him was an unusually long dispatch in which he discussed six aspects of the matter. His first proposal was immediately to select Rebel prisoners of war and make hostages of them until all the facts concerning events of April 12 were firmly in hand. In the second place, he advocated excluding Generals Forrest and Chalmers—plus all of their officers and men who had taken part in the massacre—from Lincoln's recently publicized offer of amnesty.

Grant's third point dealt with use of Rebels selected to be held in close confinement until the Tennessee affair was fully aired. These men whom he earlier had designated as hostages should be "held as hostages for the delivery up" of all Confederates involved in the massacre, he said. Such a move, according to Grant, was "justified by the laws of civilized warfare."

In the fourth place, wrote the only lieutenant general in Union forces, after a reasonable time the president should "take against the hostages above selected" punitive measures designed to protect all men in blue from "such savage barbarities as were practiced at Fort Pillow." Grant's lengthy set of analyses and recommendations placed the chief executive upon the horns of a dilemma. He could not ignore what the man he had elevated to supreme command said, yet he was not convinced that all of the facts were in hand. (OR, 120, 113)

The entire North was in an uproar, yet the South issued steadfast denials with which subtle threats were sometimes intermingled. His correspondence and informal discussions with the private secretaries upon whom he relied heavily suggest that Lincoln came very close to acting upon the advice of Grant. Some authorities say he drafted but never signed an order

Artists, who may or may not have been accurate, depicted Rebels as having ruthlessly butchered scores of black soldiers at Fort Pillow.

to seize hostages as Grant had recommended. There is no documentary support for this claim, however.

With "the evidence not yet quite ready to be laid before" him, Lincoln decided to involve his most senior advisors. On May 5 he requested each member of the cabinet to provide a written opinion concerning the course the government should take concerning Fort Pillow. (AL, 7, 328)

Opinions voiced by his high-placed civilian aides were diverse and lengthy. Most or all of them badly wanted to call upon Richmond to admit that a massacre had taken place or formally to deny it. Edwin M. Stanton, Salmon P. Chase, and Gideon Welles agreed upon another major issue. All three of them felt that captive Rebels equal in number to victims of the massacre should be set apart as hostages who would be executed if enemy leaders confessed that a massacre had taken place.

Such a course of action was opposed by Atty. Gen. Edward Bates, P.M.G. Montgomery Blair, and the relatively new secretary of the interior, John P. Usher of Indiana. Each member of this trio expressed unwillingness to sanction reprisals against innocent hostages. They were ready, however, to support the execution of any perpetrators—Forrest included—who might be captured. (Nicolay and Hay, *Lincoln*, 7, 478 ff.)

Pushed very hard by Grant but facing a divided cabinet, Lincoln said he must have time to gather more facts before deciding what punitive action to take. Hours later the Army of the Potomac launched the Wilderness campaign. Soon news of the action that began on May 5 in one of the most inhospitable areas of Virginia crowded other matters out of the minds of members of the general public. Lincoln also seems to have been greatly influenced by hourly bulletins from the Wilderness; having been diverted from the Fort Pillow issue he did not return to it.

Today, scholars generally agree that atrocities did take place at Fort Pillow, but on a far smaller scale than was initially charged. Many of them are reluctant to make scathing denunciations of Rebel actions in Tennessee because it is now well known that men in blue sometimes killed foes who had surrendered.

One of the best documented of these cases took place at Front Royal, Virginia, on September 23, 1864. Much evidence indicates that on that day, men in blue shot or hanged six prisoners in the streets of the occupied town. All of those who were executed belonged to John S. Mosby's Rangers. Shortly afterward A. C. Willis of Mosby's command was executed by Gen. William H. Powell, allegedly in retaliation for the murder of a Federal soldier by two members of Mosby's command with whom Willis had no direct connection.

Ex-Confederates who in 1899 erected a 25-foot monument to the seven rangers who were "murdered in cold blood" blamed the atrocity upon Grant's August 16 order that directed his subordinates to hang Mosby's men without trial whenever possible. Though the number of Rebels who died in the

Allegedly opposed to retaliation, Gen. Robert E. Lee repeatedly authorized the taking of hostages.

fall of 1864 after having surrendered and relinquished their weapons was small by comparison with charges leveled against Forrest at Pillow, the principle is identical. As was the case in the aftermath of Pillow, Federals and Confederates issued quite different accounts. (JSHS, 27, 250–87; OR, 90, 509.)

Attorney Lincoln, whose pre-war career had been in Illinois, was clearly willing to use hostages. That was revealed by his response to Andrew Johnson's proposal concerning nearly six dozen of them. His reluctance to act upon second- or third-hand reports about Fort Pillow means, not that he opposed use of hostages in general, but that he still had doubts about atrocity stories. In addition, he seems to have feared that dramatic seizure of many hostages might cause an escalation in the already fearful violence of the war that had been launched in order to re-unite the severed Union.

Lincoln and Johnson along with Grant and Lee had few qualms about the use of hostages. Small wonder, therefore, that scores of military leaders and civilian officials seized hundreds of hostages innocent of any offense when it appeared to them that these special captives might be useful.

26

"Little Blood-suckers" Saved Farragut

Rear Adm. E. E. Roberts is the authority for what is probably the only humorous hostage story of the Civil War. He visited New Orleans in 1907 for the first time since 1862. At that time he was a lieutenant who took part in the Federal conquest of the largest city in the Confederacy. Prior to arriving at the Crescent City for the second time, he spent a period in and about Mobile—a city he also first saw from the deck of a warship.

To New Orleans reporters he confessed that he was haunted by memories of the sinking of the USS *Tecumseh* during the battle of Mobile Bay. Since he knew many of the 94 men who went down with the ship and whose bodies were never recovered, during a recent stay in Alabama he had spent many hours in and around the harbor. There, he picked up a bizarre story of how insects saved the life of Rear Adm. David G. Farragut, under whom he fought at both New Orleans and Mobile. (*Times-Dispatch*, 1907)

Measured by any standard, Farragut was one of the most unusual and interesting key figures of the 1861–65 conflict. A native of Tennessee whose baptismal name was James, he went with his family to a plantation on Louisiana's Pascagoula River as a very small boy. His father, George, was a career U.S. Navy man who had made friends with Comdr. David Porter, Jr.

Porter several times traveled about one hundred miles from his New Orleans headquarters to visit the Farraguts. Ties between the two families became much stronger when Porter's father—also a career officer of the U.S. Navy—and Mrs. George Farragut were buried on the same day. Soon, Porter and his wife took the motherless nine-year-old boy into their home, having promised to treat him "as though he were of their own flesh and blood." For practical purposes they adopted James much as Sen. Thomas Ewing of Ohio and his wife adopted little "Cump" Sherman (William Tecumseh). There is no certainty that this process involved a formal ceremony in Ohio or in Louisiana.

Rear Adm. David E. Farragut, whose warships won monumental victories at both New Orleans and Mobile.

J. C. Buttre engraving

Eager to go to sea, James persuaded Porter to make him a midshipman shortly before his tenth birthday. While serving under his foster father aboard the USS *Essex* for three years, the little midshipman changed his name to David in honor of Porter. At age 12 he was put in command of a captured ship, possibly making him the youngest prize master in the annals of the navy. At age 14 he became a lieutenant, then waited 16 years to get his first command—the sloop *Decatur*, a member of a squadron that patrolled waters off the coast of Brazil. Confederates who planned during the spring of 1864 to make a hostage of the man who had spent most of his life on the sea probably did not know that Federal authorities were wary of him when war broke out. Washington knew all about his strong Southern roots, which they presumed had helped influence him and his wife—a native of Virginia—to make their home in Norfolk. Farragut probably knew why Gideon Welles and some of his aides were reluctant to put him in command of a warship, but he persisted in asking to fight the Rebels despite a series of rebuffs.

In a dramatic gesture intended to signal that he had cut his ties with the South, Farragut moved to Hastings-on-Hudson, located a few miles north of New York City. It was there that his foster brother, Comdr. David D. Porter, visited him and quizzed him about his feelings. Porter reputedly persuaded Farragut to say that he would not hesitate to fire on relatives who were Rebels, then returned to Washington and had several sessions with Gustavus V. Fox.

Fox, who had recently become the first assistant secretary of the Union navy, was in high favor with Abraham Lincoln and owed his post to the president. Lincoln had it created in the aftermath of Fort Sumter in order to give the man who planned the relief expedition a place worthy of his accomplishments. In post-Sumter correspondence, the chief executive noted that the failure of the Sumter expedition was of no consequence since it provoked secessionists into starting what he habitually termed an insurrection. Writing to the man to whom he felt he owed a great deal, the chief executive had said that

You and I both anticipated that the cause of the country would be advanced by making the attempt to provision Fort Sumpter even if it should fail, and it is no small consolation now to feel that our anticipation is justified by the result [of war fever in the North because the South fired first]. (Fox, *Confidential Correspondence*, 43 ff.; AL, 4, 350–51)

Porter, noted for having divorced his Southern-born wife in order to fight for the Union, persuaded Fox that his foster brother was also 100 percent loyal to the United States. With the support of the assistant secretary of the navy, it was easy to win presidential approval for Farragut to take command of the West Gulf Blockading Squadron. He soon became universally known as the man largely responsible for the capture of New Orleans in April 1862. One of the rewards heaped upon the man who went to sea at age nine was promotion to the newly created rank of rear admiral—making him the first American to hold that rank.

Men who plotted to seize Rear Admiral Farragut and use him as a hostage believed that he had come into Alabama waters, not simply to supervise routine shelling of a Confederate fortification, but to plan a naval operation against Mobile. Though their hunch was not based on hard evidence, it proved to be correct.

Having been given by Washington the assignment of taking Mobile, Farragut soon made his appearance in waters close to his target. A number of vessels belonging to the Federal blockade squadron were regularly at Sand Island in the Gulf of Mexico, not far from the entrance to Mobile Bay. Vessels armed with mortars had anchored in Mississippi Sound and from that point were engaged in shelling Fort Powell. Ostensibly in order to supervise this operation, Farragut regularly took a small boat to Dauphin Island. After crossing its narrow tip on foot, he was met by another boat that took him to the mortar fleet.

Though he was in command of the vessels that were shelling Fort Powell and was keenly interested in their operations, his real objective was Mobile Bay—the largest Confederate port in eastern waters of the Gulf of Mexico. The city of Mobile was so heavily fortified that a direct assault upon it was considered

Comdr. David D. Porter, foster brother of the rear admiral who was targeted by Rebels as a hostage.

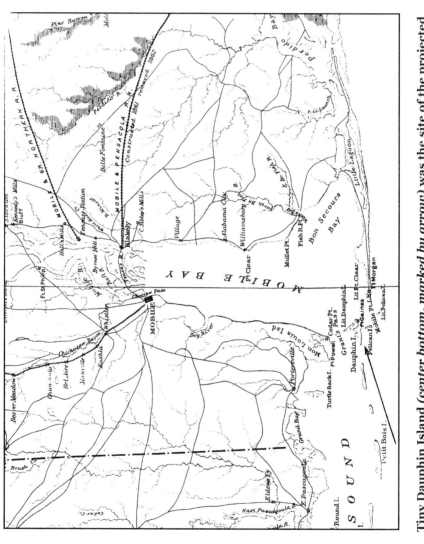

Tiny Dauphin Island *(center bottom, marked by arrow)* was the site of the projected seizure of Rear Admiral Farragut as a hostage.

Official Records, Atlas

Secessionists of New Orleans gave an angry greeting to the first contingent of Farragut's men who reached the fallen city.

U.S. Army Military History Institute

to be suicidal, but if the bay could be taken the port would be effectively closed.

On August 5, 1864, the operation that Farragut had planned in minute detail got under way. He was keenly aware that most of the bay was dotted with explosives manufactured and placed by the Torpedo Bureau that was under the supervision of Gen. Gabriel J. Rains. A narrow channel, heavily used by blockade runners and Confederate vessels, was free of mines—but was in the direct line of fire from Fort Morgan. That meant a Federal vessel trying to enter the vast harbor would be endangered by heavy guns on shore plus torpedoes in the water.

Farragut, who had spent most of his life aboard wooden vessels, was contemptuous of the new ironclads that had been brought into the U.S. Navy. His wooden flagship, the USS *Hartford*, was equipped with both sails and steam engines, however. The rear admiral—who walked the decks of wind-powered ships for decades—considered her to be one of the finest warships afloat. He believed, however, that an ironclad had a better chance than his flagship to survive hits by Rebel gunners or the impact of one of their torpedoes. Hence his attack force was led by the USS *Tecumseh* when Federal vessels headed into the channel close to Fort Morgan. This passageway site was not far from the little island planned to be used in taking Farragut as a hostage.

As the Union fleet moved into the bay shortly after 6:00 A.M., the *Tecumseh* hit a torpedo. Suddenly toppling to one side, the ironclad went down quickly and carried most of her 114 officers and men to their death.

Nearsighted but disdaining the use of glasses, the 62-year-old commander of the operation climbed into the rigging of the *Hartford's* mainmast in order to get a better view of the action. Subordinates hastily fastened a rope around him so he would not fall into the water far below.

An officer who was not identified shouted a warning about the Rebel torpedoes that abounded in the bay. At this point, tradition has it that the man whose loyalty to the Union was initially questioned by officials of the Union navy muttered an immortal order: Damn the torpedoes; full steam ahead!

Lt. John C. Kinney of the 13th Connecticut was aboard the *Hartford* as a signal officer on that eventful day. He later wrote a detailed account of the action, here summarized, that led to a dramatic Federal victory. (*Century War Book*, 271–75)

Had the plot conceived by members of the Confederate 1st Georgia succeeded, there would have been no battle of Mobile Bay in August 1864. Sgt. Wiley Wagner, Cpl. William Foster, and Pvt. Harry Savage had appointed themselves as a task force to see that the port would not be attacked. They reasoned, almost certainly correctly, that if Farragut was held as a hostage the Federal fleet would not act.

Having watched the movements of the rear admiral when he was about a mile from their post at Fort Gaines, they saw that on his frequent trips to Dauphin Island he was accompanied by only one man. That man, reasoned the Rebels who wanted Farragut as a hostage, must be either a secretary or an aide; he would be overpowered easily.

After having secured a three-day supply of water and rations, the trio of plotters moved under cover of darkness to a point very close to the path Farragut habitually took in crossing Dauphin Island. Hiding in marsh grass, they confidently expected to seize their prey and then run quickly into the cover of a nearby dense growth of trees and underbrush. Moving through the woods, they reasoned, they would be at Fort Gaines with their hostage before enemies realized that their commander was missing.

According to Roberts, the eager Rebels spent three nights and two days hiding in marsh grass but for reasons unknown Farragut did not come to the island during this period. Exposure to hordes of mosquitoes for about 60 hours proved too much for the conspirators. After their third night, all of them were so covered with marks left by mosquito bites that they dejectedly crawled back to Fort Gaines. To comrades who quizzed them about having returned without their hostage, they grimly explained that little blood suckers had forced them to give up. All three were forced to spend a solid week in what ship-oriented Roberts called Fort Gaines sick bay.

When published in the *Times Dispatch* on December 23, 1907, this yarn was entitled "How Mosquitoes Prevented Capture of Farragut." Roberts came across the story during his visit to the Mobile area 43 years after entering its harbor aboard the *Hartford*. Ending his account of the hostage taking that was thwarted by tiny bloodsuckers, the retired rear admiral said that "The very day the attempt was abandoned, Admiral Farragut resumed his visits to the mortar fleet [by way of Dauphin Island]."

27

William H. F. ("Rooney") Lee and Company

A Federal military commission convened at Cincinnati on April 22, 1863, in obedience to orders issued the previous day. Presided over by Gen. R. B. Potter, the body considered the cases of two men: William F. Corbin and T. G. McGraw, who were described as "now or late of the so-called Confederate Army." Both men were charged with having carried mail or other information from within Union lines to "persons in arms against the government." Both were also charged with having recruited men "within the lines of the Union forces for the so-called Confederate Army." Their trial was swift and perfunctory, leading to verdicts according to which the accused—both being Rebel captains—were found guilty and sentences were pronounced. They were ordered "to be shot to death at such time and place as the commanding general shall direct."

Speaking for Ambrose E. Burnside, Potter ordered that

The prisoners, now or late of the so-called Confederate Army, will be sent in irons by the proper officer and delivered into the custody of the commanding officer on Johnson's Island, depot of prisoner of war, near Sandusky, Ohio.

The commanding officer of that post will see that the sentences are duly executed at that post between the hours of 12 o'clock noon and 8 o'clock p.m. of Friday, May 15, 1863. (OR, 118, 556–57)

No one involved in a case so perfunctory that it seemed to those involved to be almost casual had the slightest idea that they were launching one of the war's most convoluted and dramatic cases in which hostages played crucial roles.

Neither was there any indication that the June 9 battle at Beverly Ford, Virginia, would have long-lasting repercussions. Now generally known as Brandy Station, the day-long contest was the biggest cavalry battle ever fought in North America. Situated on the Orange and Alexandria Railroad not far from Culpeper, the little depot seemed an unlikely spot for an epic clash.

On the previous day, Confederate Gen. J. E. B. Stuart had staged a review of his men—five brigades with almost 10,000 members—for Gen. Robert E. Lee. Their steps guided by the instruments of bandsmen, animals and men moved in near-perfect order, evoking the generous praise of Lee. No Confederate knew that Gen. Joseph E Hooker had dispatched three cavalry divisions and two infantry brigades to search for Stuart and his Rebels. At the close of a stunning spring day, Stuart relaxed in a sturdy brick house on Fleetwood Hill, a small eminence just north of the station. Even the man who had thrilled the Confederacy by riding around McClellan's entire army did not consider it important that his grand review had raised a powerful cloud of dust.

A few miles away that evening, Gen. Alfred Pleasonton's approximately 11,000 officers and men were forbidden to light fires because the cloud of dust told them that Stuart's forces were near. They were up and about long before first light, grumbling that without fires it was impossible to brew coffee. An advance guard made up of members of the 8th New York Cavalry found only a handful of pickets on duty at Beverly Ford on the Rappahannock River, so easily broke through.

Stuart heard the action that took place about daybreak and ordered reinforcements in the direction of the sounds. Gen. Wade Hampton's brigade reached a patch of trees in time to form a line of battle before they were hit by the 6th Pennsylvania Cavalry. Gen. William Henry Fitzhugh ("Rooney") Lee, second son of the commander of the Army of Northern Virginia, chose a strong position on a ridge close to the Hazel River and soon made the place formidable. Meanwhile, however, a flanking force made up of men in blue had crossed downstream and many of its members had headed straight for Brandy Station. Opposing forces soon rode headlong into battle and fought ceaselessly until the sun began to sink in the west. The Comte de Paris, an observer from France who rode with Federal forces, later wrote that "the hostile lines

At Brandy Station, Gen. Wade Hampton led a battalion that took the brunt of an assault by the 6th Pennsylvania Cavalry.
Library of Congress

were mixed in such a melee as was never before witnessed in America." Neither commander could claim a decisive win, but Pleasonton had proved that Federal cavalrymen, disparaged until that day, could hold their own against the best that Rebels had. His subordinates compiled a list of about 421 who were killed or wounded and Stuart's officers counted slightly more than three hundred who would be unable to fight again soon.

Many wounds, such as Union Capt. Henry W. Sawyer's fresh hole in his cheek, were considered by surgeons to be minor but it was probably the cause of his capture.

A map prepared later by Abner Doubleday showed Federals massed between Aquia Creek and Fredericksburg on June 9, while two-thirds of Stuart's forces were still

Captured at Brandy Station, Gen. William Henry Fitzhugh ("Rooney") Lee was a central figure in a fierce struggle about hostages.
Valentine Museum

close to Culpeper. No one in either body knew that the battle of the previous day would quickly be linked with actions taken at Cincinnati in April. Neither did anyone imagine that men in blue and in gray would converge upon the Pennsylvania hamlet of Gettysburg just one month later. (B&L, 3, 261–64)

The greatest number of casualties—more than one hundred—was suffered by the 6th Pennsylvania, but Rooney Lee's men were not far behind with 90 of their number killed, wounded, or missing. All accounts agree that one of the casualties was Robert E. Lee's son, but some say he took a bullet in his thigh and others insist that his leg was hit. Regardless of the exact location of Rooney's wound, it was serious enough for Stuart to put him on medical leave and tell him to find a spot where he could recuperate. Hence an ambulance soon took him to Hickory Hill in Hanover County, a home belonging to a relative of his wife.

Earlier, Rooney had given his loved ones quite a few sleepless nights. At age eight, with both parents away from home, he had climbed into a hayloft and experimented with a straw cutter. With it he managed to chop off a full and a partial joint from fingers of his left hand, leading his father to write that he would probably "be maimed for life."

He fell far short of his father's expectations when he went to Harvard and in 1857 quit school to become a second lieutenant in the U.S. Army. When Rooney married Charlotte Wickham in 1859, some members of the family silently worried about the fact that the two were distantly related. When Virginia seceded, he followed his father into the ranks of the state's military force. (Freeman, *Lee*, 1, 148–50, 196–98)

Though Rooney's Brandy Station wound was never considered to be critical and there was no evidence of gangrene, his mother plus his sisters Mildred and Agnes made plans to be with him while he was convalescing. Their planned journey having been described in Richmond newspapers, the three women reached Hickory Hill on Friday, June 12. Two weeks of relaxed tranquility vanished when Federal troops surrounded the place and called for Lee to surrender. Completely surprised, he offered no resistance and was hustled off to Fort Monroe at the southern tip of the Virginia peninsula.

After months of bitter fighting the capture of a Rebel general officer was so frequent an occurrence that it was taken almost casually—except by the proud force that effected it.

Confederate Gen. Simon Bolivar Buckner, taken at Fort Donelson early in 1862, was still at Fort Warren in Boston. Gen. M. Jeff Thompson was being held at Johnson's Island, despite Benjamin F. Butler's efforts to have him released on parole. (OR, 116, 350, 515)

Had he not been a son of Robert E. Lee, the June 26 capture of Rooney would not have had lasting news value. To many civilians, a June 27 call to arms by Mayor Joseph Mayo of Richmond was the chief news of the week. Officials in both capitals were concerned that Confederate Vice President Alexander H. Stephens was meddling by proposing to come to the Union capital to discuss the possibility of peace and to try to settle disputes about exchange of prisoners. (OR, 43, 74–76, 84)

Two days after Rooney was taken, Jefferson Davis voiced hope that stories that he heard about the capture were not accurate. On July 7 the commander of the Army of Northern Virginia wrote to his wife, expressing "great grief that Fitzhugh has been captured by the enemy." He was surprised, he said, that Yankees took him from his bed "& carried him off." (OR, 43, 76; Dowdey, *Wartime Papers*, 542)

Acting under orders from Gen. John A. Dix, Col. Samuel P. Spear of the 11th Pennsylvania Cavalry had led about one thousand men on a June 25 expedition along the Pamunkey River. Some members of the party having read in Richmond newspapers that several members of the Lee family would be at Hickory Hill, Spear sent a company to investigate. Men in blue soon found a wounded Rebel general, whom they mistakenly believed to be Robert E. Lee's nephew Fitz-Hugh, "recuperating at a farm house" and made him a prisoner. (OR, 43, 18–19; RR, 7, Doc #35, Doc #87)

By all odds one of the most straightforward incidents in a long and tangled hostage story, Rooney's imprisonment seemed at first to be routine in nature. When Special Order No. 160 was issued in Richmond by Gen. John H. Winder on July 4, the egg hit the fan, however. Seething at what

Benjamin Butler, satirized by Volck as playing Sancho Panza to Lincoln as Don Quixote, failed to win the release of M. Jeff Thompson from Johnson's Island.

they considered to be unjust execution by Burnside of men captured in Kentucky nearly four months earlier, Davis and his advisors had ordered Winder to take extraordinary steps. As a result, paragraph 7 of his special order directed Capt. T. P. Turner to stage a replay of the 1861 lottery held in Ligon Prison. Winder's terse directive simply told Turner "to select by lot from among the Federal captains now in his custody two of that number for execution [in retaliation for the Corbin and McGraw incident]." (OR, 119, 82)

On July 6, Turner notified Winder that

> In accordance with instructions contained in Special Orders No. 160, I have selected by lot from the entire number of Federal captains contained in this prison (not including two in hospital under medical treatment) two for execution, viz, Capt. Henry Washington Sawyer, Company K, First New Jersey Cavalry; Capt. John M. Flinn, Company F, Fifty-first Indiana Infantry.

A one-sentence referral from Winder to the secretary of war asked for "instructions as to time of execution." (OR, 119, 87)

Henry W. Halleck must have learned of the new lottery of death within hours after it took place. He presumably consulted Lincoln, then sent a July 15 dispatch to Col. William H. Ludlow at Fort Monroe saying that

> The President directs that you immediately place W. H. Lee and another officer selected by you, not below the rank of captain, prisoners of war, in close confinement and under strong guard; and that you notify Mr. R. Ould, confederate agent for exchange of prisoners of war, that if Captain H. W. Sawyer, First New-Jersey volunteer cavalry, and Captain John Flynn [whose name should have been listed as Flinn], Fifty-first Indiana volunteers, or any other officer or men in the service of the United States, not guilty of crimes punishable with death by the laws of war, shall be executed by the enemy, the afore-mentioned prisoners will be immediately hung in retaliation. It is also directed, that immediately on receiving official or other authentic information of the execution of Captain Sawyer and Captain Flynn, you will proceed to hang General Lee and the other rebel officer designated, as herein above directed.

Much the same thing was said in a July 16 dispatch to Ould in Richmond. (OR, 119, 1126; RR, 7, D, 25)

Halleck's dispatch added a bizarre postscript to the most massive cavalry encounter of the war at Brandy Station. Both Lee and Sawyer had been wounded there; now both of them were hostages. Gov. Oliver P. Morton of Indiana, who kept his ear close to the ground, had entered the imbroglio on July 11. He inquired of E. M. Stanton, Union secretary of war, whether it was correct that "Capt. John M. Flinn, of the Fifty-first Regiment Indiana Volunteers, a prisoner at Richmond, is to be executed in retaliation for a spy tried and executed by General Burnside." Not knowing that Halleck was ready to take decisive action, he added that "It would be deliberate murder if this threat is carried out, and I trust your Department will notify the rebel Government that if it is done strong retaliatory measures will be adopted." (OR, 119, 104)

On the same day that Morton wrote from Indianapolis, in Libby Prison the two Federal captains scheduled for execution appealed to Winder. They pointed out that they had been charged with no crime, and that they had "absolutely no connection with Burnsides's department of our army."

Somehow, they had discovered what they believed to be authentic information that two other Federal captains—N. T. Kendrick and D. E. Boharnace—were being held by Confederates in Atlanta "for the same persons we are held for." Hence they ended with a plea: "Innocent as we are of any offense against the rules of war, in the name of humanity we ask you if our lives are to be exacted for the alleged offense of other men in other departments of the army than that in which we served?" (OR, 119, 107)

There is no record that the two captains Sawyer and Flinn mentioned were being held in Atlanta, as they believed. But on May 22, Ould had notified Ludlow that "two captains now in our custody shall be selected for execution in retaliation" for Corbin and McGraw. Ludlow had promptly replied that "no deliveries [of prisoners of war] will be made to you under such threats." He then warned that "the United States Government will exercise their discretion in selecting such persons as they think best, whether officers or privates, for the purpose of counter retaliation." (OR, 118, 691, 702)

This exchange meant that cards were laid on the table long before Sawyer and Flinn were selected for execution. Once the two Federal captains were chosen to die, Washington did precisely what Ludlow had said; that is Rooney Lee and Capt. John H. Winder were selected as hostages in an effort to stop the cycle of retaliation. Capt. Robert H. Tyler of the 8th Virginia entered the controversy on October 6 by claiming that he had been selected as a hostage for Sawyer and Flinn. It took Col. William Hoffman a full month to notify Tyler that he was mistaken. (OR, 119, 58, 362, 488)

Robert E. Lee remained on the sideline throughout the angry sets of reprisals and exchanges of threats. He reputedly regarded Rooney's plight "as a dispensation of Providence," and took no steps designed to bring the hostage standoff to an end. Perhaps he was right to stay out of this fracas; on August 20, Ludlow notified Stanton that he was "satisfied" that Sawyer and Flinn would not be executed. At Fort Monroe, Rooney was so conspicuous that plans were made to send him to Johnson's Island, but they were canceled and he went to Fort Lafayette on November 13. Winder was the son of the Rebel provost marshal general, who was soon given oversight of all Confederate prisons. Federals gloated that their hostages were two of the officers "the Rebels want most badly." (Freeman, *Lee*, 3, 210–11; OR, 119, 219, 706)

Weeks passed with no negotiations that have been preserved. Then on February 8, 1864, Gen. Benjamin F. Butler received word at Fort Monroe that Rebels might be willing to exchange Gen. Neal Dow plus Sawyer and Flinn for "General Lee and two officers of the grade of captain." Tyler somehow knew what was taking place and immediately suggested that since he had been held for Sawyer and Flinn, he should be chosen to take part in the exchange. Tyler, who had earlier interjected himself into the intricate set of discussions, successfully managed to take the place of Winder. Butler was told to select a third captive who, with Lee and Tyler, would be exchanged for Dow, Sawyer, and Flinn. (OR, 119, 227, 975–76, 991)

Rooney was promoted soon after a formal agreement had been reached. When he walked out of Fort Lafayette the ex-hostage was the youngest major general in Confederate service. (GG, 184; Enc., 411)

Part VI

Prominent Men Were Deeply Involved

28

Former Minister to France

Charles J. Faulkner of Martinsburg, Virginia (now West Virginia) was the most distinguished diplomat to be caught in the middle of a complex hostage situation. After a long career as an attorney, Virginia legislator and congressman, in 1859 he went to France as U.S. minister. Doubtless the man from the Old Dominion thought a great deal about Thomas Jefferson, who earlier filled the same post for four years. Benjamin Franklin's role as a diplomat, in which negotiations with France were central, must have been pondered at length by Faulkner as he journeyed to his embassy.

Since he went to France during the administration of James Buchanan, he was replaced when Abraham Lincoln took office. Faulkner and his family remained in Europe long enough for his successor to arrive, then he headed to Washington in order to submit his final report. Though he had watched the growing intensity of the American sectional quarrel from a distance of three thousand miles, the Martinsburg native was not prepared for what he found when he reached the nation's capital. Suspicion dominated the time and energy of many office holders; secret police and informers swarmed throughout the capital.

Faulkner was arrested about two weeks after the battle of Bull Run by order of Simon Cameron, the secretary of war who controlled Pennsylvania's political machine. No charges were preferred and no explanation was offered. A letter of inquiry to the War Department was not answered, and he was soon transferred to the custody of the State Department. Five weeks after he was jailed, the former ambassador wrote to William H. Seward and said he had been officially informed that he was being held as a hostage for a man of whom he had never before heard—Henry S. Magraw. (OR, 115, 466, 470)

Magraw, he learned much later, was a Pennsylvania citizen who had been picked up by Rebels in the aftermath of Bull Run. In company with an old acquaintance, Arnold Harris of Kentucky, he had gone to the site of the

OUR NATIONAL BIRD AS IT APPEARED WHEN | THE IDENTICAL BIRD AS IT APPEARED A .D. 1861.
HANDED TO JAMES BUCHANAN MARCH 4 1857 |

President James Buchanan, who sent Faulkner to France, was widely ridiculed because he did not launch military action to stop secession. Note that the 1861 national bird has a wooden leg, "secession," plus a shoe, "anarchy."

battle to search for the body of Col. James Cameron, brother of Simon, who was known to have died at Bull Run. Col. J. E. B. Stuart arrested both men on suspicion and referred their case to Gen. Joseph E. Johnston.

Johnston, who seems to have known Harris, was aware that Jefferson Davis was acquainted with him. Possibly for that reason Johnston accepted the explanation that Harris and Magraw went to the battlefield without a flag of truce because Federal authorities forbade its use in such cases. Should the two men be permitted to leave Richmond, Johnston suggested, "The sea furnishes their best route." Though Harris had provided him with late and accurate information about Federal forces, Stuart objected to honoring any request made by the men he had seized. Consequently, their case was referred to the Confederate War Department. (OR, 2,995)

By July 31, both Harris and Magraw were jailed in Richmond. There they seem to have made the acquaintance of Congressman Alfred Ely of New York, who had also been arrested on the Bull Run battlefield. Ely did not know that he would later be a central actor in the Ligon Prison drama during which Rebels picked hostages for their imprisoned privateersmen. (OR, 115, 38)

Negotiations concerning Harris and Magraw got under way nearly two weeks before Faulkner was arrested in Washington. Several influential Rebels, among whom Reverdy W. Johnson was included, vouched for the Southern sentiments of Harris and requested that he be released.

Characterizing him as "no enemy to this Government," a group of five men offered to take him into their custody and said they would personally pledge that he would appear before War Department officials to face charges. (OR, 115, 1515–17)

By this time Magraw had confessed that he had a transportation contract with the Union government. In the eyes of Richmond, that made him guilty of treason since he had been apprehended behind Rebel lines. Ironically, his contract had been "extended and modified" in the spring of 1861 by none other than Joseph E. Johnston, who had been quartermaster of the Union army until his resignation on April 22. To the prisoner, it seemed self-evident that his Pennsylvania background accounted for his apparent close ties with the Union secretary of war. (OR, 115, 1516, D, 441a)

Rebel leaders did not consider Magraw's relationship with the Union government to be tenuous, however. Their reservations concerning Harris would have been strengthened had they known that Federals would later list the arrest of the Kentuckian—along with the apprehension of Ely and Faulkner—among the principal events of the summer.

Harris was also believed to be a contractor doing business with Washington. Hence his inquisitors thought that his relations with Magraw must have been close. What's more, the two contractors were at Bull Run in search of the body of the brother of Simon Cameron. Many Rebels felt that, next to Lincoln, the secretary of war was most to blame for having "sought their destruction" by launching an invasion of the Old Dominion. (OR, 115, 1, 1518)

Confederate Secretary of War L. P. Walker, who was still seething over the invasion of Virginia, explained to Davis why he was unwilling to release Harris. Walker refused to believe the prisoner's protestations that he did not have "one cent's interest in any contract with that [Federal] Government." Consequently, Walker considered him guilty of having violated "the usages of civilized warfare."

Harris responded to accusations by saying that he did not leave Washington until 24 hours after the battle of Bull Run ended. In agreeing to go with Magraw to seek the body of the slain Federal colonel, he believed he was on a humane mission and had "no intention to violate any of the usages of civilized warfare." Despite their vehemence, his personal protestations probably had far less weight than a letter that was addressed to Davis from Lexington, Kentucky.

John C. Breckinridge, a staunch Confederate who had been an 1860 nominee for the presidency of the United States, on August 18 summarized a conversation with Harris that was held in the aftermath of Bull Run. He said he knew nothing about "the enterprise for the recovery of Colonel Cameron's body." But, wrote Breckinridge in conclusion, "I think Mr. Harris was regarded in Washington as decidedly Southern in his views and sympathies." (OR, 115, 1521–22, 1524)

Whether or not the Breckinridge document tipped the scales in favor of releasing Harris is unknown. In late October, however, he was a free man and was in the city of Nashville. From that point he urged "instant reenforcement" of Gen. Felix Zollicoffer, who was trying to win Kentucky for the Confederacy. Officially neutral, the state was invaded by Rebel forces and its Unionists were recipients of large shipments of weapons from Washington.

Unable to write because of a crippled hand, Harris used the services of George N. Sanders in Nashville. Through him, the one-time prisoner suspected of having strong ties with Washington urged immediate large-scale operations in Kentucky by Confederates. He wanted at least five thousand men sent to Zollicoffer, who was later killed in the battle of Mill Springs. (OR, 115, 1524)

Faulkner was not aware that Gen. James Mansfield had accused him of having read on February 15 a letter from James M. Mason, then a member of the Virginia senate. Seward was alarmed at this news, but wanted confirmation. At his request William Chase Barney, identified simply as "a citizen of the United States," gave a deposition in Mansfield's office. According to Barney, Mason's letter urged Faulkner not to leave Paris for any reason. The Virginia lawmaker's communication was said to have informed Faulkner that the Old Dominion "would take possession of the city of Washington" on the night of March 3, 1861. To make matters worse, swore Barney, Faulkner's son had distributed secession cockades in and around the embassy.

Faulkner also did not know that two men whose names he might or might not have recognized had discussed him in New York in Astor House on August 19. One of the men was a Major Townsend of the state guard; the other was N. S. Dodge, who was associated with the Copake Iron Works in Columbia County, New York.

Dodge seems to have been a self-appointed whistle-blower or a person who had a grudge against Faulkner. After his talk with Townsend he branded the man sent to Paris by James Buchanan as a known secessionist "of the most violent character." According to him, Faulkner had turned the embassy in the French capital into "the rendezvous of all the most violent of the traitors."

The Virginia-based diplomat, said Dodge, was on intimate terms with French ministers and members of the senate and had persuaded them to express sympathy "in favor of the seceding States." Less than four weeks before writing to Seward, urged the New Yorker, a French official persuaded Col. Enrico Fardilla "to enlist at the South."

Seward apparently did not inquire about Fardilla, so was not aware that he did not cross the ocean to fight with the Confederacy. In an atmosphere of extreme tension, the Union secretary of state apparently took gossip relayed by a Federal officer and a New York resident at face value.

Gen. Felix Zollicoffer, who was trying to win Kentucky for the Confederacy, was killed at Perryville, and the state never seceded.
Frank Leslie's Illustrated Weekly

Hence he passed the Dodge letter along to the War Department and on the strength of accusations in it Faulkner was made a prisoner. (OR, 115, 465)

Though Washington clearly wanted Henry S. Magraw released in Richmond, Federal records fail to indicate that Faulkner was for a time treated as a hostage for the Pennsylvania contractor. His detention was reported in the capital's *National Intelligencer*, but no one bothered to refute or to deny repeated charges by the ex-minister that he was in jail as Magraw's counterpart. Unaware of Grant's activities in Missouri, he mistakenly believed himself to be the only hostage then held in the North or in the South. (OR, 115, 470)

In September, Mrs. Faulkner addressed a plea to Seward. Not knowing that her husband had been forwarded to Fort Lafayette, she demanded: "Why is he detained in Washington when he went there upon business with the Government feeling it his duty to give an account of his ministerial duties while at the court of France?" She assumed that the secretary of state "could not refuse to give information," but she eventually learned that her letter and most of those written by her husband got no reply. (OR, 115, 467)

The release of Harris left the case of his one-trip companion, Magraw, unresolved. Faulkner, who was a prisoner of Federals, was in the same state of limbo. From Fort Lafayette the former ambassador prevailed upon Capt. George L. Willard to deliver to Seward a lengthy memorandum of complaint. Rigors of close confinement and the denial of an opportunity to exercise, urged Faulkner, had caused his system to be "most painfully and injuriously affected." In September he was transferred from Fort Lafayette to Fort Hamilton, New York.

Almost simultaneously, Reverdy Johnson appealed to Judah P. Benjamin on behalf of Magraw. His motive in visiting the battlefield "was a humane one and however technically considered he may have rendered himself liable to arrest his is not a case for extreme rigor," Johnson urged. He also told the acting Confederate secretary of state that he was positive "that if Magraw was discharged I could at once procure the discharge of Faulkner."

This linking of the two men strongly suggests that Johnson knew that Faulkner really was hostage for Magraw. Benjamin notified Johnson that with the consent of Davis, the release of Magraw would come as soon as an especially appointed commissioner reported on the case. Formal arrangements by which he was exchanged for Cuthbert Lowe, a.k.a. Edward B. Cuthbert—about whom little is known—were perfected in May 1862. Cuthbert swore he would remain in New York City on parole until exchanged for Magraw. (OR, 115, 476–77; OR, 116, 508, 597)

Still insisting that he had not been charged with any offense, Faulkner wrote that in his many years as an attorney he had observed prison discipline closely. Even men convicted of capital offenses, he said, were seldom subjected "to a more rigid and vigilant surveillance than I have been since my arrest." He partly described the situation in which he had now placed by saying that

> The unceasing tread of armed sentinels around my door and windows leaves me not a moment in the twenty-four hours to indulge the delusion that I was born in a land of freedom, and this surveillance is observed toward a man who although imprisoned one month and the Government repeatedly called upon has not avowed to him or to the public that it has against him the shadow of a ground of accusation or complaint. (OR, 115, 468, 475–76)

Seward, to whom this plaintive letter went, broke his silence by a one-sentence order. In it he authorized Col. Martin Burke at Fort Hamilton "to allow to the Hon. Mr. Faulkner such indulgence as to air and exercise as shall be compatible with his safe-keeping and the construction and regulations of the place in which he is detained."

In a separate dispatch to Burke the secretary of state explained that his new inmate was a political prisoner "upon the ground that the authorities acting in the State of Virginia which he is understood to acknowledge and obey have inaugurated and are prosecuting by force of arms a treasonable insurrection for the overthrow of the Federal Government and the dissolution of the Union." Faulkner, he wrote, could gain his freedom "by taking and subscribing an explicit oath of allegiance to the United States excluding all express or implied reservations." (OR, 115, 469)

Though he said nothing about consequences of such an oath to a Virginian, Seward could not have failed to know what they were. Had he taken the prescribed vow, the prisoner would be turned loose but he would lose all of his property and could not return to Virginia. Statutes already in place categorized residents of the Old Dominion who espoused the Union cause as alien enemies whose entire holdings were subject to confiscation. From newspaper stories Faulkner gained a trifle of hope by reading announcements about "the probability of the speedy return of Mr. Magraw [to Washington]." (OR, 115, 471)

G. V. Lott, a son-in-law of Faulkner, secured a permit from the Department of State and made the long trip to New York in order to have a brief visit with the ex-minister. Burke, who was in command at Fort Hamilton, immediately asked Seward for specific instructions. Noting that he had often permitted "two and sometimes three interviews" to a person with a permit, he wanted to know whether Lott was entitled to other visits. Though he generally ignored Faulkner's long letters, Seward immediately replied to Burke that "No permit entitles the person to whom it was granted to more than one visit." New York resident Richard Schell applied for a permit to visit the distinguished prisoner, but did not get it. (OR, 115, 471–72)

In a lengthy and argumentative message dated September 25, Faulkner told Seward that he assumed the State Department was no longer holding him as a hostage for Magraw. He had been arrested, he charged, upon "vague understandings, beliefs, and expectations" about his personal opinions and his future conduct. Surreptitious circulation of classified material would not be called "leaking" until several generations passed. Yet in 1861 the former diplomat denounced policies that permitted journalists to print details about his situation before it was resolved. He then penned refutations of charges that he had ever "obeyed the authorities now acting in Virginia."

In what was perhaps the most vivid of numerous forceful passages from his pen while imprisoned, he roundly denounced the offer of freedom in exchange for an oath of allegiance. Of this practice, which he knew was widely followed, Faulkner wrote that

> It purposes to rivet patriotism upon me by fetters and to grind loyalty into me by the horrors of the prison. It seeks to anticipate the regular conclusions of my own reason and judgment and to make me a patriot by the potent process of the dungeon.

Gen. John Henry Winder, a West Point graduate, was heavily involved with hostages and other prisoners as Confederate provost marshal general.

Saying that he could not accept such a proposal, he roared in writing that "Arbitrary power and brute force have given you control over my body but you can exercise none over the mind." (OR, 115, 472–76)

Soon Faulkner discovered that a number of men who preceded him at Fort Warren had been released on paroles of honor. Operation of a parole varied considerably, and in the case of a civilian political prisoner usually involved his pledge to accomplish a given task or return to prison. He informed Burke that he was interested in investigating a parole for the sake of his family, but Burke had no authority to act. (OR, 115, 477–787)

Months after his arrest—a period that to Faulkner seemed much longer—he learned from newspapers that friends of Congressman Alfred Ely were besieging Lincoln with memorials. The former minister to France contacted a member of the New York delegation to Congress, asking him to submit to Lincoln his self-framed proposal to the effect that

> I will give my parole of honor with any other security deemed necessary by the Secretary of State, if permitted to proceed on to Richmond, that I will in a time to be prescribed by the Secretary of State restore Mr. Ely to his seat in Congress or deliver myself to the order of the Government in Washington City. (OR, 115, 478–79)

Acting for the president, Seward accepted the Faulkner proposal and sent him what he called a "passport enabling him to pass through the lines of the Union Army." Despite the fact that the secretary of state never said so, many clues suggest that he was delighted to get the former ambassador to France off his hands without suffering more embarrassment over the case. Though the term "hostage" was not used in the correspondence involved, for practical purposes this meant that Faulkner had now become hostage for the congressman from New York whose capture was made a few days earlier than his own. (Randall, *Constitutional*, 157)

Compilers of the *Official Records* inserted a footnote, perhaps with relief of their own at getting a lengthy and complex matter off their hands, at the end of their 16-page section on "Case of Charles J. Faulkner." They pointed out that "The exchange of Faulkner for Ely was subsequently effected, but no official statement of the fact can be found." (OR, 115, 479)

A lengthy account of Ely's imprisonment appeared, however, in the *New York Times* when he was released after 10 months in Libby Prison. According to it, when Faulkner reached Richmond 30,000 persons turned out to greet the ex-diplomat who had been held hostage for two men he had never seen. He spent an hour with Davis and the Confederate cabinet, then went to the prison to meet Ely.

"They had a pleasant interview" and on the following day Gen. John H. Winder appeared in order to present his release to the New York Congressman. Winder stayed only a short time, after which the Prison Association of which Ely was president convened and he "made a farewell address of nearly an hour in length."

About 5:00 P.M. Faulkner returned to the prison in the carriage of Gov. John Letcher. The two former prisoners soon "proceeded to the Governor's mansion, where they dined together, and parted with a mutual expression of personal good feeling." (RR, 3, Doc. #239)

29

Both Presidents Were Targeted

Union Col. Robert M. West, commanding at Fort Magruder, Virginia, conceived a daring scheme that ballooned in size as it was planned. Writing to Gen. I. J. Wistar at Yorktown on November 24, 1863, he began by stressing the plight "of our suffering soldiers in the Richmond prisons." In order to rescue them, he proposed a surprise strike against Richmond. Having contemplated such a scheme for more than a year, he had made a careful assessment of Rebel strength and reported that the aggregate force between Fort Magruder and the Confederate capital was only 1,367 men.

West urged that Federal cavalry should reach Bottom's Bridge, about ten miles from Richmond, no later than 3:00 A.M. on the night of the raid. Pointing out that "the exact locations of the prisons and prisoners are accurately known," he suggested that once men were freed they could be armed from Richmond's arsenal and aid the raiders.

"The garrison of Richmond at present is of the most ineffective troops of the so-called Confederacy," he wrote. Though he indicated willingness to command such an expedition, he realized that men of higher rank and greater prestige were available. Regardless of who might be selected to lead the raid, he urged, "Not one moment should be lost." (OR, 107, 123–24)

At Yorktown, Wistar was instantly and keenly interested in the proposal. He immediately transmitted the West plan to Butler, who was in command of the Department of Virginia and North Carolina. "I believe the plan entirely feasible, and would rejoice to assume the responsibility and conduct of the enterprise," he wrote. Almost as an afterthought, he added the first embellishment to the scheme developed at Fort Magruder:

> At the moment of entering Richmond, parties of picked men, selected from exchanged prisoners and others locally acquainted, might be detached to fire public buildings, including, if possible the Tredegar Iron Works. (OR, 107, 1282)

Richmond's Tredegar Iron Works constituted a valid and a very important reason Union officials wanted the city burned.

Library of Congress

By February 4, Butler had given his wholehearted approval to the proposed raid, and had amplified its objectives. He first agreed that it was highly desirable to free imprisoned officers and men "who must otherwise, it seems to me, of necessity be starved." Secondly, to the list of facilities to be destroyed he added "public buildings, arsenals, depots, railroad equipage, and commissary stores." His third objective, which had not entered into earlier correspondence, employed rather vague language:

> Third. To capture some of the leaders of the rebellion, so that at least we can have a means to meet their constant threats of retaliation and hanging of our men, white and black. If any of the more prominent can be brought off I believe a blow will be given to the rebellion from which it will never recover.

Almost as an afterthought, he proposed that Wistar should have a designated second in command who could take over if he should be "disabled by shell explosion or accident." Not until he wrote his personal memoirs many years later did the man whom Rebels called Beast indicate that veiled language of his third objective was meant to conceal his goal of taking Jefferson Davis as a hostage. (OR, 107, 1285–86)

Wistar instantly responded with gratitude for the opportunity to lead the raid. On the following evening, he told Butler, he would meet his two infantry commanders at Williamsburg and "go with them, map in hand, over every detail and every contingency." Every possible contingency had been considered, he said, so he had "no misgivings whatever." Some of his infantry would be on the move by 10:00 P.M. on Friday in order to be at their objective by 9:00 P.M. the following evening. He expected to "surprise Bottom's

Bridge" at 2:00 A.M., and to enter Richmond only three hours later. (OR, 107, 1286–87)

On February 5, Butler decided to brief the secretary of war about the contemplated raid. He sent a deciphered letter from Richmond's Union spy, Elizabeth Van Lew, in which she reported that Federal prisoners in the Confederate capital would soon be sent to Georgia. That being the case, he wrote, "Now, or never, is the time to strike." Wistar would lead a combined force of six thousand infantry and cavalry, he said after complaining that he could get no cooperation from Gen. John Sedgwick. From the beginning, he had counted on men under Sedgwick to create a diversion that would draw the attention of Rebels away from Richmond on the designated night. (OR, 60, 519)

Wistar issued detailed orders to his troops on the same day. Every man would carry six days' rations in his knapsack, and would be equipped with 70 cartridges instead of the standard 40. Men of the 11th Pennsylvania Cavalry were instructed to destroy the navy yard at Richmond. Their comrades of the 3rd New York were told to "attend to the Libby Prison and other public buildings." After having completed these tasks, its members were to dash to Belle Isle and liberate enlisted men who were imprisoned there. Col. Benjamin F. Onderdonk was told to take 250 men of the 1st New York Mounted Rifles and destroy both the Central Railroad depot and the

"The White House of the Confederacy," where Jefferson Davis and his family lived, was carefully pinpointed for Federal raiders.

Fredericksburg Railroad depot, "being careful to cut the telegraph the first thing."

Maj. James M. Wheelan of the same unit was entrusted with the most important aspect of the raid. With three hundred men of the 1st New York Mounted Rifles, he was told to turn right at 12th Street "and capture Jeff. Davis at his residence, corner Twelfth and Marshall streets."

Men of the 5th Pennsylvania were instructed to cooperate in the attack on Belle Island and then to "destroy the Tredegar Iron-Works and numerous public buildings, factories, and store-houses adjacent." Col. S. P. Spear, in command of the cavalry brigade, was told to take members of the 11th Pennsylvania to Capitol square in order to serve as a reserve to support the various detachments. All of them except Wheelan's were to report to Spear after completing their missions. Wheelan's men—with the president of the Confederate States as a prisoner—were told to take a back road to Bottom's Bridge and there join the infantry column stationed at that point. Wistar's orders ended by noting that all detachments would "be safe in Richmond for about three hours." During their return to their base, they could expect to be "menaced by the troops from Chaffin's farm," he added. (OR, 60, 146, 521–22)

Instead of reaching an undefended Bottom's Bridge as they had expected, raiders "found the enemy there in strong force, with infantry, cavalry, and artillery." Planks that formed the floor of the bridge had been removed, and two nearby fords known to the Federals had been closed with trees. To make things worse, "extensive earth-works and rifle-pits" had been constructed at the crucial crossing point. Men led by Spear said they counted four batteries of field artillery plus one heavy gun at Bottom's Bridge. (OR, 60, 147)

Butler and Wistar were badly disappointed at the surprise reception their forces had received. Wistar expressed his deep regret in February, and without mentioning the Confederate president by name confessed that Rebels at Bottom's Bridge had caused "the entire defeat of the real object" of the raid. Both men were sure that the raid had failed because of a leak somewhere. When Butler received a Richmond newspaper issued on the day after the failed raid, he informed the secretary of war that it said:

> Some days since a report was obtained by the authorities here from a Yankee deserter that the enemy was contemplating a raid in considerable force on Richmond. The report obtained consistency from a number of circumstances, and impressed the authorities to such a degree that a disposition of forces was made to anticipate the supposed designs of the enemy.

Having identified "conveyance of intelligence" as have caused "want of success" of the raid, Butler could not refrain from adding a self-congratulatory note. "Everything else succeeded as well as desired," he wrote concerning the raid that accomplished absolutely nothing. (OR, 60, 144)

Wistar soon briefed Butler concerning the intelligence leak. Pvt. William Boyle of the New York Mounted Rifles had been under sentence of death for murder, he reported. Precisely four days before the start of the raid, Boyle's sentinel had allowed him to escape. His life having been saved, the condemned man deserted and fled to Richmond where he was placed in Castle Thunder. There, he obviously told Rebels everything he knew about the upcoming operation.

"Boyle would have been hung long ago," Wistar noted, "but for the President's order suspending till further orders the execution of capital sentences." Butler's reaction was to fire off a telegram directed to Lincoln in which he blamed executive clemency for the failure of the raid. "I desire that you will revoke your order suspending executions in this department," he concluded. "Please answer by telegraph." There is no record that the president responded to Butler's demand, but on the day the military commander's telegram was received he suspended the execution of James Taylor. Two days later he pardoned deserter Robert Johnson and commuted the death sentence of Dennis McCarty to five years at hard labor. (OR, 60, 144; AL, 7, 172–75)

Sedgwick, who had grudgingly agreed to arrange a diversion, reported about it to Halleck on February 7. He suffered about two hundred casualties at Morton's Ford, while taking 60 prisoners and still had troops moving on Winchester. Then he put what he considered the most important part of his report into a single stinging sentence: "One result of the

"Outbreak of the Rebellion," an 1861 lithograph, helped to launch the process by which the real Abraham Lincoln became shrouded in myth.

co-operation with General Butler has been to prove that it has spoilt the best chance we had for a successful attack on the Rapidan [River]." There is no certainty that Sedgwick learned then or later that his diversion had been intended to make possible the seizure of Jefferson Davis as a hostage. (OR, 60, 532)

Forces under the command of Wistar, who had expected them to spend about three hours in the Rebel capital, never came within 10 miles of the chief executive wanted by Butler as a hostage. In Washington, the man who was already stalking Lincoln was sometimes close enough to him to have shouted a threat if he had wished to do so.

John Wilkes Booth is believed to have consulted Confederate agents in several states and Canada before perfecting a plan to make a hostage of the chief executive. About six months after Butler's men failed to take Davis, Booth was making preparations to seize Lincoln and spirit him into Confederate territory. His hostage, reasoned the actor, would give him leverage by which to secure the release of Confederate officers and men who were scattered from Camp Douglas at Chicago to Johnson's Island in Ohio and notorious Fort Delaware on the Delaware River.

To help him in capturing the chief executive, Booth is believed initially to have enlisted Samuel B. Arnold and Michael O'Laughlin as co-conspirators. Because he planned to take his hostage across the Potomac River and then to cross into the heavily prosecessionist portion of Maryland, he needed someone who knew the countryside well. George A. Atzerodt, who habitually identified himself as a resident of Maryland's Port Tobacco, seemed just the right man to serve as guide.

John H. Surratt, Lewis Paine, and David E. Herold seem to have been brought into the plot before all details about it were settled. Except for these Washington associates, Booth probably took no one except his brother into his confidence. In a lengthy letter to his brother, the chief conspirator lauded the Confederacy and said that he planned "to make for her a prisoner of this man to whom she owes so much misery." (Donald, *Lincoln*, 586–87)

His initial idea may have been to seize his hostage by means of a dramatic move that would produce headlines from every newspaper editor in the country. Samuel Arnold had apparently agreed to climb upon the stage and hold out his arms to receive the president as he was lowered from his box. After consideration, Booth decided that it would be impracticable to take his hostage in front of hundreds of spectators before riding off in the night with him. (Weichmann, *True History*, 60–61)

A clandestine meeting took place at the Lichau House on Pennsylvania Avenue on or about April 1, 1865. With four or five of his subordinates on hand, Booth explained that their purpose was "to abduct or kidnap the President and take him South for the purpose of making the Union Government have an exchange of prisoners." According to one of Mrs. Mary Surratt's boarders, the conspirators had secured a flat-bottomed boat with which

Widely admired before the assassination, dapper John Wilkes Booth was immediately portrayed as having been a tool of the devil.

J. L. Magee print, 1865

they expected to ferry their hostage across the Potomac River. (Weichmann, *True History*, 38–87, 61)

Seizure at Ford's Theatre having been discarded as impracticable, Booth and his aides decided to concentrate on the president's frequent visits to the Soldiers' Home in the outskirts of the capital. Soon they learned that on March 17 he would attend an afternoon performance of *Still Waters Run Deep* at Campbell Hospital, adjacent to the Soldiers' Home. Booth reputedly showed up at the improvised theater that afternoon, learned from actor E. L. Davenport that Lincoln was not a spectator, and stamped off in a rage.

About 4:00 P.M. on the fateful afternoon the president was at the National Hotel, where he presented to Gov. Oliver P. Morton of Indiana a flag captured at Fort Anderson, North Carolina, by men of the 140th Indiana. After this ceremony, the theater lover who had missed a performance he was scheduled to attend made a speech to assembled men of the Hoosier regiment. Some sources suggest that men of the 140th Indiana then staged a review for the president and their governor. (Miers, *Lincoln Day by Day*, 3, 321; Donald, *Lincoln*, 588)

A significant body of evidence indicates that the actor had toyed with the notion of assassination well before his kidnap scheme was foiled by an unexpected change in the president's schedule. Once he realized that it would be difficult or impossible to make a hostage of the chief executive, he seems to have turned with relish to the alternative of shooting him.

Both Jefferson Davis and Abraham Lincoln were targets of would-be hostage takers whose schemes failed, but the end results of these efforts were quite different. It may be news to some readers that a few months after Butler's raid fizzled, Davis—still hale and hearty despite defeat of the Army of Northern Virginia—fled southward from fallen Richmond. All the world knows what John Wilkes Booth did when his scheme to make a hostage of Abraham Lincoln fell apart.

30

A Cadaver as a Hostage

Big Jim Kinealy had indicated that he was about ready for his subordinates to take the train from Chicago to Springfield to pull off the biggest
job of his career. Before he gave final approval, however, through Terrence
Mullens he told Lewis Swegles to get down to the Cook County Courthouse.
"We don't make a move until we know the penalty," he explained. This decision, along with excruciatingly detailed accounts of "the Kinealy scheme,"
was later reported in voluminous contemporary accounts. Scores of stories
were published in the *Chicago Tribune, Chicago Times, New York Times,
New York World*, and other newspapers.

None of them dealt with underlying factors that made counterfeiting
easy and profitable during the last months of the Civil War and the decade
after it ended. Faced with the fact that there was not enough gold and silver
in North America to redeem paper currency needed for the Union's war
effort, Abraham Lincoln and his advisors turned to nonredeemable paper.
Because green ink was used to print one side of these novel mediums of
exchange, they were quickly dubbed "greenbacks"—a wartime term that is
still widely used.

Even in big centers such as New York City, equipment and ink used to
produce greenbacks did not always get absolutely uniform results. A fellow
who was handed his first greenback had no way of discriminating between
it and a bogus piece that to him looked exactly like it. These factors plus
huge quantities of war-born currency put into circulation created a field
day for counterfeiters. Kinealy seems to have started a major wholesale
operation in bogus bills almost as soon as the first greenbacks entered circulation in 1862.

Described as cunning and as shrewd—both terms apparently being
appropriate—the wholesale dealer in "queer," or counterfeit currency,
stayed away from personal contact with shovers whose job it was to make
passes. Kinealy figured that least was best when it came to knowledge

about operations in which dozens or scores of persons used bogus bills to make small purchases that generated a flow of genuine currency in change. Seldom having had a brush with the law, he did not want one. By relaying orders and receiving information through Mullens and others, he believed he would be shielded if anything went wrong with the most ambitious scheme he had ever devised.

With a big grin on his face, Swegles returned to The Hub, a popular saloon operated by Mullens in which Kinealy was a silent partner. He began by saying what his new boss already knew—medical schools were growing fast and were always in need of cadavers in which there was no legal market. Illinois had not modified some of its laws in years, so the most a fellow could get for grave robbing was a stay in jail and a small fine, Swegles explained. Some judges in the state did not like to bother with these petty cases and got them out of the way in a hurry. Consequently, resurrection men were busy all over Illinois except around Chicago. One of these fellows was caught from time to time, but juries who heard such cases hardly ever went for the maximum sentence.

This important matter out of the way, Big Jim focused his attention on the best way to prove he had the merchandise when he offered to exchange his hostage. He may have thought about one of the little foreign-language newspapers published in the city where Lincoln was nominated for the presidency in 1860, or an underling may have suggested using it. Whatever the exact sequence of events, he got his hands on a back issue, calculating that it would carry more weight than one just off the press.

He tore the paper into a dozen or more pieces, planning to have some segments left at the empty vault in Springfield and then use the rest to prove that his men had stolen the body of Abraham Lincoln. With the remains of the Union's Civil War commander in chief in his clutches, Kinealy figured that it would be easy to arrange a swap. After the release from prison in Joliet of his best engraver, Ben Boyd, he would turn Lincoln's body back over to the state.

It's highly unlikely that the man who supplied counterfeit gangs in several major cities with their merchandise knew that hostage taking played a major role in the Civil War. He could not have failed, however, to know at least a little about the assassination, funeral, and burial of Lincoln. Practically every adult in the nation had seen the funeral train or knew someone who viewed it or had seen pictures about the slow procession from Washington to Springfield a little more than a decade earlier.

Felled on Good Friday by a single bullet from a little derringer held by John Wilkes Booth, Lincoln had been eulogized in the pulpits of the North on Easter. Kinealy did not remember all of the details about subsequent events, but he had a fuzzy notion that for some reason the body of the dead president was moved to the White House instead of one of Washington's churches.

That recollection on the part of the master counterfeiter was correct; the remains of the man John Wilkes Booth initially planned to seize as a hostage for imprisoned Confederates were taken to the White House to be embalmed. On Tuesday, April 18, the body was dressed in the suit worn for the president's second inauguration. Then it was laid in an open cedar casket that was placed upon a catafalque in the East Room. Dr. Phineas D. Gurley delivered a funeral oration on the following day during a ceremony marked by the absence of Mary Todd Lincoln.

About the middle of the afternoon on Tuesday, the casket and the body were taken to the Capitol so members of the public could view the remains until Thursday evening. By the time disappointed persons at the tail ends of long lines of mourners saw that they would not make it inside the Capitol, the grieving widow had arranged for the body of their son Willie (William Wallace) to be dug up. Probably a victim of typhoid fever contracted from drinking Potomac River water piped into the White House, Willie had died in 1862. After a funeral service conducted by Gurley he had been buried in Georgetown's Oak Hill Cemetery. It would be fitting for him to "go home" with his father, Lincoln's widow had decided.

Edwin M. Stanton planned the route along which a special funeral train would go in order to take the president and his son back to Springfield. The train left Washington early on the morning of Friday, April 21, and went directly to Baltimore for a stop of several hours. In general following the path taken by Lincoln when he went to the capital from Springfield early in 1861, the train stopped numerous times before reaching its destination on Thursday morning, May 4.

Soon the casket, which had remained open for viewing, was closed and wrapped in lead. Then, Lincoln and Willie were taken about two miles from the heart of Springfield to tranquil Oak Ridge Cemetery. Methodist Bishop Matthew Simpson delivered still another oration, and the remains of the slain chief executive were temporarily stored in a vault. By the time Kinealy and his underlings thought of using the corpse as leverage to free a jailed engraver, the body had been moved within the cemetery several times.

Public hysteria over the assassination had waned by 1876, but veneration of the first martyred president had increased steadily. To the gang planning a body snatching, that meant they might be able to get a bundle of cash in addition to a pardon for Boyd. They figured that the corpse of Lincoln was maybe the most valued thing in the entire state of Illinois.

By the time his plan was beginning to take final shape, Kinealy saw to it that several men were involved. Herbert Nelson, a habitual purchaser from Kinealy who sold big batches of queer to dealers who dispersed them among shovers, was a natural. So was Jack Hughes, a professional who had spent his adult life shoving counterfeit currency. Lewis Swegles was a newcomer to Chicago who boasted of his exploits in thwarting the law. He

Standing on a catafalque that held the coffin, the Reverend Dr. Henry Ward Beecher paid oratorical tribute to Lincoln on April 19, 1865.

Lincoln's funeral procession on Pennsylvania Avenue.

Carried across the Hudson River by ferry, Lincoln's coffin moved in a solemn procession to the city hall in New York City.

successfully concealed from the gang the fact that he was a roper for the U.S. Secret Service who would now be called an informer or a source.

Swegeles had been told to infiltrate the band of counterfeiters because an earlier unsuccessful attempt to steal Lincoln's body had made Robert Todd Lincoln extremely jittery. The word on the streets of Chicago was that something very big was in the making and that counterfeiters were at the heart of it. Destined later to become U.S. Secretary of War and president of the Pullman Palace Car Co., the president's son enlisted the aid of John T. Stuart, one of his father's former law partners. Together they persuaded Elmer T. Washburne of the U.S. Secret Service that every possible step should be taken to protect the resting place of the Civil War president. News of the Kinealy plot justified and amplified all of the fears harbored by Lincoln's son.

Swegles, who regularly informed the Secret Service of what was going on, made a convincing case to counterfeiters for the need of a fellow who had handled horses all his life. A wagon would have to be used for the get-away, and someone who knew animals well should be the driver, he pointed out. This brought into the operation a detective on the Federal payroll, Billy Brown. He swore he would have a pair of the fastest horses in the state hitched to a light wagon modeled after a Civil War ambulance that would be able to outrun police in the unlikely event that they should give chase. In case of a clean getaway, Brown would drive leisurely into the sand dunes of Indiana and bury the body there.

Mullens, Hughes, Nelson, and Swegles should be able to handle the job of breaking into the cavernous stone building called a monument and the casket it protected. Brown would take his team as close to the monu-ment as possible and be ready to run as soon as his cargo was aboard. Each man having been briefed about his precise movements, nothing remained except to pick a night on which to pull off the job.

With America's centennial already having been celebrated by a mam-moth exposition in Philadelphia, the election of 1876 was far too close to call. Democrat Samuel J. Tilden had the backing of major political ma-chines—but Republican Rutherford B. Hayes seemed to have a slight edge of support by state and national elected officials. On the night of November 7, so many persons would be celebrating what they would believe to be a victory by their man that police everywhere would have their hands full with drunks. That meant the chance that one or more officers might wan-der into the cemetery at a crucial moment was remote.

Election night was firmly picked for the heist of the body at least as early as November 5, so information fed to authorities by Swegles put authorities into top speed. A band of operatives from Washington plus detectives from the agency founded in Chicago just before the war by Allan Pinkerton prepared stealthily to descend upon Springfield. In a move that anticipated today's surreptitious use of the media by decades, *Chicago*

At nearly every city where the funeral train stopped, artists sketched the martyred president.
Lithograph by George Koch

Tribune correspondent John English was invited to join the men whose mission was to thwart the plans of counterfeiters.

Nelson failed to get aboard the night train for Springfield on November 6, so Mullens, Hughes, and Swegles went without him. The first two had no idea that Secret Service agents and their associates rode two or three cars behind them. After checking into the tiny Saint Charles Hotel, Mullens and Hughes slept much of the day in order to be ready to go to work as soon as night fell upon streets crowded with men eager for the latest snippet of news about the contest between Tilden and Hayes.

Billy Brown, who had been ordered to go to Springfield leisurely and be there in advance, was believed to be sleeping in the stable with his horses. Swegles slipped away from his comrades in order to spend an hour with the detectives who were staying just two blocks away. As evening approached, officers fully informed about plans of coney men went into the big monument and were guided to hiding places by custodian John C. Power. Having arranged for Swegles to use a watchword when it was time for them to strike, they hunkered down and waited for grave robbers to come.

Mullens, to whom Kinealy had entrusted leadership of the undertaking, directed Hughes and Swegles to visit the cemetery in order to case the joint. They paid the customary small admission fee, wandered around inside the monument without a guide, and quickly located the target which they planned to strike.

Having learned that Lincoln's coffin was covered with lead, Mullens brought along a sack in which to carry their hostage in case the coffin proved too heavy for them. Hughes was equipped with a jimmy designed to open the exterior padlock of the monument plus an axe judged suitable for prying off the coffin lid. By 9:15 P.M. the grave robbers had opened the coffin and had discovered with surprise that "Lincoln still looked almost exactly like pictures of him."

Without telling Kinealy or the men who worked under him, Mullens had already decided that it might be wise to dump the coffin and its contents in a nearby river instead of risking a trip all the way to Indiana. Earlier, the horse handler had been instructed that once his wagon was loaded he must proceed at "a moderate normal pace" unless he was being pursued.

In Springfield, municipal officials wanted Lincoln buried at the heart of the city, so they had this tomb hastily erected, but it was never used.

Entrance to Oak Ridge Cemetery, where the Lincoln Memorial and tomb were built. Mary Todd Lincoln personally selected this burial place.

Satisfied that they had the right body, counterfeiters clumsily replaced the coffin lid and Swegles was sent to notify Billy Brown that he should get ready to move.

English, who had been designated as lookout for the Federal task force, spotted an oncoming lantern about 8:30 P.M., so detectives took off their shoes and rechecked their revolvers as best they could in the darkness. Swegles, who knew that Brown was still in Chicago, used his pretended visit to the wagon to whisper the watchword before returning to his comrades and giving them an assuring nod. With their weapons at the ready, detectives moved as silently as possible into the semicircular room that included the Lincoln vault.

One of them must have sneezed or coughed, for they quickly discovered that counterfeiters had abandoned the casket and were long gone. Racing outside, law enforcement officers reportedly exchanged a few shots with the coney men they could not see. In the confusion, Mullens and Hughes made a clean getaway. Though their identity had been known well in advance of November 7, it took two weeks to locate and apprehend Kinealy's agents who had tried to make a hostage of the nation's most revered corpse.

The trial of the two coney men did not begin until late in May 1868. Evidence against Kinealy was flimsy, so he had not been indicted. A 12-man jury composed of schoolteachers and clerks plus men who performed manual labor of one kind or another debated for only two hours before returning their verdict. Mullens and Hughes were found guilty of having attempted to steal a coffin—no law prohibiting theft of a corpse then being in effect in Illinois.

Jurors were widely divided concerning punishment. Some favored five-year prison terms, but others argued that six months would be long enough. In the end they compromised. Mullens and Hughes, who had tried to seize the most unusual hostage of the century, were sentenced to one month in solitary confinement and eleven months at hard labor.

Construction and renovations at the monument led Power and a band of assistants to dig for Lincoln a secret grave six months after the hostage trial ended. The famous corpse remained there for about 18 years until plans were developed for moving it into the section locally known as "the catacomb." At that time the maker of the cedar box in which the body lay directed the opening of the lead that covered the coffin in order to be sure that it held the body of the martyred president. Persons who had known Lincoln intimately were directed to take a look, and without exception they reported that it was his body—with features virtually unchanged from life. When the lead coffin was resealed it was lowered into a deep hole and covered with about four feet of cement.

Deterioration of the Lincoln Monument building was noticeable to visitors by the end of the century. As a result, a bigger and finer structure was erected on the same site. When it was completed, a huge and very deep hole was dug to hold the coffin that would this time be completely surrounded by steel and concrete. When the coffin was opened once more, old residents of Springfield looked into it and marveled that the corpse looked as though it might be a statue of the man who had practiced law in their city. According to some records, the body had now been moved at least 20 times since arriving at the capital of Illinois.

Failure of the last known hostage-taking attempt linked with the Civil War did not stop the flow of counterfeit greenbacks. The skill of master engraver Ben Boyd has been made obsolete by high-tech color photocopy machines. As a result, so much queer money was produced in recent times that the Bureau of Printing and Engraving has been forced to redesign $20, $50, and $100 bills—with more new designs reportedly on the way.

Even Big Jim Kinealy would today find it hard to turn out a bogus piece of currency that would not be spotted by ordinary folk. If he were alive now he would be in a different business and would have no need of a hostage to be used in bargaining for release of an engraver.

Bibliography

Primary Sources

Bates, Edward. *Diary*. Washington: Government Printing Office, 1933.

Butler, Benjamin F. *Autobiography*. Boston: Thayer, 1892.

The Charleston Daily Post/Courier, 1860–65.

The Charleston Mercury, 1860–65.

Chase, Salmon P. *Diary and Correspondence*. Washington: Government Printing Office, 1903.

The Chicago Tribune, 1886–87.

The Confederate Veteran, 40 vols., 1893–1932.

Dana, Charles A. *Recollections*. New York: Appleton, 1902.

Fox, Gustavus V. *Confidential Correspondence*. New York: De Vinne, 1918.

Grant, Ulysses S. *Personal Memoirs*. 2 vols. New York: Webster, 1895.

Johnston, Joseph E. *Narrative of Military Operations*. New York: Appleton, 1874.

Journal of the Southern Historical Society, 50 vols., 1876–1959.

Lincoln, Abraham. *Collected Works*. Roy P. Basler, ed., 9 vols. Rutgers: Rutgers University Press, 1953–55.

Longstreet, James. *From Manassas to Appomattox*. Philadelphia: Lippincott, 1903.

McClellan, George B. *McClellan's Own Story*. New York: Webster, 1886.

Meade, G. Gordon. *Life and Letters*. New York: Scribner's, 1913.

MOLLUS (Publications of the Military Order of the Loyal Legion of the United States). 68 vols. Reprint, Wilmington: Broadfoot, 1991–98.

Official Records of the Union and Confederate Navies in the War of the Rebellion. 30 vols. Washington: Government Printing Office, 1894–1927.

The New York Herald, 1860–65.

The New York Times, 1860–65, 1886–87.

The New York World, 1886–87.

The Richmond Dispatch, 1860–64.

Schurz, Carl. *Intimate Letters*. Madison: State Historical Society of Wisconsin, 1928.

Sherman, William T. *Memoirs*. 2 vols. New York: Appleton, 1875.

Sheridan, Philip H. *Personal Memoirs*. 2 vols. New York: Appleton, 1888.

Supplement to the Official Records. 12 vols. Wilmington: Broadfoot, 1981–88.

The War of the Rebellion—Official Records of the Union and Confederate Armies. 128 vols. Washington: Government Printing Office, 1880–1901.

The Washington Star, 1860–65.

Welles, Gideon. *Diary*. 3 vols. New York: Houghton Mifflin, 1911.

Secondary Sources

Anderson, Osborne P. *A Voice from Harper's Ferry*. Reprint, Freeport: Books for Libraries, 1972.

Axelrod, Alan. *The War Between the Spies*. New York: Atlantic Monthly, 1992.

Bakeless, John. *Spies of the Confederacy*. Philadelphia: Lippincott, 1970.

The Blockade Runners and Raiders. Alexandria: Time/Life, 1983.

Blue & Gray, 1980–99.

Boatner, Mark M. *The Civil War Dictionary, Revised*. New York: McKay, 1988.

Bragdon, Henry W., et al. *History of a Free Nation*. New York: McGraw-Hill, 1998.

Brooks, Noah. *Washington in Lincoln's Time*. New York: Century, 1895.

Brown, Dee A. *Morgan's Raiders*. New York: Konecky, 1959.

The Century War Book. New York: Century, 1894.

Civil War. 1–48.

Civil War Times Illustrated. 1960–99.

Dahlgren, John A. *Memoir*. Boston: Osgood, 1882.

Davis, Jefferson. *The Rise and Fall of the Confederate Government*. Richmond: Garrett and Massie, 1881.

———. *Short History of the C.S.A.* New York: Bedford, 1890.

Davis, William C. *Brother Against Brother*. Alexandria: Time/Life, 1983.

Denney, Robert E. *Civil War Prisons & Escapes*. New York: Sterling, 1993.

Donald, David H. *Lincoln*. London: Jonathan Cape, 1995.

Dowdey, Clifford, ed. *The Wartime Papers of Robert E. Lee*. Boston: Little, Brown, 1961.

Dyer, Frederick H. *A Compendium of the War of the Rebellion*. 3 vols. Reprint, New York: Yoseloff, 1959.

Evans, Clement A., ed. *Confederate Military History*. 14 vols., extended edition. Wilmington: Broadfoot, 1987.

Faust, Patricia, ed. *Historical Times Illustrated Encyclopedia of the Civil War*. New York: Harper, 1986.

Foote, Shelby. *The Civil War*. 4 vols. New York: Random House, 1958–74.

Freeman, Douglas S. *Lee's Lieutenant's*. 3 vols. New York: Scribner's, 1942.

——. *R. E. Lee*. 4 vols. New York: Scribner's, 1934–35.

Garraty, John A. *The Story of America*. New York: Holt, Rhinehart, Winston, 1991.

Hay, John. *Lincoln and the Civil War*. New York: Dodd, Meade, 1931.

Hertz, Emanuel. *Abraham Lincoln*. 2 vols. New York: Liveright, 1931.

The John Brown Invasion. Boston: James Campbell, 1860.

Johnson, Robert Underwood, and Clarence Clough, eds. *Battles and Leaders of the Civil War: Being for the Most Part Contributions by Union and Confederate Officers*. 4 vols. New York: Century, 1887.

Kettell, Thomas P. *History of the Great Rebellion*. Hartford: Stebbins & Howe, 1866.

Lewis, Lloyd. *Myths After Lincoln*. New York: Blue Ribbon, 1929.

——. *Sherman*. New York: Harcourt, Brace, 1932.

Long, E. B., and Barbara Long. *The Civil War Day by Day*. Garden City: Doubleday, 1971.

Lord, Francis A. *They Fought for the Union*. Harrisburg: Stackpole, 1960.

Lossing, Benson J. *Pictorial Field Book of the Civil War*. 3 vols. Baltimore: Johns Hopkins, 1997.

Lossing, Benson J., ed. *Harper's Encyclopedia of United States History*. 10 vols. New York: Harper, 1905.

Markle, Donald E. *Spies and Spymasters of the Civil War*. New York: Hippocrene, 1994.

Miers, Earl S., ed. *Lincoln Day by Day*. Vol. 3. Washington: Lincoln Sesquicentennial Commission, 1960.

Miller, Francis T., ed. *Photographic History of the Civil War*. 10 vols. New York: Review of Reviews, 1910.

Moore, Frank, ed. *Rebellion Record.* 10 vols. Reprint, New York: Arno, 1977.

Neely, Mark E., Jr. *The Fate of Liberty.* New York: Oxford, 1991.

Nevins, Allan. *Ordeal of the Union.* 2 vols. New York: Scribner's, 1947.

———. *The War for the Union.* 4 vols. New York: Scribner's, 1971.

Nicolay, John G., and John Hay. *Abraham Lincoln.* 10 vols. New York: Century, 1886.

Paludan, Phillip S. *A Covenant with Death.* Urbana: University of Illinois, 1975.

Power, John C. *Attempt to Steal the Body of Lincoln.* Springfield: Rokker, 1890.

Quinn, S. J. *History of the City of Fredericksburg, Virginia.* Richmond: Hermitage, 1908.

Randall, J. G. *Constitutional Problems Under Lincoln.* Urbana: University of Illinois, 1951.

Seward, Frederick W. *Seward at Washington.* 2 vols. New York: Derby and Miller, 1891.

Sifikas, Stewart. *Who Was Who in the Civil War.* New York: Facts on file, 1988.

Warner, Ezra J. *Generals in Blue.* Baton Rouge: Louisiana State University, 1964.

———. *Generals in Gray.* Baton Rouge: Louisiana State University, 1959.

Weichmann, Louis J. *A True History of the Assassination of Abraham Lincoln.* New York: Knopf, 1975.

Wood, Leonard, et al. *America.* New York: Harcourt Brace Jovanovich, 1985.

Index

(Page numbers in *italics* refer to the illustrations.)